E P I C

STORIES OF SURVIVAL FROM
THE WORLD'S HIGHEST PEAKS

EPIC

STORIES OF SURVIVAL FROM THE WORLD'S HIGHEST PEAKS

EDITED BY CLINT WILLIS

A Balliett & Fitzgerald Book

Thunder's Mouth Press
New York

First Edition

Book design: Sue Canavan
Frontispiece photo: Prayer flags in western Nepal © 1997 Beth Wald

Published by
Thunder's Mouth Press
632 Broadway, 7th Floor
New York, NY 10012

Distributed by
Publishers Group West
4065 Hollis Street
Emeryville, CA 94608
800/788-3123

A Balliett & Fitzgerald Book
Editorial director: Will Balliett
Managing editor/Art director: Sue Canavan
Associate editor: Maria Fernandez
Editoral Assistants: Rachel Florman, Margaret Hanscom, Aram Song,
       Ben Welsh, Paige Wilder

ISBN: 1-56025-154-9

Library of Congress Card Catalog Number 97-61889

For Jennifer, Harper and Abner
May you be free of fear

c o n t e n t s

p h o t o g r a p h s

introduction

Traditional epics recount heroic achievement. When climbers talk about an epic, they are talking about a climb that went wrong. The party got lost; an avalanche destroyed their camp; a storm kept them tentbound for six days; someone dropped the water bottle; a climber broke his femur or skied into a crevasse or both.

The stories in this book are epics in both senses. They include heroic achievement; they also include disasters and near disasters—avalanches, storms, altitude sickness, falls, crevasses, blood clots, spiritual crises, broken ice picks, and homicidal military bureaucrats.

I didn't set out to edit a collection of adventures gone wrong. My self-appointed task was to collect samples of first-rate writing that happens to be about climbing. As it turned out, much of the climbing writing I liked best describes difficult situations in the mountains. It's not that people can't write badly about those situations; they can. But good writers write especially well about life-threatening experience.

The climbing anthologies I've read include a lot of bad writing. Often, a poorly written magazine piece or book excerpt makes the cut because it's by a famous climber or describes a famous climb. Anthologies also have neglected the best climbing writing, which is typically found in book-length accounts of expeditions such as David Roberts' *Mountain of My Fear* and Tom Hornbein's *Everest: The West Ridge*. I have devoted most of this collection to long excerpts from such books. Some of the books are out of print or otherwise neglected. The bibliography on page 342 will help you find them.

This book includes nothing that can't stand on its merits as prose. Robert Bates, Peter Boardman, Greg Child, John Climaco, Art Davidson, Maurice Herzog, Tom Hornbein, Eric Shipton, Joe Tasker, H. W. Tilman and Stephen Venables are all climbers who write very well. Jon Krakauer and David Roberts are superb writers who climb. Peter Matthiessen is another fine writer who has spent time in the mountains and plays for high stakes. Alfred Lansing is a writer who got hold of a wonderful story—Shackleton's—and did it justice.

I admire them all and I am grateful to them; their work has helped me to see the world more clearly. And I now have my answer to the question people ask mountaineers: These men climb—and write—to be more fully themselves.

This collection is for readers who love good writing. It helps if you love the mountains, too.

—*Clint Willis*

The Devils Thumb

by Jon Krakauer

Jon Krakauer (b. 1954) is best known as the author of Into Thin Air, *his first-hand account of the 1996 Everest disaster. The book's enormous success reflected the public's interest in the story it reports. But it didn't hurt that Krakauer is one of our best writers—thoughtful, honest, artful and painstaking—as well as a bold climber. This essay recounts a solo trip the young Krakauer took to a remote Alaskan peak in 1977.*

B y the time I reached the interstate I was having trouble keeping my eyes open. I'd been okay on the two lane twisting blacktop between Fort Collins and Laramie, but when the Pontiac eased onto the smooth, unswerving pavement of I-80, the soporific hiss of the tires began to gnaw at my wakefulness like ants in a dead tree.

That afternoon, after nine hours of humping 2x10s and pounding recalcitrant nails, I'd told my boss I was quitting: "No, not in a couple of weeks, Steve; right now was more like what I had in mind." It took me three more hours to clear my tools and other belongings out of the rust-stained construction trailer that had served as my home in Boulder. I loaded everything into the car, drove up Pearl Street to Tom's Tavern, and downed a ceremonial beer. Then I was gone.

At 1 am, 30 miles east of Rawlins, the strain of the day caught up to me. The euphoria that had flowed so freely in the wake of my quick escape gave way to overpowering fatigue; suddenly I felt tired to the bone. The highway stretched straight and empty to the horizon and beyond. Outside the car the night air was cold, and the stark Wyoming plains glowed in the moonlight like Rousseau's painting of the sleeping gypsy. I wanted very badly just then to be that gypsy, conked out on my back beneath the stars. I shut my eyes—just for a second, but it was a second of bliss. It seemed to revive me, if only briefly. The Pontiac, a sturdy behemoth from the Eisenhower years, floated down the road on it's long-gone shocks like a raft on an ocean swell. The lights of an oil rig twinkled reassuringly in the distance. I closed my eyes a second time, and kept them closed a few moments longer. The sensation was sweeter than sex.

A few minutes later I let my eyelids fall again. I'm not sure how long I nodded off this time—it might have been for five seconds, it might have been for 30—but when I awoke it was to the rude sensation of the Pontiac bucking violently along the dirt shoulder at 70 miles per hour. By all rights, the car should have sailed off into the rabbitbrush and rolled. The rear wheels fishtailed wildly six or seven times, but I eventually managed to guide the unruly machine back on to the pavement without so much as blowing a tire, and let it coast gradually to a stop. I loosened my death grip on the wheel, took several deep breaths to quiet the pounding in my chest, then slipped the shifter back into drive and continued down the highway.

Pulling over to sleep would have been the sensible thing to do, but I was on my way to Alaska to change my life, and patience was a concept well beyond my 23-year-old ken.

Sixteen months earlier I'd graduated from college with little distinction and even less in the way of marketable skills. In the interim an off-again, on-again four-year relationship—the first serious romance of my life—had come to a messy, long-overdue end; nearly a year later, my love life was still zip. To support myself I worked on a house-framing crew, grunting under crippling loads of plywood, counting the minutes until the next coffee break, scratching in vain at the sawdust stuck *in perpetuum* to the sweat on the back of my neck. Somehow, blighting the Colorado landscape with condominiums and tract houses for $3.50 an hour wasn't the sort of career I'd dreamed of as a boy.

Late one evening I was mulling all this over on a bar stool at Tom's, picking unhappily at my existential scabs, when an idea came to me, a scheme for righting what was wrong in my life. It was wonderfully uncomplicated, and the more I thought about it, the better the plan sounded. By the bottom of the pitcher its merits seemed unassailable. The plan consisted, in its entirety, of climbing a mountain in Alaska called the Devils Thumb.

The Devils Thumb is a prong of exfoliated diorite that presents an imposing profile from any point of the compass, but especially so from the north: its great north wall, which had never been climbed, rises sheer and clean for six thousand vertical feet from the glacier at its base. Twice the height of Yosemite's El Capitan, the north face of the Thumb is one of the biggest granitic walls on the continent; it may well be one of the biggest in the world. I would go to Alaska, ski across the Stikine Icecap to the Devils Thumb, and make the first ascent of its notorious Nordwand. It seemed, midway through the second pitcher, like a particularly good idea to do all of this solo.

Writing these words more than a dozen years later, it's no longer entirely clear just *how* I thought soloing the Devils Thumb would transform my life. It had something to do with the fact that climbing was the first and only thing that I'd ever been good at. My reasoning, such as it was, was fueled by the scattershot passions of youth, and a literary diet overly rich in the words of Nietzsche, Kerouac, and John Menlove Edwards—the latter a deeply troubled writer/psychiatrist who, before putting an end to his life with a cyanide capsule in 1958, had been one of the preeminent British rock climbers of the day.

Dr. Edwards regarded climbing as a "psycho-neurotic tendency" rather than sport; he climbed not for fun but to find refuge from the inner torment that characterized his existence. I remember that spring of 1977, being especially taken by a passage from an Edwards short story titled "Letter From a Man":

> *So, as you would imagine, I grew up exuberant in body but with a nervy, craving mind. It was wanting something more,*

something tangible. It sought for reality intensely, always if it were not there. . . .

But you see at once what I do. I climb.

To one enamored of this sort of prose, the Thumb beckoned like a beacon. My belief in the plan became unshakable. I was dimly aware that I might be getting in over my head, but if I could somehow get to the top of the Devils Thumb, I was convinced, everything that followed would turn out all right. And thus did I push the accelerator a little closer to the floor and, buoyed by the jolt of adrenaline that followed the Pontiac's brush with destruction, speed west into the night.

You can't actually get very close to the Devils Thumb by car. The peak stands in the Boundary Ranges on the Alaska-British Columbia border, not far from the fishing village of Petersburg, a place accessible only by boat or plane. There is regular jet service to Petersburg, but the sum of my liquid assets amounted to the Pontiac and $200 in cash, not even enough for one-way airfare, so I took the car as far as Gig Harbor, Washington, then hitched a ride on a northbound seine boat that was short on crew. Five days out, when the Ocean Queen pulled into Petersburg to take on fuel and water, I jumped ship, shouldered my backpack, and walked down the dock in the Alaskan rain.

Back in Boulder, without exception, every person with whom I'd shared my plans about the Thumb had been blunt and to the point: I'd been smoking too much pot, they said; it was a monumentally bad idea. I was grossly overestimating my abilities as a climber, I'd never be able to hack a month completely by myself, I would fall into a crevasse and die.

The residents of Petersburg reacted differently. Being Alaskans, they were accustomed to people with screwball ideas; a sizeable percentage of the state's population, after all, was sitting on half-baked schemes to mine uranium in the Brooks Range, or sell icebergs to the Japanese, or market mail-order moose droppings. Most of the Alaskans I met, if they reacted at all, simply asked how much money there was in climbing a mountain like the Devils Thumb.

In any case, one of the appealing things about climbing the Thumb—and one of the appealing things about the sport of mountain climbing in general—was that it didn't matter a rat's ass what anyone else thought. Getting the scheme off the ground didn't hinge on winning the approval of some personnel director, admissions committee, licensing board, or panel of stern-faced judges; if I felt like taking a shot at some unclimbed alpine wall, all I had to do was get myself to the foot of the mountain and start swinging my ice axes.

Petersburg sits on an island, the Devils Thumb rises from the mainland. To get myself to the foot of the Thumb it was first necessary to cross 25 miles of salt water. For most of a day I walked the docks, trying without success to hire a boat to ferry me across Frederick Sound. Then I bumped into Bart and Benjamin.

Bart and Benjamin were ponytailed constituents of a Woodstock Nation tree-planting collective called the Hodads. We struck up a conversation. I mentioned that I, too, had once worked as a tree planter. The Hodads allowed that they had chartered a floatplane to fly them to their camp on the mainland the next morning. "It's your lucky day, kid," Bart told me. "For 20 bucks you can ride over with us. Get to your fuckin' mountain in style." On May 3, a day and a half after arriving in Petersburg, I stepped off the Hodads' Cessna, waded onto the tidal flats at the head of Thomas Bay, and began the long trudge inland.

The Devils Thumb pokes up out of the Stikine Icecap, an immense, labyrinthine network of glaciers that hugs the crest of the Alaskan panhandle like an octopus, with myriad tentacles that snake down, down to the sea from the craggy uplands along the Canadian frontier. In putting ashore at Thomas Bay I was gambling that one of these frozen arms, the Baird Glacier, would lead me safely to the bottom of the Thumb, 30 miles distant.

An hour of gravel beach led to the tortured blue tongue of the Baird. A logger in Petersburg had suggested I keep an eye out for grizzlies along this stretch of shore. "Them bears over there is just waking up this time of year," he smiled. "Tend to be kinda cantankerous after not eatin' all winter. But you keep your gun handy, you shouldn't have no problem." Problem was, I didn't have a gun. As it turned out, my only encounter with hostile wildlife involved a flock of gulls who dive-bombed my head with Hitchcockian fury. Between the avian assault and my ursine anxiety, it was with no small amount of relief that I turned my back to the beach, donned crampons, and scrambled up on to the glacier's broad, lifeless snout.

After three or four miles I came to the snow line, where I exchanged crampons for skis. Putting the boards on my feet cut 15 pounds from the awful load on my back and made the going much faster besides. But now that the ice was covered with snow, many of the glacier's crevasses were hidden, making solitary travel extremely dangerous.

In Seattle, anticipating this hazard, I'd stopped at a hardware store and purchased a pair of stout aluminum curtain rods, each ten feet long. Upon reaching the snowline, I lashed the rods together at right angles, then strapped the arrangement to the hip belt on my backpack so the poles extended horizontally over the snow. Staggering slowly up the glacier with my overloaded backpack, bearing the queer tin cross, I felt like some kind of strange *Penitente*. Were I to break through the veneer of snow over a hidden crevasse, though, the curtain rods would—I hoped mightily—span the slot and keep me from dropping into the chilly bowels of the Baird.

The first climbers to venture onto the Stikine Icecap were Bestor Robinson and Fritz Wiessner, the legendary German-American alpinist, who spent a stormy month in the Boundary Ranges in 1937 but failed to reach any major summits. Wiessner returned in 1946 with Donald Brown and Fred Beckey to attempt the Devils Thumb, the nastiest-look-ing peak in the Stikine. On that trip Fritz mangled a knee during a fall on the hike in and limped home in disgust, but Beckey went back that same summer with Bob Craig and Cliff Schmidtke. On August 25, after several aborted tries and some exceedingly hairy climbing on the peak's east ridge, Beckey and company sat on the Thumb's wafer-thin summit tower in a tired, giddy daze. It was far and away the most technical ascent ever done in Alaska, an important milestone in the history of American mountaineering.

In the ensuing decades three other teams also made it to the top of the Thumb, but all steered clear of the big north face. Reading accounts of these expeditions, I had wondered why none of them had approached the peak by what appeared, from the map at least, to be the easiest and most logical route, the Baird. I wondered a little less after coming across an article by Beckey in which the distinguished mountaineer cautioned, "Long, steep icefalls block the route from the Baird Glacier to the icecap near Devils Thumb," but after studying aerial photographs I decided that Beckey was mistaken, that the icefalls weren't so big or so bad. The Baird, I was certain, really was the best way to reach the mountain.

For two days I slogged steadily up the glacier without incident, congratulating myself for discovering such a clever path to the Thumb. On the third day, I arrived beneath the Stikine Icecap proper, where the long arm of the Baird joins the main body of ice. Here, the glacier spills abruptly over the edge of a high plateau, dropping seaward through the gap between two peaks in a phantasmagoria of shattered ice. Seeing the icefall in the flesh left a different impression than the photos had. As I stared at the tumult from a mile away, for the first time since leaving Colorado the thought crossed my mind that maybe this Devils Thumb trip wasn't the best idea I ever had.

The icefall was a maze of crevasses and teetering seracs. From afar it brought to mind a bad train wreck, as if scores of ghostly white boxcars had derailed at the lip of the icecap and tumbled down the slope willy-nilly. The closer I got, the more unpleasant it looked. My ten-foot curtain rods seemed a poor defense against crevasses that were 40 feet across and 250 feet deep. Before I could finish figuring out a course through the icefall, the wind came up and snow began to slant hard out of the clouds, stinging my face and reducing visibility to almost nothing.

In my impetuosity, I decided to carry on anyway. For the better part of the day I groped blindly through the labyrinth in the white-out, retracing my steps from one dead end to another. Time after time I'd think I'd found my way out, only to wind up in a deep blue cul-de-sac, or stranded atop a detached pillar of ice. My efforts were lent a sense of urgency by the noises emanating underfoot. A madrigal of creaks and sharp reports—the sort of protests a large fir limb makes when it's slowly bent to the breaking point—served as a reminder that it is the nature of glaciers to move, the habit of seracs to topple.

As much as I feared being flattened by a wall of collapsing ice, I was even more afraid of falling into a crevasse, a fear that intensified when I put a foot through a snow bridge over a slot so deep I couldn't see the bottom of it. A little later I broke through another bridge to my waist; the poles kept me out of the hundred-foot hole, but after I extricated myself I was bent double with dry heaves thinking about what it would be like to be lying in a pile at the bottom of the crevasse, waiting for death to come, with nobody even aware of how or where I'd met my end.

Night had nearly fallen by the time I emerged from the top of the serac slope onto the empty, wind-scoured expanse of the high glacial plateau. In shock and chilled to the core, I skied far enough past the icefall to put its rumblings out of earshot, pitched the tent, crawled into my sleeping bag, and shivered myself to a fitful sleep.

Although my plan to climb the Devils Thumb wasn't fully hatched until the spring of 1977, the mountain had been lurking in the recesses of my mind for about 15 years—since April 12, 1962, to be exact. The occasion was my eighth birthday. When it came time to open birthday presents, my parents announced that they were offering me a choice of gifts: According to my wishes, they would either escort me to the new Seattle World's Fair to ride the Monorail and see the Space Needle, or give me an introductory taste of mountain climbing by taking me up the third highest peak in Oregon, a long-dormant volcano called the South Sister that, on clear days, was visible from my bedroom window. It was a tough call. I thought the matter over at length, then settled on the climb.

To prepare me for the rigors of the ascent, my father handed over a copy of *Mountaineering: The Freedom of the Hills*, the leading how-to manual of the day, a thick tome that weighed only slightly less than a bowling ball. Thenceforth I spent most of my waking hours poring over its pages, memorizing the intricacies of pitoncraft and bolt place-ment, the shoulder stand and the tension traverse. None of which, as it happened, was of any use on my inaugural ascent, for the South Sister turned out to be a decidedly less than extreme climb that demanded nothing more in the way of technical skill than energetic walking, and was in fact ascended by hundreds of farmers, house pets, and small children every summer.

Which is not to suggest that my parents and I conquered the mighty volcano: From the pages and pages of perilous situations depicted in *Mountaineering: The Freedom of the Hills*, I had concluded that climbing was a life-and-death matter, always. Halfway up the South Sister I sud-denly remembered this. In the middle of a 20-degree snow slope that would be impossible to fall from if you tried, I decided I was in mor-tal jeopardy and burst into tears, bringing the ascent to a halt.

Perversely, after the South Sister debacle my interest in climbing only intensified. I resumed my obsessive studies of *Mountaineering*. There was something about the scariness of the activities portrayed in those pages that just wouldn't leave me alone. In addition to the scores of line drawings—most of them cartoons of a little man in a jaunty Tyrolean cap—employed to illustrate arcana like the boot-axe belay and the Bilgeri rescue, the book contained 16 black-and-white plates of notable peaks in the Pacific Northwest and Alaska. All the photographs were striking, but the one on page 147 was much, much more than that: it made my skin crawl. An aerial photo by glaciologist Maynard Miller, it showed a singularly sinister tower of ice-plastered black rock. There wasn't a place on the entire mountain that looked safe or secure; I couldn't imagine anyone climbing it. At the bottom of the page the mountain was identified as the Devils Thumb.

From the first time I saw it, the picture—a portrait of the Thumb's north wall—held an almost pornographic fascination for me. On hundreds—no, make that thousands—of occasions over the decade-and-a-half that followed I took my copy of *Mountaineering* down from the shelf, opened it to page 147 and quietly stared. How would it feel, I wondered over and over, to be on that thumbnail-thin summit ridge, worrying over the storm clouds building on the horizon, hunched against the wind and dunning cold, contemplating the horrible drop on either side? How could anyone keep it together? Would I, if I found myself on the north wall, clinging to that frozen rock, even attempt to keep it together? Or would I simply decide to surrender to the inevitable straightaway, and jump?

I had planned on spending between three weeks and a month on the Stikine Icecap. Not relishing the prospect of carrying a four-week load of food, heavy winter camping gear, and a small mountain of climbing hardware all the way up the Baird on my back, before leaving Petersburg I paid a bush pilot $150—the last of my cash—to have six cardboard cartons of supplies dropped from an airplane when I reached the foot of the Thumb. I showed the pilot exactly where, on his map, I intended to be, and told him to give me three days to get there; he promised to fly over and make the drop as soon thereafter as the weather permitted.

On May 6 I set up a base camp on the icecap just northeast of the Thumb and waited for the airdrop. For the next four days it snowed, nixing any chance for flight. Too terrified of crevasses to wander far from camp, I occasionally went out for a short ski to kill time, but mostly I lay silently in the tent—the ceiling was too low to sit upright—with my thoughts, fighting a rising chorus of doubts.

As the days passed, I grew increasingly anxious. I had no radio, nor any other means of communicating with the outside world. It had been many years since anyone had visited this part of the Stikine Icecap, and many more would likely pass before anyone did so again. I was nearly out of stove fuel, and down to a single chunk of cheese, my last package of ramen noodles, and half a box of Cocoa Puffs. This, I figured, could sustain me for three or more days if need be, but then what would I do?

It would only take two days to ski back down the Baird to Thomas Bay, but then a week or more might easily pass before a fisherman happened by who could give me a lift back to Petersburg (the Hodads with whom I'd ridden over were camped 15 miles down the impassable, headland-studded coast, and could be reached only by boat or plane).

When I went to bed on the evening of May 10 it was still snowing and blowing hard. I was going back and forth on whether to head for the coast in the morning or stick it out on the icecap, gambling that the pilot would show before I starved or died of thirst, when, just for a moment, I heard a faint whine, like a mosquito. I tore open the tent door. Most of the clouds had lifted, but there was no airplane in sight. The whine returned, louder this time. Then I saw it: a tiny red-and-white speck, high in the western sky, droning my way.

A few minutes later the plane passed directly overhead. The pilot, however, was unaccustomed to glacier flying and he'd badly misjudged the scale of the terrain. Worried about winding up too low and getting nailed by unexpected turbulence, he flew a good thousand feet above me—believing all the while that he was just off the deck—and never saw my tent in the flat evening light. My waving and screaming were to no avail; from that altitude I was indistinguishable from a pile of rocks. For the next hour he circled the icecap, scanning its barren contours without success. But the pilot, to his credit, appreciated the gravity of my predicament and didn't give up. Frantic, I tied my sleeping bag to the end of one of the crevasse poles and waived for all I was worth. When the plane banked sharply and began to fly straight at me, I felt tears of joy well in my eyes.

The pilot buzzed my tent three times in quick succession, dropping two boxes on each pass, then the airplane disappeared over a ridge and I was alone. As silence again settled over the glacier I felt abandoned, vulnerable, lost. I realized that I was sobbing. Embarrassed, I halted the blubbering by screaming obscenities until I grew hoarse.

I awoke early on May 11 to clear skies and the relatively warm temperature of 20 degrees Fahrenheit. Startled by the good weather, mentally unprepared to commence the actual climb, I hurriedly packed up a rucksack nonetheless, and began skiing towards the base of the Thumb. Two previous Alaskan expeditions had taught me that, ready or not, you simply can't afford to waste a day of perfect weather if you expect to get up anything.

A small hanging glacier extends out from the lip of the icecap, leading up and across the north face of the Thumb like a catwalk. My plan was to follow this catwalk to a prominent rock prow in the center of the wall, and thereby execute an end run around the ugly, avalanche-swept lower half of the face.

The catwalk turned out to be a series of 50-degree ice fields blanketed with knee-deep powder snow and riddled with crevasses. The depth of the snow made the going slow and exhausting; by the time I front-pointed up the overhanging wall of the uppermost bergschrund, some three or four hours after leaving camp, I was whipped. And I hadn't even gotten to the "real" climbing yet. That would begin immediately above, where the hanging glacier gave way to vertical rock.

The rock, exhibiting a dearth of holds and coated with six inches of crumbly rime, did not look promising, but just left of the main prow was an inside corner—what climbers call an open book—glazed with frozen melt water. This ribbon of ice led straight up for 200 or 300 feet, and if the ice proved substantial enough to support the picks of my axes, the line might go. I hacked out a small platform in the snow slope, the last flat ground I expected to feel underfoot for some time, and stopped to eat a candy bar and collect my thoughts. Fifteen minutes later I shouldered my pack and inched over to the bottom of the corner. Gingerly, I swung my right axe into the two-inch-thick ice. It was solid, plastic—a little thinner than what I would have liked but otherwise perfect. I was on my way.

The climbing was steep and spectacular, so exposed it made my head spin. Beneath my boot soles, the wall fell away for three thousand feet to the dirty, avalanche-scarred cirque of the Witches Cauldron Glacier. Above, the prow soared with authority toward the summit ridge, a vertical half-mile above. Each time I planted one of my ice axes, that distance shrank by another 20 inches.

The higher I climbed the more comfortable I became. All that held me to the mountainside, all that held me to the world, were six thin spikes of chrome-molybdenum stuck half an inch into a smear of frozen water, yet I began to feel invincible, weightless, like those lizards that live on the ceilings of cheap Mexican hotels. Early on a difficult climb, especially a difficult solo climb, you're hyperaware of the abyss pulling at your back. You constantly feel its call, its immense hunger. To resist takes a tremendous conscious effort; you don't dare let your guard down for an instant. The siren song of the void puts you on edge, it makes your movements tentative, clumsy, herky-jerky. But as the climb goes on, you grow accustomed to the exposure, you get used to rubbing shoulders with doom, you come to believe in the reliability of your hands and feet and head. You learn to trust your self-control.

By and by, your attention becomes so intensely focused that you no longer notice the raw knuckles, the cramping thighs, the strain of maintaining nonstop concentration. A trance-like state settles over your efforts, the climb becomes a clear-eyed dream. Hours slide by like minutes. The accrued guilt and clutter of day-to-day existence—the lapses of conscience, the unpaid bills, the bungled opportunities, the dust under the couch, the festering familial sores, the inescapable prison of your genes—all of it is temporarily forgotten, crowded from your thoughts by an overpowering sense of purpose, and by the seriousness of the task at hand.

At such moments something like happiness stirs in your chest, but it isn't the sort of emotion you want to lean on very hard. In solo climbing, the whole enterprise is held together by little more than chutzpa, not the most reliable adhesive. Late in the day on the north face of the Thumb, I felt the glue disintegrate with a single swing of an ice axe.

I'd gained nearly 700 feet of altitude since stepping off the hanging glacier, all of it on crampon front-points and the picks of my axes. The ribbon of frozen melt water had ended 300 feet up, and was followed by a crumbly armor of frost feathers. Though just barely substantial enough to support body weight, the rime was plastered over the rock to a thickness of two or three feet, so I kept plugging upward. The wall however, had been growing imperceptibly steeper, and as it did so the frost feathers became thinner. I'd fallen into a slow, hypnotic rhythm— swing, swing; kick, kick; swing, swing; kick, kick—when my left ice axe slammed into a slab of diorite a few inches beneath the rime.

I tried left, then right, but kept striking rock. The frost feathers holding me up, it became apparent, were maybe five inches thick and had the structural integrity of stale cornbread. Below was 3,700 feet of air, and I was balanced atop a house of cards. Waves of panic rose in my throat. My eyesight blurred, I began to hyperventilate, my calves started to vibrate. I shuffled a few feet farther to the right, hoping to find thicker ice, but managed only to bend an ice axe on the rock.

Awkwardly, stiff with fear, I started working my way back down. The rime gradually thickened, and after descending about 80 feet I got back on reasonably solid ground. I stopped for a long time to let my nerves settle, then leaned back from my tools and stared at the face above, searching for a hint of solid ice, for some variation in the underlying rock strata, for anything that would allow passage over the frosted slabs. I looked until my neck ached, but nothing appeared. The climb was over. The only place to go was down.

Heavy snow and incessant winds kept me inside the tent for most of the next three days. The hours passed slowly. In the attempt to hurry them along I chain-smoked for as long as my supply of cigarettes held out, and read. I'd made a number of bad decisions on the trip, there was no getting around it, and one of them concerned the reading matter I'd chosen to pack along: three back issues of *The Village Voice*, and Joan Didion's latest novel, *A Book of Common Prayer*. The *Voice* was amusing enough—there on the icecap, the subject matter took on an edge, a certain sense of the absurd, from which the paper (through no fault of its own) benefited greatly—but in that tent, under those circumstances, Didion's necrotic take on the world hit a little too close to home.

Near the end of *Common Prayer*, one of Didion's characters says to another, "You don't get any real points for staying here, Charlotte." Charlotte replies, "I can't seem to tell what you do get real points for, so I guess I'll stick around here for a while."

When I ran out of things to read, I was reduced to studying the rip-stop pattern woven into the tent ceiling. This I did for hours on end, flat on my back, while engaging in an extended and very heated self-debate: Should I leave for the coast as soon as the weather broke, or stay put long enough to make another attempt on the mountain? In truth, my little escapade on the north face had left me badly shaken, and I didn't want to go up on the Thumb again at all. On the other hand, the thought of returning to Boulder in defeat—of parking the Pontiac behind the trailer, buckling on my tool belt, and going back to the same brain-dead drill I'd so triumphantly walked away from just a month before—that wasn't very appealing, either. Most of all, I couldn't stomach the thought of having to endure the smug expressions of condolence from all the chumps and nimrods who were certain I'd fail right from the get-go.

By the third afternoon of the storm I couldn't stand it any longer: the lumps of frozen snow poking me in the back, the clammy nylon walls brushing against my face, the incredible smell drifting up from the depths of my sleeping bag. I pawed through the mess at my feet until I located a small green stuff sack, in which there was a metal film can containing the makings of what I'd hoped would be a sort of victory cigar. I'd intended to save it for my return from the summit, but what the hey, it wasn't looking like I'd be visiting the top any time soon. I poured most of the can's contents onto a leaf of cigarette paper, rolled it into a crooked, sorry-looking joint, and promptly smoked it down to the roach.

The reefer, of course, only made the tent seem even more cramped, more suffocating, more impossible to bear. It also made me terribly hungry. I decided a little oatmeal would put things right. Making it, however, was a long, ridiculously involved process: a potful of snow had to be gathered outside in the tempest, the stove assembled and lit, the oatmeal and sugar located, the remnants of yesterday's dinner scraped from my bowl. I'd gotten the stove going and was melting the snow when I smelled something burning. A thorough check of the stove and its environs revealed nothing. Mystified, I was ready to chalk it up to my chemically enhanced imagination when I heard something crackle directly behind me.

I whirled around in time to see a bag of garbage, into which I'd tossed the match I'd used to light the stove, flare up into a conflagration. Beating on the fire with my hands, I had it out in a few seconds, but not before a large section of the tent's inner wall vaporized before my eyes. The tent's built-in rainfly escaped the flames, so the shelter was still more or less waterproof; now, however, it was approximately 30 degrees cooler inside. My left palm began to sting. Examining it, I noticed the pink welt of a burn. What troubled me most, though, was that the tent wasn't even mine—I'd borrowed the shelter from my father. An expensive Early Winters Omnipo tent, it had been brand new before my trip—the hang-tags were still attached—and had been loaned reluctantly. For several minutes I sat dumbstruck, staring at the wreckage of the shelter's once-graceful form amid the acrid scent of singed hair and melted nylon. You had to hand it to me, I thought: I had a real knack for living up to the old man's worst expectations.

The fire sent me into a funk that no drug known to man could have alleviated. By the time I'd finished cooking the oatmeal my mind was made up: the moment the storm was over, I was breaking camp and booking for Thomas Bay.

Twenty-four hours later, I was huddled inside a bivouac sack under the lip of the bergschrund on the Thumb's north face. The weather was as bad as I'd seen it. It was snowing hard, probably an inch every hour. Spindrift avalanches hissed down from the wall above and washed over me like surf, completely burying the sack every 20 minutes.

The day had begun well enough. When I emerged from the tent, clouds still clung to the ridge tops but the wind was down and the ice-cap was speckled with sunbreaks. A patch of sunlight, almost blinding in its brilliance, slid lazily over the camp. I put down a foam sleeping mat and sprawled on the glacier in my long johns. Wallowing in the radiant heat, I felt the gratitude of a prisoner whose sentence has just been commuted.

As I lay there, a narrow chimney that curved up the east half of the Thumb's north face, well to left of the route I'd tried before the storm, caught my eye. I twisted a telephoto lens onto my camera. Through it I could make out a smear of shiny grey ice—solid, trustworthy, hard-frozen ice—plastered to the back of the cleft. The alignment of the chimney made it impossible to discern if the ice continued in an unbroken line from top to bottom. If it did, the chimney might well provide passage over the rime-covered slabs that had foiled my first attempt. Lying there in the sun, I began to think about how much I'd hate myself a month hence if I threw in the towel after a single try, if I scrapped the whole expedition on account of a little bad weather. Within the hour I had assembled my gear and was skiing toward the base of the wall.

The ice in the chimney did in fact prove to be continuous, but it was very, very thin—just a gossamer film of verglas. Additionally, the cleft was a natural funnel for any debris that happened to slough off the wall; as I scratched my way up the chimney I was hosed by a continuous stream of powder snow, ice chips, and small stones. One hundred twenty feet up the groove the last remnants of my composure flaked away like old plaster, and I turned around.

Instead of descending all the way to base camp, I decided to spend the night in the 'schrund beneath the chimney, on the off chance that my head would be more together the next morning. The fair skies that had ushered in the day, however, turned out to be but a momentary lull in a five-day gale. By midafternoon the storm was back in all its glory, and my bivouac site became a less than pleasant place to hang around. The ledge on which I was crouched was continually swept by small spindrift avalanches. Five times my bivvy sack—a thin nylon envelope, shaped exactly like a Baggies brand sandwich bag, only bigger—was buried up to the level of the breathing slit. After digging myself out the fifth time, I decided I'd had enough. I threw all my gear in my pack and made a break for base camp.

The descent was terrifying. Between the clouds, the ground blizzard, and the flat, fading light, I couldn't tell snow from sky, nor whether a slope went up or down. I worried, with ample reason, that I might step blindly off the top of a serac and end up at the bottom of the Witches Cauldron, a half-mile below. When I finally arrived on the frozen plain of the icecap, I found that my tracks had long since drifted over. I didn't have a clue how to locate the tent on the featureless glacial plateau. I skied in circles for an hour or so, hoping I'd get lucky and stumble across camp, until I put a foot into a small crevasse and realized I was acting like an idiot—that I should hunker down right where I was and wait out the storm.

I dug a shallow hole, wrapped myself in the bivvy bag, and sat on my pack in the swirling snow. Drifts piled up around me. My feet became numb. A damp chill crept down my chest from the base of my neck, where spindrift had gotten inside my parka and soaked my shirt. If only I had a cigarette, I thought, a single cigarette, I could summon the strength of character to put a good face on this fucked-up situation, on the whole fucked-up trip. "If we had some ham, we could have ham and eggs, if we had some eggs." I remembered my friend Nate uttering that line in a similar storm, two years before, high on another Alaskan peak, the Mooses Tooth. It had struck me as hilarious at the time; I'd actually laughed out loud. Recalling the line now, it no longer seemed funny. I pulled the bivvy sack tighter around my shoulders. The wind ripped at my back. Beyond shame, I cradled my head in my arms and embarked on an orgy of self-pity.

I knew that people sometimes died when climbing mountains. But at the age of 23 personal mortality—the idea of my own death—was still largely outside my conceptual grasp; it was as abstract a notion as non-Euclidian geometry or marriage. When I decamped from Boulder in April, 1977, my head swimming with visions of glory and redemption on the Devils Thumb, it didn't occur to me that I might be bound by the same cause-effect relationships that governed the actions of others. I'd never heard of hubris. Because I wanted to climb the mountain so badly, because I had thought about the Thumb so intensely for so long, it seemed beyond the realm of possibility that some minor obstacle like the weather or crevasses or rime-covered rock might ultimately thwart my will.

At sunset the wind died and the ceiling lifted 150 feet off the glacier, enabling me to locate the base camp. I made it back to the tent intact, but it was no longer possible to ignore the fact that the Thumb had made hash of my plans. I was forced to acknowledge that volition alone, however powerful, was not going to get me up the north wall. I saw, finally, that nothing was.

There still existed an opportunity for salvaging the expedition, however. A week earlier I'd skied over to the southeast side of the mountain to take a look at the route Fred Beckey had pioneered in 1946—the route by which I'd intended to descend the peak after climbing the north wall. During that reconnaissance I'd noticed an obvious unclimbed line to the left of the Beckey route—a patchy network of ice angling across the southeast face—that struck me as a relatively easy way to achieve the summit. At the time, I'd considered this route unworthy of my attentions. Now, on the rebound from my calamitous entanglement with the *nordwand*, I was prepared to lower my sights.

On the afternoon of May 15, when the blizzard finally petered out, I returned to the southeast face and climbed to the top of a slender ridge that abutted the upper peak like a flying buttress on a gothic cathedral. I decided to spend the night there, on the airy, knife-edged ridge crest, 1,600 feet below the summit. The evening sky was cold and cloudless. I could see all the way to tidewater and beyond. At dusk I watched, transfixed, as the house lights of Petersburg blinked on in the west. The closest thing I'd had to human contact since the airdrop, the distant lights set off a flood of emotion that caught me completely off guard. I imagined people watching the Red Sox on the tube, eating fried chicken in brightly lit kitchens, drinking beer, making love. When

I lay down to sleep I was overcome by a soul-wrenching loneliness. I'd never felt so alone, ever.

That night I had troubled dreams, of cops and vampires and a gang-land-style execution. I heard someone whisper, "He's in there. As soon as he comes out, waste him." I sat bolt upright and opened my eyes. The sun was about to rise. The entire sky was scarlet. It was still clear, but wisps of high cirrus were streaming in from the southwest, and a dark line was visible just above the horizon. I pulled on my boots and hurriedly strapped on my crampons. Five minutes after waking up, I was front-pointing away from the bivouac.

I carried no rope, no tent or bivouac gear, no hardware save my ice axes. My plan was to go ultralight and ultrafast, to hit the summit and make it back down before the weather turned. Pushing myself, continually out of breath, I scurried up and to the left across small snowfields linked by narrow runnels of verglas and short rock bands. The climbing was almost fun—the rock was covered with large, in-cut holds, and the ice, though thin, never got steep enough to feel extreme—but I was anxious about the bands of clouds racing in from the Pacific, covering the sky.

In what seemed like no time (I didn't have a watch on the trip) I was on the distinctive final ice field. By now the sky was completely overcast. It looked easier to keep angling to the left, but quicker to go straight for the top. Paranoid about being caught by a storm high on the peak without any kind of shelter, I opted for the direct route. The ice steepened, then steepened some more, and as it did so it grew thin. I swung my left ice axe and struck rock. I aimed for another spot, and once again it glanced off unyielding diorite with a dull, sickening clank. And again, and again: It was a reprise on my first attempt on the north face. Looking between my legs, I stole a glance at the glacier, more than two thousand feet below. My stomach churned. I felt my poise slipping away like smoke in the wind.

Forty-five feet above, the wall eased back onto the sloping summit shoulder. Forty-five more feet, half the distance between third base and home plate, and the mountain would be mine. I clung stiffly to my axes, unmoving, paralyzed with fear and indecision. I looked down at the dizzying drop to the glacier again, then up, then scraped away the film of ice above my head. I hooked the pin of my left axe on a nickel-thin lip of rock, and weighted it. It held. I pulled my right axe from the ice, reached up, and twisted the crook into a half-inch crack until it jammed. Barely breathing now, I moved my feet up, scrabbling my crampon points across the verglas. Reaching as high as I could with my left arm, I swung the axe gently at the shiny, opaque surface, not knowing what I'd hit beneath it. The pick went in with a heartening THUNK! A few minutes later I was standing on a broad, rounded ledge. The summit proper, a series of slender fins sprouting a grotesque meringue of atmospheric ice, stood 20 feet directly above.

The insubstantial frost feathers ensured that those last 20 feet remained hard, scary, onerous. But then, suddenly, there was no place higher to go. It wasn't possible, I couldn't believe it. I felt my cracked lips stretch into a huge, painful grin. I was on top of the Devils Thumb.

Fittingly, the summit was a surreal, malevolent place, an improbably slender fan of rock and rime no wider than a filing cabinet. It did not encourage loitering. As I straddled the highest point, the north face fell away beneath my left boot for six thousand feet; beneath my right boot the south face dropped off for 2,500. I took some pictures to prove I'd been there, and spent a few minutes trying to straighten a bent pick. Then I stood up, carefully turned around, and headed for home.

Five days later I was camped in the rain by the sea, marveling at the sight of moss, willows, mosquitoes. Two days after that, a small skiff motored into Thomas Bay and pulled up on the beach not far from my tent. The man introduced himself as Jim Freeman, a timber faller from Petersburg. It was his day off, he said, and he'd made the trip to show his family the glacier, and to look for bears. He asked me if I'd "been huntin' or what?"

"No," I replied sheepishly. "Actually, I just climbed the Devils Thumb. I've been over here 20 days."

Freeman kept fiddling with the cleat on the boat, and didn't say anything for a while. Then he looked at me real hard and spat, "You wouldn't be givin' me double talk now, wouldja, friend?" Taken aback, I stammered out a denial. Freeman, it was obvious, didn't believe me for a minute. Nor did he seem wild about my snarled shoulder-length hair or the way I smelled. When I asked if he could give me a lift back to town, however, he offered a grudging, "I don't see why not."

The water was choppy, and the ride across Frederick Sound took two hours. The more we talked, the more Freeman warmed up. He still didn't believe I'd climbed the Thumb, but by the time he steered the skiff into Wrangell Narrows he pretended to. When we got off the boat he insisted on buying me a cheeseburger. That night he even let me sleep in a derelict step-van parked in his backyard.

I lay down in the rear of the old truck for a while but couldn't sleep, so I got up and walked to a bar called Kito's Kave. The euphoria, the overwhelming sense of relief, that had initially accompanied my return to Petersburg faded, and an unexpected melancholy took its place. The people I chatted with in Kito's didn't seem to doubt that I'd been to the top of the Thumb, they just didn't much care. As the night wore on, the place emptied except for me and an Indian at a back table. I drank alone, putting quarters in the jukebox, playing the same five songs over and over, until the barmaid yelled angrily, "Hey! Give it a fucking rest, kid!" I mumbled an apology, quickly headed for the door, and lurched back to Freedman's step-van. There, surrounded by the sweet scent of motor oil, I lay down on the floorboards next to a gutted transmission and passed out.

It is easy when you are young, to believe that what you desire is no less than what you deserve, to assume that if you want something badly enough it is your God-given right to have it. Less than a month after sitting on the summit of the Thumb I was back in Boulder, nailing up siding on the Spruce Street Townhouses, the same condos I'd been framing when I left for Alaska. I got a raise, to four dollars an hour, and at the end of the summer moved out of the job-site trailer to a studio apartment on West Pearl, but little else in my life seemed to change. Somehow, it didn't add up to the glorious transformation I'd imagined in April.

Climbing the Devils Thumb, however, had nudged me a little further away from the obdurate innocence of childhood. It taught me something about what mountains can and can't do, about the limits of dreams. I didn't recognize that at the time, of course, but I'm grateful for it now.

from Thin Air: Encounters in the Himalayas
by Greg Child

Greg Child, who was born in Sydney, Australia in 1957, and now lives in Seattle, has made many formidable ascents. They include K2's North Ridge (1990), a new route on Trango Tower's South Face (1992), Everest's North Ridge (1995) and the first ascent of Shipton Spire (1996). In 1983, Child and partner Peter Thexton attempted Broad Peak in Pakistan's Karakoram Range; at 26,400 feet, it is the world's 12th-highest mountain. This was Child's first encounter with the rigors of extreme altitude, and it was a brutal one.

Throughout the calm, clear morning of 25 June we watched the figures of Alan, Andy, Roger, and Jean leave their high bivouacs and head towards the summit of Broad Peak. A thousand feet below them, the two Polish women followed their tracks. Even through an 800 millimetre lens they appeared as mere specks beneath the rocky black pyramid of the main summit. The slant of the sun highlighted their tracks as they zigzagged across the great snowy terrace. They negotiated a small serac, then a steep chute, then gained the col at 25,591 feet between the main and central summits.

"They'll be on the summit in two hours," Doug forecasts.

As the figures move south on the long summit ridge they disappear behind a rocky promontory. Below them we see the Polish women turn around and descend from 24,500 feet, evidently deciding that the time is not ripe for them to push on. As the women descend they sway and stumble with fatigue. From a distant part of the mountain a savage crack rents the air as a huge avalanche cuts loose and blows up a thick cloud of debris.

Soon it will be time for us to leave for Broad Peak too. Pete and I decide to leave in the later afternoon to climb Broad Peak's initial couloirs by moonlight and reach Camp One while the snow is firmly frozen. Doug and Steve, with Don and Gohar, decide to leave at dawn on the 26th, after a full night's sleep. An hour before sunset, as the afternoon begins to gather and the light on the peaks around base camp softens to a gentle glow, Pete kisses Beth goodbye and we bid the camp farewell, heading across the glacier. Out in the centre of the icy wastes I pause to photograph K2, majestic and clear in the twilight.

"There'll be plenty of time for that," Pete says, hurrying me along toward the base of the three-crowned giant ahead of us.

Between base camp and the foot of Broad Peak lie two miles of glacier, crevassed and forested with a maze of ice towers, or *penitentes*. As Pete and I pick our path across suspect snow patches, moving from one rubbly island to another, we probe the snow with our ice axes to check for crevasses. We talk of the route ahead and check off items to ensure that nothing has been forgotten. As we make our way we talk about Lobsang. Yes—it had been perfection, and there would be more. We spoke of more climbs—he'd come to Yosemite and we'd climb El Capitan; I'd visit the Alps in winter; and maybe, just maybe, if Broad Peak went well, we'd find ourselves together on K2. A great warmth radiated from Pete onto me, like the alpenglow clinging to the mountains. His small kindnesses and carefully chosen words told me that I was at last breaking through the carefully guarded barrier with which he surrounded himself.

At a snow patch I probe forward, poking my ice axe shaft into the snow ahead. The snow feels firm. Nothing thuds or tinkles to imply a hollow surface. I deem it safe, but the very moment I assure Pete it is so and move forward, the surface gives way with a crash and I drop into a slot.

"Crevasse," I understate in the sudden quiet that follows smashed mirrors and glassware. I had the foolish surprise one would feel standing on a glass-topped table that had suddenly shattered. More surprising was that the crevasse had a false floor and I had stopped just a bodylength down. Beneath me I could see cracks in the floor that dropped into a black emptiness.

"Thought I'd lost you already," Pete said, seating himself on his pack as I extricated myself. Scalpel-sharp fins of ice had sliced hairline cuts into my arms and face. I looked as if I'd had a tussle with a wildcat.

Pete points over his shoulder. "You'll be pleased to know you've got an audience. Some trekkers watched the whole display from their camp a few hundred feet away."

"How embarrassing."

"Don't worry," Pete added impishly, "no one from our camp saw it."

As we enter the forest of *penitentes* the sun drops, leaving the air breathless and the summit rocks of K2 burning orange. The gurgle and rush of streams fall suddenly silent, choked by night's freeze. As we emerge from the icemaze, Broad Peak stands suddenly before us, its silhouette well defined as the Baltoro grows quickly black with night. On a bed of scree beneath the mountain we pause for a drink and a bite to eat. On the scree lies a cluster of old wooden wedges and hemp slings. We fiddle with these artifacts left by some predecessor, perhaps the Austrians Hermann Buhl, Kurt Diemberger, Fritz Winterstellar, and Marcus Schmuck, who pioneered the first ascent of Broad Peak in 1957 or, perhaps, they belonged to the tragic Polish expedition who'd made the first ascent of the 26,247-foot high Central Peak.

In late July 1975, six Poles set off up the face above us, climbing a more direct variation of the Austrian Route to the 25,591-foot col between the Main and Central summits. That variation has become the *voie* normal, but from the col they planned to climb the South Ridge of the Central Summit. Snow conditions were poor, the going slow. Beneath the col, as night and storm approached, one man, Roman Bebak, descended, leaving five to complete the climb. As the storm grew stronger and the five rushed to complete the route, three men—Bohdan Nowaczyk, Marek Kesicki, and Andrej Sikorski—took shelter from the wind on the final rock step below the summit, while Kazimierz Glazek and Janusz Kulis persevered to the top. At 7:30 pm Glazek and Kulis reached the summit, then descended to the others. The storm was now upon them. As the last man, Nowaczyk, made the final abseil to the col, the anchor pulled and he fell to his death, taking the vital ropes with him. Trapped in a raging storm and with no way to descend the steep, avalanche-prone chute beneath the col, the climbers bivouacked out, wearing only the clothes on their backs.

At first light they resumed their search for Nowaczyk and the ropes. Nothing was found. In desperation, they tied all their slings and harnesses together to construct a makeshift rope. In the afternoon Glazek descended the gully to the snow-fields and 300 feet down found a site for a bivouac. But behind him the weakened Sikorski slipped, knocking Kesicki and Kulis from the face. Sikorski fell 600 feet; Kesicki slid down the snow-fields and plummetted thousands of feet over the huge seracs; Kulis, the only one of the three to survive the fall, stopped 150 feet below Glazek. Glazek and Kulis endured a second terrible night in a snowhole, then continued down next morning, their fingers and feet frostbitten. Kulis would subsequently lose most of his fingers and toes. On the descent they found Sikorski, partially buried in snow. Attempts to revive him proved fruitless: He was dead. The only traces of Kesicki were a few tufts of hair and some bloodstains on the snow.

As we enter the first couloirs of Broad Peak the full moon rounds the mountain and douses the West Face in a silvery light that bounces bright as daylight off the snow. We crampon our way quickly over the firm, crystalline surface until a rocky promontory appears, at 18,543 feet. Here sits a small tent—Camp One, established by the Polish women. Anna and Krystyna were climbing the mountain in siege style, placing fixed camps along the route, each stocked with bivvy gear, food, and fuel. We rest here an hour, make tea, then continue into the moonlight.

Step after step, breath after breath, every hour the atmosphere just a little thinner. Behind us, the first hint of dawn turns the Karakoram every shade of blue and gold imaginable, while the moon sits fixed in the sky, great and white, refusing to evaporate. The mountains glow, changing colour by the minute, like a horizon of chameleons. With this view over our shoulders, we zigzag through the gullies and towers of yellow limestone. As we reach the crest of a rocky spur at about 20,000 feet, blinding daylight and heat flood the mountain. Day reveals further relics of past expeditions; shredded tents, bits of fixed rope, and an old oxygen cylinder poking out of the snow. I pick up the steel cylinder to feel what it would be like to hump its weight up a mountain. Weighing at least 20 pounds, it feels like an unexploded bomb, but my lungs wish they could have a taste of the cylinder's juicy contents.

The half-melted tracks of our four members above pit the slope. As I slot my feet into their footsteps I play a brief game of pretend that I am following Buhl's tracks, back in 1957, the year of my birth, and the year too that he died, on Chogolisa. Heat dries our throats so we keep chewing handfuls of snow. Tiny black gnats, blown in from the plains, dot the surface of the snow. At first they look dead, but as the sun warms them they spring to life and crawl around.

At about 20,500 feet on the morning of 26 June we meet Alan, Andy, Roger, and Jean, returning from their successful ascent of the previous day. They look tired, almost aged.

"Well done," Pete says to Andy and Alan, who reach us first and describe their windless summit day.

"It's no punter's peak up there," Alan says. "The summit ridge is at 26,000 feet and is bloody long. Technical too. Andy felt sick all the way along the ridge. And Roger nearly bought it on the descent—he tried to glissade down from the col, got out of control, lost his ice-axe, and went sliding down. By a miracle he stopped in some soft snow."

Andy considers us wearily. "Now I know what they mean when people say '8,000 metres.' " And down they go, sucking at the atmosphere that grew thicker with each step.

From our position on the spur, we can see the jet-black Central and Main summits far above. To the north is K2. To our left, the 300-foot-tall ice cliffs at the foot of the West Face's great snow terrace, above which our route will skirt, appear to threaten our path. This is, however, an optical illusion, for the cliffs are far to the side. Even so, whenever there is a crack and rumble of falling ice we look up in alarm.

At about 21,600 feet Pete stops and points ahead. "Hey—I see numbers!"

"What? You're hallucinating!"

"No. Look—on the side of the Central Peak—three numbers—666."

I scan the wall and just as I feel certain that Pete is succumbing to hypoxia I too see a chance play of sunlight on white snow and black rock that bears a perfect resemblance to three sixes.

"Looks as though Crowley left his mark here too," says Pete, referring to Aleister Crowley, the Irish mountaineer and Satanist who'd been on the flanks of K2 in 1902.

Crowley believed that the number 666 had magical powers. On K2's Northeast Ridge his party had reached 20,000 feet with a contingent of Balti porters but steep ice had halted them. Disappointed at the decision to retreat Crowley, who referred to himself as "The Great Beast," got into a violent quarrel with his partner, Guy Knowles, and threatened him with a revolver that he pulled from his pack. A fight ensued that almost dragged the two men over the precipice until Knowles wrested the weapon from Crowley. Seventy-six years later, a strong American expedition climbed the Northeast Ridge, shortly after a Polish team had pioneered the route to over 8,000 metres.

We reach Camp Two at 21,998 feet, late that morning, just as the heat becomes stifling and the snow turns to mush. Here stands another tent left in place by the Polish women. We slip into it and begin to melt snow to fend off dehydration. Doug and Steve reach us in the early afternoon and pitch a tent nearby while we begin to sleep off our long night-shift.

The next morning, 27 June, is again clear. We climb a long, low-angled spur of snow and ice until noon, when at 22,802 feet we find a third ragged and fluttering Polish tent. Here, we all rest and brew up for an hour. Wind cuts fiercely across the slope and rams into the tent's nylon walls. As we set off again Don and Gohar arrive. Don moves in spritely fashion for all his 50 years. These two decide to bivvy here, while Doug, Steve, Pete, and I set off to camp higher. We agree that while we go to the summit the next day, Don and Gohar will move up and occupy our high camp for their own summit bid the following day.

"Better keep climbing if we're going to make it up this hill," Doug says, and we set off.

As we gain elevation K2 disappears behind Broad Peak's squarish Central Summit. Occasional clouds now wander across our path, engulfing us and creating eerie contrasts of diffuse light over the stark neutrals of white snow and black rock. We spread out over the slope, carving a diagonal route upwards, Doug striding powerfully in front, then Steve, me, and finally Pete. At 3:00 pm, at the site of Alan's and Andy's bivouac, we pause for another brew. Their snow cave resembles less a cave than a rabbit hole. Steve checks the altimeter.

"24,300 feet," he announces. It is the highest Steve and I have ever been, short of flying.

We set off again, trudging and gasping at the altitude until twilight begins to darken the mountain. At 24,500 feet, near a jumble of 100-foot-tall seracs, I clear a platform to place our tent, light the stove to melt a pan of snow, and await Pete. Doug and Steve climb through the serac and bivvy 300 feet above. Twenty minutes pass. Pete approaches slowly, coughing raucously.

"Hurry up Pete—you've got the tent!" I call, feeling the cold night bite into my fingers and toes. He staggers up to me, panting at the unsubstantial air, then dumps his pack, and sits on it. I hand him a hot brew. He guzzles it and quickly revives.

"How are you feeling?" I ask.

"Just tired. I'll be better with a rest."

It is late into the night before we finish melting snow for drink. Even then we feel we could have consumed a gallon more. Our stomachs feel queasy with altitude. Out of the sweets, chocolate, Grain Bars and tinned fish we carry, it is a salty can of sardines that sates us most; with the huge fluid loss through breathing and exertion at altitude our body salts are dropping low. Pete's cough disappears as he rehydrates, then sleep descends on us. I begin to realize the deficit in sleep we have amassed by climbing around the clock for so many hours and by pushing ourselves up the mountain so late into the day.

During that night the altitude creeps into our heads. By morning it is bashing away from inside our skulls. Waking is a long and difficult process, cloudy and drug-like. The crack of wind on the tent walls and the crinkle of our frost-covered Gore-Tex sleeping bags are soon accompanied by the hiss of the stove. While I melt snow I hear Pete mumbling in his sleep, in between the sporadic gasping of Cheynes-Stokes breathing.

"What about this rope then?" he asks.

"Rope? Our rope is in the pack."

"Noooo, not that rope," he chides.

"Then what rope?"

"The rope we're all tied into."

"We're not tied in Pete, we're in the tent, Camp Four, Broad Peak."

"Noooo, you don't understand," and I began to feel like a thick-headed schoolboy giving all the wrong answers. I plied him for more clues to his sleepy riddle and got this:

"It's the rope that all of us are tied to."

"Fixed rope?"

"Noooo," he whined.

"Umbilical cord?" Any wild guess now.

"Noooo!"

"Then you must be speaking of a metaphysical rope eh, one that everyone is tied to but no one is tied to?" But before I can get an answer the smell of sweet tea wakes him. "How is your head?" I ask, as I try to force some hot oatmeal down my throat.

"Terrible." Both of us squint from the pounding pain in our temples.

"Mine too. Maybe we should go down."

"No. Mornings are always the worst. We're nearly there. Give me some aspirin. We'll be OK"

We quaff down three aspirin each and set off, carrying nothing in our packs but a stove. The steep ice of the serac gets our blood flowing and clears our heads. As I pull onto the slope above the serac I see Doug and Steve stomping out the last few feet of the final chute to the col. Following their tracks I enter the steep chute two hours later, wade through soft snow, and arrive at the 25,591-foot col. Here, on Broad Peak's first ascent in 1957, Buhl had almost given up, slumping in the snow until his doggedness and Diemberger's enthusiasm had urged him onto his feet and on to the summit. A strong wind gusts from the north, splashing spindrift over the summit ridge. Ahead, the prow-like summit juts toward Sinkiang China. Beneath me, in Sinkiang, lie the North Gasherbrum Glacier, and deep within a fold of valley, the Shaksgam River. China's rust-coloured landscape contrasts sharply with the blinding white of the Godwin-Austen Glacier and the peaks of the Karakoram.

Pete labours up to me via the chute the Austrians in '57 had found to be verglassed, the Poles in '75 a bed of ice, and we in '83 a ribbon of steep snow. While awaiting Pete I'd fallen asleep long enough for the lump of ice I'd dumped in the pan to melt and boil. As I make a brew, Doug and Steve wave from their position on the ridge a few hundred feet away. We signal back. All is well, the summit a few hours away, and within sight. The sky is intensely clear all across Baltistan. Nanga Parbat, 150 miles away, stands on the southwest horizon. Straddling the border of Pakistan and China, as Broad Peak itself does, lies the pyramidal Gasherbrum IV, immediately to our south, and visible to the left of Broad Peak's Main Summit. Gasherbrum IV is an impressive sight, with its unclimbed Northwest Ridge directly before us and the Northeast Ridge of the first ascent on the left. I recall that an American team is working on the Northwest Ridge and wonder if they are gasping away somewhere on the final rocky headwall capping the mountain.

"That's a beautiful mountain down there," Pete remarks of Gasherbrum IV. "We ought to give that Northwest Ridge a shot next season, if it isn't climbed this year."

I agree and we set off along Broad Peak's mile-long summit ridge at ten o'clock.

Along the summit ridge lies the most technical climbing yet; short steps of compact snow interspersed with rock outcrops. We rope up and move together, pausing to belay over tricky sections. The first difficulties of the ridge lie in skirting a large limestone block, across which an old piece of bleached rope is strung, knotted to a rusting piton. As I lead across, in crampons, mitts, and down suit, I squint at the rock and check my eyes to be sure I'm not hallucinating, for the rock over which I climb is pitted with the fossils of sea-shells. Eons ago, this piece of the earth lay on the ocean floor; now it stands at 8,000 metres.

As we near the summit the strain of altitude grows. Each step becomes increasingly harsh. When we pass through the door of 8,000 metres and enter the region climbers call the "death zone," disorientation and fatigue take an exponential leap. At perhaps one o'clock Doug and Steve pass us on their return from the summit.

"We summited at 11:30 am. It's even windier and colder up there," Doug says, shouting above the wind. Plumes of spindrift curl over the ridge ahead.

"How far away?" I ask.

"An hour."

"Doug, let's go. I can't feel my feet," shouts Steve.

Doug yells into my ear: "We'll get as far down the mountain tonight as we can. Good luck, kid." They move off, their steps jerky and tired. Pete and I are now as alone as we will ever be.

Moving at 8,000 metres is like wading through treacle. I gradually become aware of a peculiar sense of disassociation with myself, as if a part of me is external to my body, yet is looking on. I feel this most when setting up boot-axe belays or making difficult moves, a strong feeling as if someone is peering over my shoulder keeping an eye on me, or even as if I have a second invisible head on my shoulders.

We traverse for another half-hour to the False Summit, an icy, corniced dome at 26,382 feet. There we sit, looking toward the tantalizingly close Main Summit. By now those sensations of disassociation are punctuated by feelings of total absence: momentary blackouts, when neither I nor the guy over my shoulder seem to be around. I emerge from these absences a few paces from where they struck me, leading to a concern over stepping off the narrow ridge. "Like a dream," I mutter to Pete, but the wind snatches my words away before he hears them.

I look ahead: The corniced ridge dips down and curves left in a final long, easy slope to the summit, only 18 feet higher than our position. We are nearly there, 30 minutes away. But my fears about what is happening to me double. A vicious headache rings in my ears and pounds at my temples, and a tingling in my arms grows so intense that my fingers curl into a tight fist, making it hard to grip my ice axe. My last shred of rational consciousness raises a cry of concern over the possibility of a stroke, or cerebral edema. But to articulate this to Pete is difficult, as speech and thought seem to have no link in my mind. Exhaustion I can understand, and given that alone I might have crawled to the summit, but something alien is going on within me and I am not prepared to push my luck with it. I get it out that I want down. Pete kneels beside me and gazes at the summit, so near yet so far.

"Go down? But we're so close! Just half an hour!"

The idea of turning away from success when it is so close is maddening to me too, and Pete's ever present determination nearly gets me going. I try to ascertain whether the sensations I feel are imaginary, or are really the beginning of some short circuiting of my body chemistry. There is a state of mind that sometimes infests climbers in which the end result achieves a significance beyond anything that the future may hold. For a few minutes or hours one casts aside all that has been previously held as worth living for, and focuses on one risky move or stretch of ground that becomes the only thing that has ever mattered. This state of mind is what is both fantastic and reckless about the game. Since everything is at stake in these moments, one had better be sure to recognize them and have no illusions about what lies on the other side of luck. It is one of those times. I have to weigh up what is important and what is most important.

"It'd be nice to reach the top, you and I," Pete says. And so it would, to stand up there with this man who had become such a strong friend in such a short time.

"Didn't you say that summits are important?" he adds. Those are my words he is throwing back at me, shouting above the wind and his own breathlessness, harking back to my determination of a few weeks before that we should succeed on Lobsang Spire. I struggle to compose an intelligible sentence.

"Only important when you're in control . . . Lost control . . . Too high, too fast. You go on. I'll wait below."

"No—we stay together," he replies.

Strain is written on Pete's face as much as mine. In 60 hours we'd climbed from 15,500 feet to over 26,000 feet. We had found our limits. The decision to descend comes without a word. We just get up and begin the long path down, seeing that those red hills in China are now covered in cotton wool clouds, encircling K2 and lapping at Broad Peak's East Face.

A few hundred feet from our high point I feel a sensation like a light blank out in my brain. I have just enough time to kneel down before I slump backwards onto a patch of snow, then black out into a half-world of semi-consciousness and inaction. . . .

"So this is it," I think with a strangely detached curiosity as the day turns pitch; "this is where the plunge into senselessness and apathy begins, where the shades of death descend." Yet at the same time I am conscious of my swaying head and my incoherent mumbling. I think of Salley, whom I have no right to inflict such folly upon. "Get up you idiot, get up," I keep telling myself, until vision gradually returns. How long had I been out? I cannot tell.

Next to me sits Pete, observing my state as a good doctor should. He wears a white lab coat with a stethoscope draped around his neck; I double-check; nonsense. He is wearing his red high-altitude suit. I am beginning to imagine things. A minute later I regain control of myself, as suddenly as I'd lost it. Pete puts a brew of hot grape drink in my hands. As soon as I drink the liquid I throw it up.

"See . . . told you I was sick." The purple stain in the snow forms intricate arabesque designs that grow onto the snow crystals glinting in the afternoon light. I could have watched these hallucinations all day, but Pete urges us onto our feet. Rapidly I begin to improve. My strength and mental faculties return. I'd made it back through the 8,000 metre door before it slammed shut and locked me in. But I'd cut it close.

In the warm glow of evening I take Pete's photo as we reach the col:
The summit stands behind him. Had we made the right decision?
Should we go on? Would we have the strength to return later? I feel
remorse at having let Pete down, but then the tables suddenly turn:
Pete appears over a crest on the col, lagging on the end of the rope. He
takes short steps and looks stressed.

"I can't breathe properly," he says in a whisper. "It feels as if my
diaphragm has collapsed."

A bolt of fear runs up my spine.

"Are my lips blue?" he asks.

"Yes," I say, noting the indication of oxygen starvation.

We stare at each other.

"We'll get down," I blurt out, and we turn and crunch tracks to the
edge of the wind-blown col. Things were wrong, very wrong. We had to
shed altitude, and fast, but a snail's pace was the best Pete could manage
in this thin soup of air. We reach the steep chute that we'd climbed to
reach the col. The hour is late, about 7:00 pm, but we seem outside of
time: we are simply there. I wrap a sling around a spike, double our
short rope, and I abseil 60 feet to the start of the snowfield. Pete follows.

On the snowfield wind and driving snow had covered all sign of our
tracks. "I'll go ahead and break trail. Follow as fast as you can," I say and
Pete nods in response. Dragging the rope behind me I begin loping
down the slope. After 300 feet I turn to see that Pete has barely moved.

"Pete!"

No answer.

By the time I fight my way back through the soft snow the last gleam
of twilight peters out in the sky and night is upon us. Where had the
hours gone? Pete has his headlamp on. It shines out to the windy
night. He doesn't speak. When I turn toward the glacier I see a pinpoint
of light shining up from base camp, 11,000 feet below. It's Beth, his
girlfriend far below, giving the eight o'clock signal as arranged, and
Pete is returning it.

Conversation is superfluous. We know we're going to be on the
move all night, very high, and in rising wind and storm. Already,

clouds are blocking out the stars. I tie the rope to Pete's harness and begin belaying him down, length after length, till his strength begins to ebb. Then I talk him down, ordering and cajoling every step out of him. At about 10:00 pm he collapses in the snow and whispers he can no longer see. So I guide him by direction, telling him to traverse 45-degrees right, or straight down. Even on the easiest ground he has to face in. Without tracks it's all instinct anyway. And all the time wind and spindrift swirl across the slope, and the bastard moon shines everywhere but on the upper slopes of Broad Peak. There is no time to think of what might happen to us, but only that we must move down, move down, move down.

The hours melt into a pastiche of endless, dreamlike movement. Pete becomes too weak to walk, so somehow I support him, dragging him, lowering him, whatever it takes to move. The sensation of being outside of myself is more prevalent than ever. My watcher checks my every move and decision. I keep turning around, expecting to see some-one. As I mechanically work toward getting us down, part of my mind begins to wander. I find myself thinking of that first ascent of the Central Summit, by the Poles. The account I'd read called their stormy descent a "struggle for survival." Accompanying the story was a photo of Broad Peak, littered with crosses where the climbers had perished. Those crosses were now underfoot, and the ghosts of history were hid-ing in the shadows. I find that agnostics also pray.

The slope steepens, indicating that somewhere nearby is the band of ice cliffs we'd climbed that morning. We need to find the low spot in them by which we'd ascended, but where that was was anyone's guess. We link arms and shuffle towards what I hope was our earlier position. The wind howls and Pete inches around uncertainly.

"If only I could see . . ."

"I'm your eyes, Pete—move right ten steps!"

And he does.

It soon becomes too steep to blunder about as we are, so I begin making 20-foot leads, shoving my axe into the soft snow and belaying Pete in to me. At the last belay he lets go of everything and swings

down to the edge of the ice cliff. The shaft of my axe droops alarmingly. I lose my cool and yell a mouthful of curses at him as I haul him
back up.

"Sorry," he whispers calmly. Throughout the ordeal he had remained
composed, conserving his energy for matters of survival, rather than letting fear take hold. I clip him to his axe and wrap his arms around it.

"Just don't lose it now, brother. Please."

The wind attacks with unprecedented malice. Waves of spindrift hiss
down around us, burning our faces. If my back-tracking is correct, then
somewhere in the darkness at the bottom of the ice cliff is our tent,
and if things have gone as planned, Don and Gohar are in it. I call till
my throat is raw, then shove my ice-axe in to the hilt, from which to
lower Pete. Confusion reigns in the seconds it takes to lower him, he
is so disoriented that he cannot tell whether he is at the bottom of the
cliff or not, I am blinded by spindrift, and feel the axe shifting out of
the snow. I wrap the rope around my arm to distribute some of the
weight while holding the axe in with my knee. Pete gasps in distress as
the rope pinches his waist.

"Are you down?"

"Can't . . . tell."

"For God's sake, you gotta be down!"

He comes to a stop and digs his hands into the snow. I abseil off my
second short tool, moving quickly before it slides out. At the bottom
of the serac we again link arms to negotiate some broken ground. I
glance about, searching with my headlamp for a familiar lump of ice
to tell me that we have descended the ice cliffs in the right spot. Then,
suddenly, a light appears, illuminating the form of a tent.

"We've got a sick man here, Don," I call to the light. Pete crawls a
few feet along a crest of snow then stops completely. A bobbing headlamp approaches. It is Gohar, himself groggy, woken from a deep sleep.
I lie on my back, sit Pete on my shoulders, and slide us down the last
60 feet to the tent, while Gohar belays us. As Don drags Pete into the
tent it comes around to 2:00 am. We have been moving for 22 hours.

In the quiet of the tent we lie, all crammed in together, rubbing each other's limbs and melting snow to get vital fluids back into us. Feeling takes a long time to return to my hands and feet, and Pete's are ice cold, yet remarkably, not frostbitten. Warm liquid perks him up.

"How are you, Gregor?" Pete asks with a hopeful spark in his voice.

"Done in. Rest a couple of hours till dawn, then we'll head on down."

"I'll watch him, lad," Don says.

I stagger out to repitch our tent, the tent that Pete and I had collapsed and weighted with snow blocks that morning so it wouldn't blow away. It is filled with snow and the foam pads are gone. I throw the rope down for insulation and crawl into my sleeping bag. It seems that a million years have passed since we set out. We've gone beyond mental and physical barriers that we didn't even know existed within us. We'd become a single entity, fighting to survive. Nothing could stop us from getting down now. In a couple of days this would be just an experience we would have shared to become closer. All the bullshit of ethics, ego, competition, and the glamour of big summits have been scraped aside to reveal that in the end everything boils down to one thing—life! My eyelids close under the weight of exhaustion and I dream of grassy places.

But those words of Pete's were the last we ever share. Two hours later, at dawn on 29 June, he awoke to ask Gohar for water. Gohar pressed a cup of warm liquid to Pete's lips, but Pete didn't drink from it. Don and Gohar looked at each other for a few seconds then called me. I awoke with a throbbing headache. "Dead," they were saying. But that was impossible! We'd made it through that hellish descent! We were going to make it down! Then sense prevailed like a sledge-hammer. I rushed into the tent and tried to force life into him, through his mouth, with mine, forcing my own thin, tired air into him. His lungs gurgled loudly, saturated with the fluid of pulmonary edema. I tore his jacket open and rhythmically pounded my palms against his chest to squeeze a beat from his heart, but he would have none of it. He would only lie there with an expression of sublime rest on his face, as if dreaming the same grassy dream I had dreamed.

We sat in silence, our heads full of sad thoughts, our eyes registering that the unthinkable had happened. Don lay back on one elbow, looking at Pete.

"It's always the good blokes that go," Don said.

Suddenly I hated this mountain and its heartless geology. What about the people at home and below who loved Pete, what about them? Tears filled my eyes. Outside, the Karakoram was ablaze with a clear and calm light.

"Notice that the wind has suddenly dropped?" asked Don. "Not a breath. It's always the same when death is about, always a lot of noise and wind, but as soon as it gets what it's after it quietens down. I've seen it before and it's always the same."

I'm still thinking about that, still wondering.

The wind returned a few minutes later, stronger than before, and threatened to tear the tent apart with its claws, like an evil predator, now searching for us. I sat staring at Pete. He couldn't be dead. I wouldn't accept it. But he had gone and I knew it. I closed his partially opened eyelids with my hand and wrapped his sleeping bag around him. Gohar clenched my arm. "Greg Sahib, we must go," he said with a look of natural fear. I looked around thinking there must be something we should do—a place to bury him—some words—or get him down the mountain for . . . for what?

"We've got to see to ourselves now," said Don sternly. "You're in a terrible state, youth."

One last glance at Pete. Gohar's lips moved as he softly spoke a prayer in Urdu, then we bade our friend farewell. I crawled out of the tent, zipped it shut, turned into the maelstrom of blowing snow, and started down. We left everything as it was. Gear lay strewn about, none of it possessed of value any longer. It was a long descent, with every step full of a great sense of loss and perhaps a strange feeling of guilt at having to leave our friend as we did. But the snow would soon settle over him and set firm as earth. The snow-field would inch inexorably to the icecliffs and peel away in bursts of avalanche to the glacier, which would carry him within it to the fast-flowing Braldu. His journey would outlive us and no ashes could be scattered more thoroughly, nor a monument exist more lasting than Broad Peak.

Weary legs took us down to the Polish tent at 23,000 feet by late morning. Doug and Steve, two specks 3,000 feet below, moved down ahead of us. We tumbled into the tent, laying about.

"I thought he'd make it," I said for the tenth time.

"No. I could tell the moment I laid eyes on him that he was bad," said Don. I kept thinking of what death meant, of how none of us would ever know Pete again. Then there were voices outside the tent. A party of Swiss, heading up, appeared and greeted us happily. I formed words to explain the tragedy, but somehow words had no feeling, no reality. One of the Swiss looked at us with pity. "Yes, I was on Everest last year and lost a member. We also had to leave him on the mountain . . ." By God, that's not a member who has died, that's a man, a friend. I cursed his practicality, but what could he say?

The Swiss had a radio. They called their base camp and carried the message to ours. In a few hours Doug, himself just off the mountain, would break the news to Beth and she would burst into tears. Then the Polish women arrived. I told them too, but the news didn't seem to sink in. They could only complain that Don had accidentally taken one of their stoves from Camp One and when he'd realized his mistake had left it in Camp Two. They harped about this, while I mouthed words to try and make them see exactly what had happened above.

"But don't you think it's important that there be a stove in every camp?" one of them asked rhetorically. I tossed them our stove and set off down the mountain. Words. They had meaning no longer. No one really understands what we've been telling them. No one is thinking correctly. Nothing is the same up here. It's the thin air.

On 30 June we trace our way down the final narrow couloir of the mountain. Slipping clumsily with snow balling up under our feet, we see four figures on the glacier below. Andy, Alan, Roger, and Nebi look up and count four figures descending—we have been joined by one of the Swiss—and hope beyond hope that a mistake has been made and we are all coming down alive. I lope through soft snow across the final stretch, sinking up to my thigh with each step.

It is Alan who comes forward to meet me halfway. We look at each other, point-blank. Our gazes penetrate more than flesh and blood.

"Then you know . . . ," I say.

"Yeah. Pete is dead."

I throw my axe on the scree. I can no longer contain myself. Roger supports me and holds me tightly. "It's not worth it, it's not bloody worth it," I say.

"No. It's not," Roger answers . . .

As the afternoon fell on that last day of June we looked into one another's eyes and for the first time knew each other. I had learned the real rule of this beautiful, reckless, terrible game, the only rule: The mountains are beautiful but they are not worth dying for.

from Everest: Alone at the Summit
by Stephen Venables

Stephen Venables (b. 1954), one of England's most distinguished climbers, has written five books. In 1988, he and three Americans set out to climb Everest's formidable Kangshung Face. Venables arrived alone at the summit after a 16-hour climb from his top camp. Every mountaineer knows that the descent can be the crux of a climb, and so it was for Venables on this occasion.

allowed myself ten minutes on the summit. Now, writing three months later, I find it almost impossible to recall the emotions of those precious moments. Even at the time, I found it hard to know exactly what I was feeling. There was a dreamlike sense of disbelief at being in this special place, sitting so utterly alone beside the three yellow French oxygen cylinders which the Asian expedition had left upright in the snow. The empty cylinders were labelled CNJ for China-Nepal-Japan and were decorated with the prayer flags that I had mistaken for hats. The cylinders and bits of discarded radio equipment were the only signs that people had ever been here. When I could find the strength to stand up again I looked down the West Ridge, which disappeared into swirling clouds. There was no sign of the British Services Expedition. Then I turned to the right, where the Northeast Ridge—the "Mallory Route"—also dropped away into the clouds. I could not see the Rongbuk Glacier, nor the Kama valley and to the south there were yet more clouds, completely hiding Lhotse from view. It was like being alone on the apex of some huge grey roof. At this point on the ridge the ground drops away slightly to the giant cornices overhanging the Kang-shung Face, so that one can keep well clear of danger, yet stand right on the crest of the ridge, on a real unequivocal summit.

I had work to do. First I had to photograph myself. I took off the camera belt, removed the big camera, cocked the self-timer, and, gasping with the effort, knelt down to prop it on its case about three metres from the summit. I was too tired to lie right down and frame the picture in the viewfinder, so I just put the zoom on wide-angle and pointed it in the general direction of the summit. Then, as the self-timer whirred, I stepped back up and sat by the ornamental oxygen bottles. I thought that I heard the shutter click. I knew that I should take more frames, bracketing the exposures for safety, but I did not have the mental or physical energy to reset the camera.

Robert had the summit flags and trinkets from Norbu, but there was one small ritual for me to carry out. I reached into one of my inside pockets and pulled out a tiny polythene bag. Inside it were the two miniature envelopes given to me in Bombay by Nawang and Sonam. I carefully took out the flower petals and scattered them in the snow, then placed the two envelopes beside the oxygen bottles. Then, panting with the effort of concentration, I took two pictures on the compact camera.

The film in the SLR with the self-portrait was either not wound on properly or was lost on the journey home, for I was never to see the photo of myself on the summit. However, I do have a picture showing the little envelopes. Each envelope is decorated with the face of one of the teachers at Geeta's ashram in Pondicherri, staring up from amongst the radio boxes, yellow cylinders and wisps of prayer flag on the summit of Everest.

I rested again, slumped in the snow. The air temperature in this second week of May had been getting steadily warmer and even at 8,848 metres there was still very little wind. I felt comfortable and I was almost tempted to linger, for I was aware that this was a terribly important event in my life and I wanted to savour that precious moment, storing away what memories I could in my feeble oxygen-starved brain. It would be nice to say that it was the happiest moment of my life and that I was overwhelmed by euphoria, but that would be a gross exaggeration, for at the time there was only a rather dazed feeling of—"Isn't this strange? You really have done it, after all those weeks of watching and waiting and worrying. It would have been better if everyone had made it but at least someone has actually reached the summit—and a rather special summit. . . . So this is what it's like."

It was a turning point. Even in my befuddled state I knew that this would inevitably alter my life. But I also knew that it was far more urgently critical as a turning point in the climb, the point where I no longer had to struggle upwards but had to start down immediately fleeing from this bewitching dreamlike place and hurrying back down to Earth before it was too late. It was now 3:50 pm, Nepalese time. I was just ahead of schedule, but the clouds were closing in fast and in three hours it would be dark. I stood up, took the ice axe in my mittened hand, had one last look down Mallory's ridge, then hurried away back south.

After descending a short way I stopped for my final summit task. Just below the top there was an exposed outcrop of shattered rock where I knelt down to collect some pieces of limestone and stuff them in a pocket.

The wind was mounting now, starting to blow spindrift in my face. I hurried on, using gravity to speed myself back towards the Hillary Step. As I came over the last hump the clouds enveloped me completely. Suddenly I realised that I was heading too far to the right, down towards the Southwest Face. I headed back up to the left, peering through my iced-up sunglasses at the swirling greyness. I was utterly alone in the cloud and there was no sign of the South Summit. I felt disorientated and frightened, remembering the tragedy of 1975 when Mick Burke, the last person to complete the Southwest Face, went alone to the summit and never came back. Somewhere up here, in conditions like this, blinded behind iced glasses, even more myopic than me, he had made an unlucky mistake, probably falling through one of those fragile cornices overhanging the Kangshung Face. I suddenly noticed the dim outline of one of those bulbous overhangs just in front of me and veered back right. For God's sake don't do a Mick Burke. Just concentrate. You've gone too far left now. Head for that rock—must be solid ground there. Now I could pick out some tracks—my tracks almost filled with spindrift already, but tracks nonetheless. This is right. But it's so difficult. Must have a rest. I sank down and sat in the snow. Then I continued wearily, too slowly, legs sagging, head bowed. I stopped after only a few paces but forced myself not to sit down, leaning instead on my ice axe. Then I took a few steps again, willing my legs not to sag and crumple.

It was snowing now, stinging my face and encrusting my glasses. I had to wipe them with a clumsy mitten, clearing a hole to peer through, searching for landmarks. I recognised clumps of rock and followed them to the pinnacle above the Hillary Step. Then came the hard part, taking off mittens, pulling up some slack in the fixed rope and clipping it into my waist belt carabiner with an Italian hitch. I pulled mittens back on and started to abseil down the cliff. Even though I was moving downhill it was exhausting. Possibly the waist belt was pulling up and constricting my diaphragm, for I had to slump and rest during the 20-metre abseil, gasping for breath. I continued in a frantic blind struggle to the bottom of the Step where I fell over and collapsed on the side of the ridge, hyperventilating furiously.

It had never happened before and I was terrified. This was quite new—this ultra-rapid panting, like a fish out of water incapable of getting oxygen into its gills. I panted harder and harder, clutching at the air, frantic to refill my lungs. But nothing seemed to get beyond my throat and for a ghastly moment I thought that I was going to suffocate. Then the air started to get through, and I gasped great sobs of relief as my breathing slowed to normal again.

I had to move. Get off that rope and continue. Take mittens off and unclip from the rope. Now, quickly get those mittens back on again. The first one is always easy but the second one won't go. I can't grip it— can't make those useless numb fingers work. It's all too difficult, I'll

never get it on and my fingers will freeze solid. No more piano playing. But I must get that mitten on or I'll never get down. Concentrate.
That's it, ease it up the wrist.

I slumped over again, gasping with exhaustion. The wind was fling-
ing snow at me and I was starting to shiver. I was completely blind and
tore at my sunglasses, letting them hang down round my neck by their
safety leash. At least I could see a little now, only blurred shapes, but
better than nothing. There's a bit of a clearing. That's the South Summit up there on the far side of the bridge. No sign of Robert or Ed.
They must have gone down by now. Crazy to continue to the top in
these conditions and no reason to wait for me. There's no-one to help
me. Either I get myself down or I die. It would be so easy to die—just
lie down here and rest and soon the wind would kill me. It would be
the easiest thing in the world but I'd look so bloody silly. No use to
anyone climbing Everest then lying down to die. No, pull yourself
together and move. It's not possible to get out the other pair of glasses
without taking off mittens again, so we'll just have to move very carefully on half vision.

My invisible companion, the old man, had reappeared and together
we moved forward, determined not to die. We stumbled half-blind
along the ridge, crouched over the ice axe, peering anxiously through
the driving snow, almost on all fours, laboriously dragging ourselves
across the rocks, clinging carefully to avoid the death slide down the
Southwest Face. Fear and instinct kept me moving over the rocks. Then
I recognised the dry hollow by the overhanging rock where Boardman
and Pertemba had waited in vain for Mick Burke to return. I wondered
briefly whether I should bivouac there, but decided to continue, determined to get right back across the bridge to the South Summit. That was
the critical point beyond which I was confident that I could survive.

The visibility was still atrocious and I strayed too close to the crest
on the left. Suddenly my left leg shot down into a hole and I collapsed
in another fit of hyperventilation. I may have trodden on the cornice
fracture line, but I think it was just a deep snowdrift. Whatever it was,
the jolt almost suffocated me; but I regained my breath and forced

myself on up the 15-metre climb to the South Summit. I collapsed again and this time, as I regained my breath in great anguished gasps, I was filled with pity for the poor old man who was finding it all a bit too much.

We floundered eventually up to the crest of the South Summit where my mind must have gone almost blank, for I can only recall blurred images of snow and cloud and the gloom of dusk. I can remember nothing of the descent of the knife-edge ridge, I only have the vaguest recollection of slithering back over the bergschrund and then I was back on the big snowslope, sitting down to slide, because it is easier to sit than to stand.

We were racing the darkness, using gravity to hurry down towards the safety of the South Col. But even sliding is hard work, because you have to brace your legs and brake with your ice axe. It was somewhere down here that Peter Habeler, during his phenomenal one-hour descent from the summit to the South Col, spurred on by his fear of permanent brain damage, almost flew out of control down the Kang-shung Face. I was anxious about the big slope below me and kept stopping to walk further right towards the ridge. Then on one slide the old man became very frightened. We were gathering speed in a blinding flurry of powder snow. The surface underneath felt hollow and unstable and seemed to be breaking off in avalanches. We were sliding faster and faster down to the east and the old man was hating it. He had suddenly become a musician. Musicians hate this. The composer is sliding on his cello, riding the avalanche to his death. Please stop! Now!

I dug my heels in and leant over hard on my ice axe, dragging the ferrule deep into the snow, and came to a halt. We were about to collapse and had to rest as soon as possible, but we could not sit down here. Too steep and insecure. Quick, cut a ledge. Ice axe and burrowing hand—that's it. Quick. Just enough of a hollow to sit down. Must rest. Must have a pee. The old man says do it in your pants—it'll keep you warm.

I could wait no longer and with one last frantic effort I plunged the ice axe deep into the snow and used it to heave myself up onto the ledge. Then my strength gave out and I collapsed, wetting myself and suffocating in another fit of hyperventilation.

Poor old man . . . that's better now, he's breathing again. He just needs to rest. What was all that business about music—cello music? What has that got to do with avalanches? Who is this composer? Dvorak wrote a cello concerto. Kate plays the cello—but she's a woman. It's all too confusing. Better to concentrate on reality—on me sitting here on this precarious ledge in the snow. And why did I believe that nonsense about peeing in my pants? All wet now. It must have been the shock.

I was getting chronically exhausted and it was now virtually dark so I decided to stay where I was. I sat there for about an hour, shivering as the cold pressed through from the snow. Then I decided that my precarious perch was too dangerous and that I should try to continue down to the South Col where Ed and Robert would be waiting in the tents. I lowered myself to my feet, faced into the slope and started kicking steps carefully across the snow, back towards the crest of the ridge. There I tried to orientate myself, climbing backwards and forwards over the rocks, trying to recognise individual outcrops from the morning. But it was dark, there was no moon and, although the afternoon storm had blown over, there were still drifting clouds to confuse my vision. Even after putting on glasses and switching on my headtorch, I found it very difficult to judge shapes and distances. I started to worry that perhaps my glissade had taken me lower than I thought and that I was now below the point where I had to turn right into the couloir.

After about half an hour of wandering about, the old man suggested that we should stop here for the night and wait for daylight to re-orientate ourselves. I decided that he would be warmest sitting on a rock and soon I found a ledge on the ridge where we could sit down. But it was precarious and sloping and we both longed to lean back properly, so we traversed back out onto the snow and dug a horizontal ledge where we could lie down properly. At about 9 pm we settled down for the night.

The emergency bivouac had many precedents. During the American traverse of Everest in 1963 Willi Unsoeld and Tom Hornbein completed the first ascent of the West Ridge, reaching the summit just before dark at 6:15. Two companions had reached the summit by the normal route the same afternoon and were waiting near the South Summit when Unsoeld and Hornbein started to descend the Southeast Ridge. When they met, Hornbein tried to persuade the other three to continue down to the top camp but they soon became lost in the dark and had to resign themselves to a night out in the open at about 8,500 metres. They survived the intense cold and descended safely the next day, but afterwards Unsoeld had to have nine frostbitten toes amputated and one of the Southeast Ridge duo, Barry Bishop, lost all his toes.

In 1976 two British soldiers, Bronco Lane and Brummie Stokes, were also forced to bivouac on the same slope just below the South Summit, descending in bad weather. Twelve years later in Kathmandu, Stokes was to show me his mutilated toeless feet. Lane had to have fingers as well as toes amputated, but at least both of them were alive, unlike the German climber, Hannelore Schmatz, who in 1979 insisted on stopping to bivouac before dark, even though her Sherpas were urging her to carry on down to the safety of their top camp. She died sitting in the snow and for several years her frozen body was a grisly landmark on the Southeast ridge, until it was recently buried or swept away by an avalanche. I also knew about the Bulgarian climber who had died whilst descending the difficult West Ridge in 1984. Meena Agrawal, who had been doctor to another Everest expedition that year, had later told me how she had talked to the Bulgarian on the radio, trying to comfort him and persuade him to live through the night; but eventually the man had been unable to hold up the receiver any longer and had presumably died soon afterwards.

I had no intention of dying that night. I was alone just above 8,500 metres (about 28,000 feet) but the wind which had frightened me so much by the Hillary Step had now died away and the air temperature was probably not much lower than minus 20 degrees centigrade. I was lucky with the conditions and I knew that I could survive in the excellent clothes I wore, but I had to resign myself to the probable loss of toes. Six months earlier, caught out high on Shisha Pangma, Luke and I had dug a snowhole and crawled inside to take off boots and warm each other's toes. But now I was nearly a thousand metres higher, I was alone and I barely had the strength to cut a ledge, let alone a proper cave where I could safely take off boots. I had climbed with the specific intention of not bivouacking, so I had no stove to melt snow. Only a trickle of half-frozen juice remained in my water bottle and in the last 24 hours I had drunk less than a litre. Dehydration was thickening my blood, already viscous with the concentration of red blood cells necessary to survive at altitude, and circulation was sluggish to the remote outposts of the vascular system, particularly my toes.

If the weather had been worse, I would probably have found new reserves of strength, either to dig a snowhole or to search harder for the correct descent route. But as the air was calm I lay inert, huddled up in the snow with my spare mittens providing meagre insulation under my hips and my ice axe plunged into the slope in front of me, like a retaining fence post.

I was not really alone. The old man was still with me and now there were other people as well, crowding my tiny ledge. Sometimes they offered to look after parts of my body. At one stage during the long night the old man became rather patronising towards a girl who was keeping one of my hands warm. Perhaps it was then that Eric Shipton, the distinguished explorer so closely involved with the history of Everest, took over warming my hands. At the end of the ledge my feet kept nearly falling off where I had failed to dig a thorough hollow in the snow. I was aware of several people crowding out the feet, but also trying to look after them. They were being organised by Mike Scott.

I had never met Mike Scott but I knew his father, Doug, who had bivouacked even higher than this, right up on the South Summit in 1975. He and Dougal Haston had been half-prepared for an emergency bivouac, carrying a tent sack and a stove. When they emerged from the Southwest Face late in the day, they had started digging a cave and had made a hot brew before climbing the final ridge to the sum-

mit. After photographing the magical sunset from the summit they
returned to the snowcave where their oxygen ran out and they settled
down for the highest bivouac ever. Scott had no down gear—only the
tent sack and a rucksack to sit on, yet on that bitterly cold autumn
night he had the strength not only to survive but to concentrate on
"the quality of survival", warming and talking to his feet throughout
the night. When he and Haston descended to the haven of Camp 6 the
next day, neither of them had any frostbite.

I drifted in and out of reality, occasionally reminding myself that I
was actually alone, before returning to my confused hallucinations.
Towards dawn, as I started to long for warmth, my companions teased
me by announcing that there were some yak herders camping just
round the corner with tents and food and hot fires. They left me alone
with the old man and went to investigate. It was good to be left in
peace for a while and I reminded myself that yak herders could not
possibly be living up here at 8,500 metres; but later the people
returned to tell me that while the insidious cold of the snow had been
creeping through my body they had been enjoying hot baths and food.
Now I longed even more desperately to be warm.

At some stage during the night I stood up to enlarge my ledge. After
that I felt slightly more comfortable and less precarious. Eventually I
think that I must have slept, for I remember an actual awakening and
sudden realisation that the long night was finally over.

I sat up shivering. There was pastel light in the sky and only a soft
blanket of grey cloud remained in the valley far below. All the people,
even the old man, had gone but I had survived my night out. My body
was stiff and my feet were dead, but my fingers were still alive inside
their down mittens. The hairs on my eyebrows, moustache and beard
were stuck together with great lumps of ice and a frozen film encased
my wooden nose. My iced sunglasses still hung useless round my neck,
but my other glasses were clear, so that I could see the route down.

I could not believe that it had all seemed so strange in the dark, now
that I could see the shoulder just below me, with the little dip where
one had to turn right into the couloir. If only I had seen better in the

dark I could perhaps have descended to Camp 3 and saved myself all that shivering!

The sun was rising over Kangchenjunga as I stood up shakily, picked up my ice axe and set off wobbling and sliding down the slope. Soon I was back in the couloir, daring myself to sit down and slide wherever possible. Once I went too fast and gave myself another alarming attack of hyperventilating, but after that I stayed in control. The world was sparkling in morning sunlight and life was wonderful. I was alive and warm again, I had climbed Everest and soon I would be back in the valley.

Suddenly I saw two people in the couloir, down by the Dunlop tent. It took a while for my dulled mind to realise that they must be Ed and Robert, who had also failed to reach the South Col in the dark and had taken shelter in the Asians' abandoned tent. They turned round and saw me sliding towards them and a few minutes later we were reunited. I cannot remember what we said. Only a few words were spoken and they were probably banal; but I remember vividly Ed and Robert's relief at seeing me alive and a deep warmth of friendship as the three of us roped together for the final descent to the South Col.

Dangerous Liaisons
by John Climaco

Foreign climbers who venture to the Himalayas have long depended upon porters and other local inhabitants to help them achieve their goals. Climbers often must accept the supervision of "liaison officers" assigned by the host country's bureaucracy. A liaison officer can make or break a trip, as John Climaco (b. 1968) and a partner learned on a 1995 expedition to Pakistan's 25,112-foot Chogolisa.

The guns pointed at me were not toys and the soldiers holding them, despite their mismatched uniforms, were not clowns. I hadn't expected AK 47s to be the biggest danger on the Baltoro, but then nothing on this expedition happened as I expected. When our liaison officer finished screaming at me and the soldiers finally left, I sat down and held my head in my hands. The expedition had gone down the drain, I was going to jail, and we hadn't even reached basecamp.

Suneeb, one of our porters, sat down next to me. "This liaison officer," he said, "is a crazy man, very bad man." I nodded. "You," he continued in a different tone, "are a good leader for us, care for the Balti people. He has insulted you, so tonight, *Inshallah*, we shall kill him. We will slit his pig throat."

I can pinpoint exactly when the mess that became our expedition to Chogolisa began: October 24, 1993. I was sitting below the west face of Cholatse, having just made the second ascent of that peak's Southwest Ridge. I was feeling pretty good about myself, a little too good in fact. I wished in my journal for a bigger, harder version of what we'd just done, something like Chogolisa.

Eighteen months later Andrew Brash and I were in Rawalpindi sitting face to face with the man who over the next two months would turn my wish into a nightmare: Captain Mohammed Ayub, our liaison officer. Ayub immediately informed me that in Pakistan his army rank meant great status, something I could not possibly have as a civilian. "You," he said with an extravagant wave of his hand, "are nothing here." Captain Ayub had just returned from six months duty on the Siachen Glacier, the front line in the border war with India, the highest battleground in history. It is not what military men consider a choice posting, and I had to wonder privately about Ayub's real status. He made no secret of his displeasure about returning to the "God-forsaken hell of the North," as he called the Karakoram Range.

"Many peoples have died in these snows," he explained while Andrew and I unpacked the $2000 of kit the regulations required we buy for him. "They are having parts of their bodies chopped off due from cold. This, I think should not be happening to me." Reasonable enough. "So these," he continued as he pushed away a pair of brand-new plastic boots, "are substandard. I will not go to the mountains in these. And this," he held aloft a new down jacket, "have you not brought another color? I am captain in Pakistan army. This is not smart looking." Andrew rolled his eyes. Though we'd only known the captain for ten minutes, things already looked bleak. Then, dismissing our carefully thought out schedule, Ayub announced, "We cannot possibly rush up into the mountains tomorrow. I must have perhaps one week to buy the proper equipment, which you will pay for. Then, perhaps, we shall move from this place."

As Ayub stood there with his scrawny arms akimbo, I felt the Italian temper that has caused so much trouble in the past welling up inside me. With a conscious effort of will I controlled a feeling I would come to know well in the weeks ahead: the desire to throttle Captain Ayub.

Instead, I pleaded that the current good weather would enable us to fly to Skardu and thus avoid the death-trap Karakoram Highway. I suggested that the extra cost of the hotel, food, and of course the captain's extra salary during the delay was more than we could afford. "Rule and regulation clearly tell expedition to come prepared to stay in Rawalpindi for two weeks," barked Ayub. "Two weeks! If you have not brought sufficient funds, then the expedition must be canceled immediately." I shut up.

I for one was not spending even one week in the sweltering hell-hole of Rawalpindi and I had only to glance at Andrew's widening eyes to know how he felt about the matter. We mentioned to the captain that we wanted to go to Peshawar and play tourists. He replied that we could not leave the hotel without his permission, and that visiting Peshawar, about four hours west toward the Afghan border, was totally out of the question. Again came the urge to throttle. I said nothing until the next morning when I asked permission to go shopping. After noting his benevolence, Captain Ayub gave his blessing; we promptly left the hotel and went shopping . . . in Peshawar.

Andrew was nervous about Peshawar from the beginning. A worker at the U.S. consulate there had recently been held at gunpoint for an hour in broad daylight and was only saved when her captor, still holding the gun to her head, was shot by a USDEA sniper. In Peshawar, the conduit for weaponry heading to the Afghan freedom fighters, every type of artillery and ammunition known to man is freely available on the streets. I thought it would be exciting, though I had second thoughts as we passed signs at the entrance to the city announcing, "You are now leaving the area where the Government of Pakistan can guarantee your safety."

Smoggy, crowded, and even hotter than Rawalpindi, the city itself turned out to be dull. The taxi ride home was not. Our driver was fluent in English and we took the opportunity to whine about the asshole ruining our trip. "I hate the army, the police, the ISI (Pakistan's KGB)—all of those hooligans," the driver announced. "They killed my brother because he refused to pay their bribes. Would you like to see a photo of him?"

As we pulled into the police checkpoint, and the machine-gun-toting officer approached the car to demand his bribe, the driver handed back a photo. His brother, lying on a steel table, was missing the back half of his head, his eyes and much of his chest. We didn't leave Rawalpindi again.

About a week later Captain Ayub finally exhausted his last excuse to delay us. Of course, the stable high pressure that had been parked over Pakistan since our arrival was also exhausted. As the rain poured down in sheets, flights to Skardu were grounded, which meant only one thing: the Karakoram Highway.

Careening through rain-slick turns 500 feet above the Indus River, I thought over all I'd read about the highway. Some have written it is the most beautiful road in the world, winding as it does past Nanga Parbat. Others have said it's the most exciting, entertaining part of an expedition to Pakistan. Those people are idiots. In many places the "highway" is nothing more than a shelf blasted into the sheer wall of the gorge. More than once a timely deceleration saved us from being crushed under a falling boulder. This I can only attribute to divine intervention, since in his hash-induced trance our driver seemed unable to locate the brake pedal. It appeared at times as though he was trying to physically outrun Death up the highway. I suppose in a race like that, the speed limit is simply as fast as whatever grossly overloaded vehicle you're unlucky enough to be in can go. As it turned out Death must have taken a rest day during our 24-hour heat. Judging by the number of burnt buses scattered below the highway, it was well earned.

Arrival in Skardu was hardly a release from our troubles. On a bed at the K2 motel we spread out what was left of the expedition finances. Thanks in large part to Captain Ayub and his at-our-expense account, our once Himalayan pile of rupees was down to a molehill. We'd been informed that the road to Askole—dubious in the best conditions—had been wiped out in 14 landslides triggered by the continuing rain. With Jeeps trapped between some of the slides, it was conceivable that we could shuttle loads over the debris. We figured we could afford two extra porter stages and still get back from basecamp. The porters, now camped outside the gates of the motel, would be our responsibility as soon as we started walking and we had to pay them every day whether we covered any ground or not.

When to leave Skardu thus became a critical decision. Captain Ayub, interested only in lounging about the motel as long as possible, was of no help. After conferring with Phil Powers, leader of an expedition to Hidden Peak, and Issaq, our cook, we agreed to caravan the two expeditions together and make a dash for Askole the moment the rain stopped.

About the time it seemed we'd be taking an ark to Chogolisa, the rain finally turned to drizzle. Two hours later eight climbers, 90 porters, three cooks, two liaison officers, and 2,250 kilos of stuff were on there way to Askole.

"Have you any dynamite?" Captain Butt asked me during a fuel stop. "Why?" I asked.

"To blow up the road, of course," he laughed as he walked away to buy some. Captain Monte Butt, the Hidden Peak liaison officer, was the antithesis of Captain Ayub. Monte, who spoke flawless English, became our source for advice on everything from handling the porters to fixing the road. As the five Jeeps rumbled along, Monte kicked back on the roof of one, grooving to London techno on his Walkman, while Ayub sat in the cab barking orders at the driver.

Caravanning worked well. The extra manpower allowed us to quickly fix bits of the road and keep moving. Our only significant delay was at the final police checkpost at Dasso, a windblasted cluster of police barracks sitting next to the last road bridge over the Braldu River. "This is bogus!" the officer yelled as he thrust my peak permit for Chogolisa back at me. "You have made this up on your typewriter in America. You must go back to Islamabad and get another." I thought I was about to have a seizure and Andrew looked like he was ready to slit his wrists before following that order. It was, of course, a subtle way of requesting compensation for his plight, stuck guarding Dasso Bridge. Captain Ayub spotted this amateur quickly and stepped in to settle the matter. If any money was to be bled out of the Chogolisa expedition, it was going into his pocket, not some bridge guard's.

Shortly after Dasso we came to a landslide that no amount of effort was going to fix. Monte surveyed the scene and walked away in defeat, holding his dynamite like a child with a broken toy. We'd made excellent progress in the Jeeps, but it was still three-and-a-half extra porter stages to Askole, one-and-a-half more than we could afford. That was a problem. Fortunately, it was one we wouldn't have to deal with until later. We started walking the next day in steady rain and pounded our way to Askole. Along the way we crossed paths with a soaking wet Alan Hinkes, just returning from the summit of K2. "You should bloody well turn around now, lads," he said bitterly. "There's nothing up there worth this fucking walk." It was the best advice anyone could have given us. Of course, we ignored it.

The first few days of the approach proper turned out to be beautiful. We'd split off from the Hidden Peak expedition at Korophon, wishing them well and promising to visit them at their basecamp. The rain had finally abated and as we followed the Braldu River toward its source at the Baltoro Glacier, we actually began to feel as though our luck had changed. Of course, we were still in Pakistan, so when a porter carrying kerosene burned all the skin off his back, I was up all night cleaning what was left of his skin, dressing up his wounds and trying to explain to him that if he carried his load the next day he would die. Ultimately, only the threat of arrest from the irredoubtable Captain Ayub sent this man and his son packing toward the hospital, four days down valley. Still, this and other ongoing catastrophes—like the fixing rope some soldiers relieved us of at the Drumordu River crossing—failed to dampen our new enthusiasm.

"This is a disgrace to Pakistan army." Ayub announced when we reported the rope incident to him. "Why have they not come with rope of their own? And this bridge man; he has no right to charge a toll whatsoever. I will write each one of these men in my report and *Inshallah* they will be hanged for this." Capital punishment seemed a bit stern to me but who was I to question Pakistani justice. After all, Captain Ayub for once seemed to be on *our* side.

Two days later we reached the campsite of rDukus, where the view across the Baltoro toward the Trango group is surely one of the most impressive in the mountain world. Unfortunately, we couldn't sit outside and enjoy it because of the flies attracted by the stinking heaps of excrement and garbage dumped there. As we camped in what amounted to an open-air toilet, the phrase "Throne Room of the Mountain Gods" took on new meaning.

rDukus is important for another reason. When you step off the grassy moraine onto the ice and rock of the Baltoro, it is likely the last step you'll take on solid ground until you return. This is especially significant to the porters, who usually insist on a cash payment in lieu of foam pads, shoes, or other equipment. They march onto the glacier unequipped to live on the ice, though large numbers suffer hypothermia or trench foot. It is not surprising then that the porters prefer to spend as few nights camped on the Baltoro as possible, which was fine with us. We decided to follow their pace to basecamp, having no idea when we left rDukus how much this choice would affect us.

On the six-hour walk from rDukus to Gore II, an army camp on the glacier and our destination for day eight of the approach, we were awestruck. Masherbrum, Gasherbrum IV, Broad Peak, and Mustagh Tower all came into view. The weather was brilliant and Andrew and I lagged behind the porters and Captain Ayub, absorbed in a photographic orgy. After about four hours of the walk we met one of our porters coming down the glacier from Gore II. He proudly announced that all the loads had reached Gore II and, as it was still early in the day and they were running low on food, the porters requested permission to continue on to Concordia. We sent him back to deliver our permission; this would mean reaching basecamp a day early and that would save the porters an extra night on the ice and, we hoped, prevent them from going hungry. It seemed like a great idea, so we were surprised to find all the porters sitting next to their loads when we reached Gore II.

The mystery cleared itself up when I saw Captain Ayub's feet sticking out of his tent, the only one set up. Gore II is at roughly 14,000 feet and he was totally spent from the walk. Whatever bullshit he was about to offer, this was the real reason for not moving on. Captain Ayub rose from the tent and announced, "We will only be doing whatsoever-absolutely it states in Rule and Regulation. You have said we will be camping at this Gore II and this is where we will camp."

"Yes, but the porters have said they are running out of food and need to get back home quickly," I offered in response.

"This is not *my* fuck-up!" Ayub snarled. "This is *your* fuck-up." Of course the one English phrase we'd added to his lexicon was "fuck-up." How appropriate, I thought. "Who are you? I have told you, and told you that you are nothing." I felt my violent urges returning. "These Johnnies"—he waved toward the porters—"they do not know what is good for themselves." Beating his chest, he said, "I know what is good for them . . . and if I have to beat them to make them do what is best then I will beat each and every one of them."

After an hour-long harangue, I finally managed to slip my copy of the dreaded Rule and Regulation book in front of the captain, wherein he read that if I, as leader, put my reasons for disagreeing with him in writing, my decision was final. We were going to Concordia.

Or so I thought. I walked back to the porters and announced my victory. "Now it is too late John," Issaq told me. "It will be dark soon and there are crevasses. We will go tomorrow." I threw up my hands, and turned around to go tell the Captain. He was busy supervising the disassembly of his tent when I told him we'd be staying at Gore II.

For a moment, there was silence. He stood up, turned around, and stared hard at me. In that instant my whole world collapsed to the small place between us. Then he started to shake; they were small tremors at first, but soon his whole body vibrated. His eyes bulged, his teeth started to gnash, and he seemed to transform into pure hate. I was scared.

"You-are-*joking*-with-*me*!" he screamed. He was beating his chest. "I am captain in Pakistan Army. Government of Pakistan has given me three stars. You do not treat me like slave!"

Spit and foam flew from his mouth as he continued screaming and beating his chest. Captain Ayub had gone insane. I tried to explain that I was only doing what the porters wanted. "It does not matter what they want. Why have you not asked me?" he spat his response. "Always asking this cook or Butt, never *me*. I am Liaison Officer. I am in command."

His screaming was so loud that our audience of porters was soon joined by a group of soldiers, from the nearby army camp. They hadn't left their guns behind. Ayub saw them before I did and after a quick order they surrounded us and those guns were leveled in my direction.

Suddenly I had no desire to argue. I felt sick. My mind was filled with images of a taxi driver with half his head blown off. Was Ayub angry enough to kill us? There was no one for a hundred miles in any direction to stop him. I apologized but it was too late. The soldiers stood by as he continued his tirade. "You will not be allowed to leave Pakistan until the ISI has interrogated you about your crimes."

"Crimes?" I asked.

"You have called Pakistan Army a disgrace at the Drumordu River. You have photographed army camps and this is a treason, a violation of Official Secrets Act. This-is-punishable-by-death."

It was Ayub who'd called the rope-theft incident at the Drumordu River disgraceful, and the photos I'd taken were of mountains near various army camps. That was the truth, but we stood in a world where truth didn't matter. "I will now write your confession and you will surrender all of your film to Pakistan Army," Ayub said.

While I waited for my "confession" to be drafted, I returned to my tent and spooled up some unexposed film. I might have been terrified but I wasn't stupid: Somewhere in the 50 rolls I'd exposed there was sure to be something objectionable, and I couldn't take any chances. When I returned, the captain was still quivering with anger and he handed me the most bizarre document I had ever seen. Written in the first person in my name was a confession of several crimes against Pakistan. I was supposedly admitting to photographing military installations, bridges, and aircraft. I had repeatedly insulted the Pakistani Army, the Government of Pakistan, and Islam. I had disobeyed direct orders from a Pakistani Army officer. At the bottom was a space for my signature. It was tantamount to a death certificate.

"I can't sign this," I said shakily. "It's not true."

"It is true," Ayub replied. "I have said it is true, so it is true. You will sign!"

"No, I will not!"

During the tense hour that followed we went back and forth repeatedly. Finally, when the soldier's guns began to droop and Captain Ayub felt he was losing face, he snatched the paper and announced he would sign it for me. I watched in stunned silence as he put my name to the paper, folded it up and walked away toward the army camp to have tea.

I sat down and tried to clear my spinning head. What had just happened? How had a simple misunderstanding spiraled into a confession of *treason*? What was going to happen next? It wasn't long before Suneeb sat down to answer my last question. *Murder* was what was going to happen next, because the expedition was completely out of control.

I'd been thinking it might come to this from the moment the guns came out. Ayub was serious, and seriously deranged. If he chose to, he could kill Andrew and me and the only thing our families would ever know was that we disappeared while attempting Chogolisa. It wasn't so far-fetched. People disappear every season in the Himalayas. It would have been easy for him to kill us.

Or, I began to think, for us to kill him. The thought scared me. I was seriously considering killing Captain Ayub. It was insane: the whole place, the whole situation, and I had absorbed some of it. Ayub must have sensed this. He came back over and tried to make me sign a contract taking full responsibility for anything that might happen to him, including accident or poisoning. He knew we couldn't stay camped next to his soldiers forever. I thought I recognized some of my fear in his eyes. Again I refused to sign.

The expedition, as far as I was concerned, was over. The only way to solve our problems was to return to Islamabad and get inside the U.S. Embassy as soon as possible. Andrew was disappointed but he understood: It wasn't his name on the confession.

"We're going back to Islamabad tomorrow," I announced.

Ayub looked surprised. "No, we must continue. Fuck-up is finished. ISI will deal with you when you return."

Why was he arguing to continue the same expedition he'd done so much to destroy? Andrew figured it out: Ayub was being paid by the day. Inadvertently, I'd called his bluff and now had a bargaining chip.

"Tear up the confession," I said, "and we continue."

"Not today," Ayub answered, "but if you behave on the climb I will return your film and rip up your confession." It was a bizarre blackmail deal, but it defused a situation where violence still hung in the air. It is disturbing to admit now, but I wasn't thinking of killing Ayub as right or wrong. It was a purely practical decision. There was a chance that we could get out of our mess peacefully, and a dead liaison officer would mean a lot of questions. I decided, at least for the time being it wouldn't help. "Please don't kill him tonight," I told Suneeb later. "Wait."

The next day we reached Concordia, where we ran into some trekkers on their way out of the mountains. I decided to dispatch a letter with them. I didn't want to alarm my family but at the same time I wanted them to take some precautions for me. If I was tossed in jail when we returned from the mountains, I didn't want to spend one extra minute there. Captain Ayub was suspicious of everything, so I waited until dark before quietly slipping the letter to a beautiful Swiss woman named Maria, and told her to mail it from Geneva. It was ridiculous; I felt like a B-movie James Bond.

The following morning the laziest of the porters started suggesting locations for basecamp only 30 minutes out of Concordia. Andrew and I used every bit of charm we had to coax six hours of walking out of them. When they finally refused to go any further without pay for a full extra stage, we established basecamp. Of course, this meant it was time to face up to an old problem: money, or more specifically, the lack thereof. At Concordia we confirmed our earlier suspicions that after paying these porters we wouldn't have enough cash left to pay for the return trip to Skardu. The concept of credit does not exist on the Baltoro, and if even one of our porters found out how broke we were, no one from Baltistan would come and retrieve us and our gear.

The payoff went smoothly except for the moment when I saw Ayub stuff a wad of our rupees into his pocket. He just didn't quit. When questioned he insisted it was his money, but offered no explanation of how it came to be in *our* pile of porter wages. As soon as the porters were paid, they took off down the glacier, apparently unsuspecting that they had our last rupees.

I woke up early the next morning to have a look at the spot that would be home for the next month. Though I couldn't see the northeast face—our proposed route—Chogolisa's summit was clearly visible 9,000 feet above. I started daydreaming about walking across that perfect flat summit ridge at 25,000 feet.

Issaq was soon standing next to me and brought me back to reality by handing in his resignation. I had never heard of a cook *quitting* an expedition, throwing away what might be his only opportunity all year to earn hard currency. Issaq claimed he was ill but it was clear that he just couldn't take another minute of Captain Ayub. When Ayub heard of the resignation he realized he would soon be in a camp alone with Andrew and me, and immediately announced that it was his duty to leave and find another cook. An hour later, Andrew and I were alone.

That afternoon Andrew also decided to leave, but only to visit the Hidden Peak team for a couple of days. I stayed behind to start a recon, while carrying gear up to the base. When I reached the bottom of the face the next morning it looked huge, and totally different from the ten-year-old photos we had. It looked suicidal. Andrew came to the same conclusion at Hidden Peak basecamp, and both of us started looking at the Northeast Ridge, an elegant line that had only seen one ascent, a huge siege that used 10,000 feet of fixed rope. An alpine-style ascent would be incredible.

Andrew returned two days later, as did Captain Ayub with our new cook, Gulham. I was a bit suspicious of Gulham, whom Ayub had found just hanging around Concordia. When I went to shake Gulham's hand, he thrust out a page from Jim Curran's book *K2: Triumph and Tragedy* that had his picture on it. The caption read, "Gulham: film porter impossible, opportunist." I'd had Curran to my house for dinner years before and remembered a story of a porter in 1986 who'd tried to slip out of K2 basecamp with Kurt Diemberger's tent and personal belongings after it was assumed, wrongly of course, that Kurt was dead. *It can't be the same guy,* I thought.

A week later, when Gulham's kitchen contained, among other things, one of my sleeping bags, a pack, my spare boots, Andrew's ski poles, spare hat, socks, gloves, and down jacket, I revised my thinking. Of all the men in Baltistan Captain Ayub could have possibly found to replace Issaq, he picked the only one documented in mountaineering literature as a kleptomaniac.

Despite Gulham's best efforts, Andrew and I were able to scrape together enough of our equipment for our first attempt on August 13. The unlucky date lived up to its reputation. At our bivy at the bottom of the route the stove refused to light. After four hours of effort Andrew booted it across the ice and we returned to fetch the spare. We spent the 14th in basecamp under crystal-blue skies. It was the best weather of the trip and, looking at the summit of K2, we were sure that people were going for it. What we didn't know was that seven people would die for it that day, among them one of Andrew's good friends, Jeff Lakes.

The spare stove also refused to work and so on the 16th we were back at the bottom of the route with a fire-spitting conglomeration of every working stove part we had. It was dangerous as hell but at least it burned. We'd planned to climb at night, so just as the sun set we started through the icefall. It was such a chaotic mess that there was no way we could reach the clean northern branch of the ridge taken by the Spanish in '86. We opted instead for the southern branch and its 6,000 feet of virgin terrain.

The initial climbing was easy and straightforward. We found a great bivy on the ridge proper and spent the day looking up at what we figured would be the crux of the route. Three thousand feet above, at about 20,000 feet, the ridge rose dramatically into a vertical ice cliff. There seemed to be a way around it, by threading through a narrow slot between an ice cliff and a huge serac hanging off the ridge. Barring that, it would be a direct attack.

The next night, as we set out, the moon was a little smaller, the air a little colder, and we found some of the scariest terrain either of us had ever encountered. Somehow the ridge itself was split by crevasses every hundred meters. We'd never seen anything like it. Climbing along a 60-degree arête of rotten snow we'd suddenly find our tools and feet popping through into space. The view through the holes to the glacier below was sickening. At one point I had to tunnel more than a body length into the slope to find ice for a screw. All Andrew could see from 50 meters below was the weak glow of my headlamp coming out of my little mineshaft. The pitch after that, he tried a similar belay excavation, and tunneled right through the ridge into thin air.

It was 2 am before we reached the bottom of the ice cliff. We reckoned it was near vertical for close to 400 feet without any appreciable breaks. Andrew leads Grade 6 water ice, so when he said forget it, I forgot it. The alternative didn't look much better. We headed for a slot we'd seen from below, a huge partly-filled crevasse formed by a serac that had calved from the ice cliff. Andrew led a brilliant pitch across a gaping crevasse which split the ridge with a hundred-foot deep gash. He swung his way over stacked blocks and an overhanging snow mushroom to gain the slot. I led across the floor of the slot next, expecting every step in the deep snow to collapse. At the end of the rope I saw a small gap in the ice cliff and began to head toward it. The snow was terrible and we were moving at a crawl. Soon it became apparent that in order to reach the gap we would have to spend an hour or more wallowing away under some enormous overhanging seracs perched above the ice cliff. It was too dangerous, but it was also too late. It was 3:45 am, we'd been climbing for 11 hours, and we had to find a bivy. As we couldn't get out of the slot and onto the ridge above, the only option was to bivy *on* the serac. We climbed up, chopped out a platform, and crashed until 10 am. When we awoke we had a whole day ahead to sit on our little perch. Looking around, we realized we occupied the only island of safety on the entire slope below the ridge.

After a nerve-wrecking day waiting for *something* bad to happen, we finally started climbing at about 6 pm. The plan was to regain the ridge via a diagonal end-run around the ice cliff and the seracs. After eight steep pitches, we regained the ridge—and the crevasses. Andrew stepped through the ridge crest into a gaping hole. The hard work of slithering across the slot was followed by the even more tiring climb up the steep, sugar-snow arête on the opposite side. We continued upward on the ridge for another three or four pitches of terrible snow to a small, filled-in crevasse, where we prepared a bivouac without discussion.

When we woke later in the morning it was snowing, and clearly had been since we'd gone to bed. If there was one thing the Northeast Ridge of Chogolisa didn't need, it was more snow. The following morning, August 18th, it was still snowing and a thick fog had rolled in from Kondus Saddle. Was this the same fog that engulfed the Duke of Abruzzi in 1909, the same fog in which Herman Buhl disappeared in 1957? It sure was the same mountain in damn near the same spot. We were getting scared.

At 2 pm, we tuned in our radio and caught Phil Powers' end of a call to Broad Peak. I heard Phil's voice crackling, "can you tell us about the accident." We jumped into the conversation. Seven people were dead. Jeff Lakes was dead. It was the final blow.

Jeff had really wanted to go to the Karakoram that year and asked Andrew if he could join us. We'd politely turned him down: we wanted to try as a team of two. So Jeff found his way onto a K2 expedition.

It didn't take a lot of talking to decide our climb was over. Descending what we'd climbed was impossible with our three screws and three pickets, forcing us onto the concave face between our line and the Spanish route. It took two days to get down, and the day after we reached basecamp the entire face slid, scouring clean all of our tracks.

During the six days we were gone, Ayub and Ghulam had been falling over each other to see who could steal the most. The shortwave radio, a camera, medicines, boots—they'd grabbed it all. We had to politely ask for individual items back as we discovered them missing. The only thing we really wanted now was to get the hell out of the mountains, and we sent Ghulam to find some porters. Not wanting to be alone with us, Ayub also took off for Concordia, promising to return with porters.

Ten days later the porters arrived, and two days after that I was again walking past Gore II, revisiting all the bad memories of that place. I couldn't wait to reach a shower and a bed, but I wondered if I'd be enjoying those amenities in a jail cell. As I passed by the last of the rag-tag army tents, a lone porter, coming up the valley, stopped me.

"Mr. John, from Chogolisa expedition?"

"Yes?"

"I have Federal Express for you." He pulled a large red, white, and blue box from his pack. It was probably the highest and most remote delivery in the company's history, and certainly the most important package I'd ever received. Beside *Playboy* and *Penthouse* magazines was a letter from my father. My letter had reached him from Geneva just the week before, and per my instructions he'd contacted my friend Eshun Khan, son of retired Admiral Sahid Khan, former Chief of Staff of the Pakistan Navy and currently Pakistan's Ambassador to the Hague.

According to the letter, Admiral Khan was mad as hell that we'd been treated so disrespectfully. He expected a phone call as soon as possible. I was laughing like a lunatic before I'd finished reading.

We broke the news to Captain Ayub that evening by asking him if he could help us arrange a trip to Karachi, where the Admiral lived. "It is much too dangerous there," he told us. "You cannot go."

"I think my friend can ensure our safety," I responded, handing him the letter. I watched the color drain from Ayub's face as he scanned the page.

"Admiral . . . Sahid Khan?" His voice quivered.

"Yes," I explained, "his son and I were great friends at university."

Ayub looked ill. He retired to his tent and we didn't hear from him until the next morning when he woke us with breakfast in bed. It was pathetic. The entire journey back to Skardu became one attempt after another by Ayub to make up to us.

When we reached the road, we told the porters we were broke. They took it surprisingly well; Ayub appointed one porter as representative to go with us to the bank in Skardu for the porters' money. The day after we arrived in Skardu, one seat opened on a flight out. Andrew and I agreed that I should take it and call the ambassador. I walked out onto the tarmac, leaving Ayub screaming at airport security to stop the plane.

"What would you like me to do to this man?" These were the first words I heard through the phone receiver after I finished my story. The casual power in Ambassador Sahid's voice stopped me cold. As soon as he'd answered my phone call, I had felt safe. The passion and urgency of the days on the Baltoro evaporated. On the verge of winning the game of Pakistani justice that I'd been preparing for two months to lose, I hesitated. Captain Ayub had stolen from me, threatened me, and in many ways he'd ruined our expedition. But was that reason enough to do to him what I suspected the ambassador could do? The silence on the line began to be uncomfortable.

"I just don't think that he should be allowed to do this again." That was all I could say, and as the words came out of my mouth I felt sorry for Captain Ayub.

Seven months to the day after leaving Pakistan, I was tromping down from Point Five Gully on Ben Nevis, Scotland, and ran into an English climber I'd met at Concordia at the end of our expedition. He filled me in on what happened to Captain Ayub.

"It was in all the papers after you left. Dishonorable discharge, lost his pension, court martial. Probably in jail by now."

I shook my head and kept walking. So that was it, the end of the story. It wasn't the way I'd have chosen to win.

In 1978, Joe Tasker (b. 1948; d. 1982) and three partners were turned back from K2's unclimbed West Ridge. One climber left for home, and the others tackled the mountain's less difficult, but still imposing, Abruzzi Ridge. Tasker's gripping account of that attempt, which almost killed him and his teammates, conveys a sense of the man who, with his long-time friend and partner Peter Boardman, disappeared in 1982 on Everest's unclimbed Northeast Ridge.

ackling a mountain as big and difficult as K2 in a party of only three should have been a daunting concept but we had reached this point gradually so it seemed only a logical development. At Base Camp, back at the spot from where the porters had left, we amended our plans. Gohar and Ali were still with us, two mail runners periodically arrived after a round trip of ten days with news from home, and Major Sarwat was proving to be an encouraging and valued supporter of our efforts to climb the mountain.

Since the days when I had been perturbed by his serious demeanour and attention to the smallest of rules, I had begun to realise that he was wholeheartedly in favour of our expedition. In arguing with the porters he had worn himself out on our behalf to spur them on to help us. His job now was unenviable. He had to wait in attendance at Base Camp until we had finished the climb, however long it took. There was little for him to do, but he occupied his time reading and doing odd jobs about the camp. The vast pile of debris nearby from the previous year's French expedition provided a rich source of pickings for him. He unearthed several huge cylinders of gaz and put together a stove from discarded parts, providing for Ali a cleaner and easier means of cooking than the paraffin stoves we had brought. Sarwat always managed to appear immaculately clean when we were dishevelled and grubby. On the walk-in he wore a green tracksuit, appearing as neat and dapper as an athlete on a track. He preserved the ability to look neat and well cleaned throughout the three months of the expedition.

Ali had won his place as cook on the strength of his avowal that he had worked in an army mess. By the time we discovered that he had only been a waiter, we had not the heart to change our minds. The meals he cooked were excellent and he was always cheerful. Only when an aching tooth bothered him was he anything but busy and willing at every moment of the day. Gohar came to borrow some pliers to remove the aching tooth but we gave him some pain-killers and promised to send Ali to the Base Camp of a Japanese expedition three days away if the pain did not let up.

Dick had gradually come to accept that meals would be cooked for him. Ali as cook and Gohar as a general help liberated us from the daily chores and allowed us to concentrate our energies on the mountain. They were also company for Sarwat who, unlike many Liaison Officers, refused to slip back to wait in warmer quarters at Askole, insisting that his duty lay at Base Camp, to be on hand lest his help be needed. One day I noticed Dick, instead of jumping to do the job himself, passing a tube of Araldite to Gohar who was looking for some way to mend the cracked washing-up bowl. Misunderstanding Dick's instructions and gestures of mixing the substances together, Gohar started squeezing the tubes into the soup which Ali was busy stirring. The soup was rescued before harm was done.

We were waiting for a clearing in the weather before going back on the mountain. Little information could be obtained from the radio which Sarwat tuned in to each evening. A one-sentence forecast described the weather pattern for the whole of the country and we were having to make our own judgements.

On descending from the West Ridge, we had found Major Sarwat to be in a state of great distress. He was pleased to have our company again but it was a full day before he could be made to divulge what was upsetting him. I had developed a joking relationship with him, often being wildly outrageous in my comments so that he could see I was not serious. It was good for him to see that there were differences between the three of us so that when Pete took Sarwat's side in disapproval of some extravagant statement I had made, Sarwat could see that he was not an outsider to the group, that we regarded his opinion as of equal validity to any of our own. When the mail arrived and he received letters I used to tease him that his wife should still be writing and not have run off with someone else, an event which was a near impossibility in a well-regulated Muslim state. I remembered to enquire again what had upset him; he had not wanted to mar our return immediately by his own troubles.

He described the amazing confrontation he had had with Ghirardini, who had visited our Base Camp whilst we were away, and the arguments he had had with him. It seemed hardly credible to us that such antagonisms could have arisen to spoil the atmosphere of a region so remote that any encounter should be a welcome one of people who have a love of the mountains.

The same day that he recounted this tale we were visited by two American friends who had come to climb the neighbouring peak of Skyang Kangri. They had made their camp near to us and their jovial Liaison Officer, Tim, turned out to be an old friend of Major Sarwat's. We were sitting inside our large dining tent reminiscing and swapping yarns when Gohar's face fell, and a strange dismay seemed to possess him as two figures approached our tent. It was the Frenchman and his wife.

The ensuing scene was bedlam. The Frenchman vociferously insisted that he was prepared to forget the earlier arguments if the Liaison Officers would let him climb K2 on his own, and his wife offered her opinion and supported her husband's demands in a strident French which it was difficult to comprehend.

The scene seemed starkly out of place amongst the mountains, this confrontation and dispute, and the forcing upon us of a dilemma which had nothing to do with us but into which we were inevitably drawn.

Ghirardini wanted us to say that we did not mind him climbing K2 and he seemed to think he could manoeuvre the Liaison Officer into turning a blind eye to his activities. He intended to follow the ropes left in place by the French party the previous year. But we told him that we had no authority even to say that he could climb the mountain. We were in a foreign country and had agreed to accept its laws, whatever we thought of them.

The Frenchman had no time for such restrictions: "If I see a beautiful mountain, I want to climb it. It is my natural response."

There was some point in his assertions but his attitude was very simplistic and his peremptory manner did not inspire sympathy for himself or his views. Even Dick was moved to voice his disapproval of the man's attitude. In a quiet and sincere voice he said: "But we all know what the rules are before we come."

"I have no time for rules. They make me sick. I don't like coming to places with such rules."

"Well there you are then. Don't come if you don't like it."

"O.K."

The man and his wife left to camp some distance away without saying whether he was going on the mountain or not. What should have been a period of rest before our return to the mountain had been more exhausting than if we had stayed high up in the worst of storms. I was keen to get back on the mountain but I felt annoyed at the waste of time and energy which had sprung from both meetings with the man. He was certainly an odd character and seemed to have the ability to introduce tensions and discord where none should have existed.

On 2 July Dick, Pete and I returned to the Abruzzi Ridge. Ali and Gohar came with us to the foot of the ridge, relieving us of the full weight of our loads until the climbing proper started. The trek round to the ridge took two hours, up through the complex maze of ice towers on the Godwin Austen glacier. There was debris from the camps of earlier expeditions at the foot of the ridge, including some oxygen cylinders and a decayed breathing mask. Pete turned on a bottle of oxygen to test if it still worked and sniffed at the oxygen: "Smells good, do you want a sniff?" But Dick and I refused and Pete felt outlawed by our refusal even to sample the invigorating gas.

Ali and Gohar turned back from the small platform a few hundred feet up a rocky slope from the glacier. It had been on this platform that we had spent three nights confined inside our tents by storms during our first foray on the ridge. This second time we benefited from the knowledge gained during the earlier attempt and reached a camp-site on a snow shelf at the head of a couloir at 20,000 feet.

Our movements were slow and weary. We had expected ourselves to be fitter on this new attempt but it was six weeks since we had first reached Base Camp and although we were well acclimatised, the effect of living at altitude and making strenuous efforts on the mountain must have had a debilitating effect. Our rucksacks were heavy too. We carried 50 pounds each, bringing up food for a prolonged assault and spare rope to fasten over awkward steps to facilitate our eventual descent.

Since the route had been almost climbed in 1939 and 1953, then finally succeeded on in 1954, we did not expect the difficulties to be too great. We reasoned that our technical skills were probably greater with the general rise in climbing standards since those days; the modern mentality now encouraged a more mobile attack on a mountain and our equipment was correspondingly lighter and better suited to this sort of approach. We could carry everything we needed for survival on our backs and, once fit and acclimatised, given that no obstacles caused long delays, we were now expecting to be able to start from the bottom of K2 and reach its summit in a matter of days.

We were not doing justice to the early pioneers. The route was extraordinarily difficult. Low down on the ridge, broken rocky slopes and snow couloirs were interspersed with awkward steps of rock. This was not unusual for the lower reaches of any route but on this ridge the difficulties increased as we climbed higher. Frayed remnants of ropes, sometimes over 25 years old, marked the route in places. Though only three expeditions had succeeded in climbing the ridge, the history of attempts, tragic accidents and hopeless retreats had left relics of former struggles along the way. We could always climb sections but were overawed by the perseverance which must have been needed in the days when ropes were made from hemp and when boots were heavy with the nails in the sole for friction. Our loads felt terribly heavy but they would lighten as we went on, as we consumed the food and left ropes on difficult passages. In those early days one rope alone would have weighed ten pounds, and much more when damp.

In theory, now that we were as acclimatised as we would ever be, we should have been able to climb the mountain in five or six days, even though it was the second highest in the world. We had worked out our projected camping spots on photographs and the stages into which we planned to break up the ascent.

In practice the difficulties were too great and our loads too heavy to make such methodical progress. The weather too played a major part and we became resigned to languishing in our tents for days at a time until the ferocious winds should diminish and the snow stop falling. We came to accept that we would have to climb in weather worse than we would normally have contemplated if we were to make any progress at all. Thus if it was possible to move we would climb up into the cloud, hoods drawn tight against the storm to explore the next section, fix short lengths of rope where necessary and dump food and gear up high ready for the next day when we would move up ourselves with the tents.

At 23,000 feet we spent four nights in the tents which were beaten flat by the winds, but the alloy tubes, forming hoops inside each tent, would spring upright once again when the storm allowed. Snow formed drifts against the tents but this was a welcome supply for melting into water.

We had with us two tents, weighing six pounds each. All three of us could squeeze into one but we carried a second lest one became damaged. During the enforced halt I had a tent to myself and Pete and Dick shared the other. I used to lie during the day with my rucksack packed, ready to evacuate the tent at any moment as the roof flattened against my body under the impact of the wind. I had used one rope to hold the tent in place, wrapping it round the poles and anchoring it to stakes driven into the snow. Pete and Dick thought I was better off than they and would shout to me to make them drinks of tea. For my part I believed my tent was more exposed and acted as a windbreak for them, whom I considered to have the advantage, expecting them to do the tea-making.

We had radio contact with Base Camp via a tiny, lightweight walkie-talkie. Major Sarwat could be relied on absolutely to pass on any information he could glean from the sparse weather reports on the radio. But K2 seemed to create its own weather pattern and the benefit of the walkie-talkie was the psychological advantage of a link with our Base. We had radio calls at 7:00 am and 5:00 pm as a regular schedule, with a fall-back call time every half hour after those times lest something prevented either party speaking then. We had brought lightweight walkie-talkies after realising on Kangchenjunga, when we had been separated and out of touch, just how useful they could be.

There were times when Sarwat was encouraging us on when the weather was clear at Base Camp and he could not suspect that the cloud, which he could see enveloping the mountain, was more than a light mist. From inside the cloud, for our part, we could not believe that the ferocity of the storms we were experiencing was having no effect at Base Camp only a few miles away.

On 8 July the weather allowed us to make our third camp. The ground was steep, complex and loose. The fresh snow further hampered us. We stopped earlier than intended as ledges large enough for a tent were infrequent. The third camp-site itself was only large enough for one of the tents. From there, however, we had a magnificent view across the border into the Sinkiang province of China and of Broad Peak, in profile, capped by plumes of cloud and coloured pink by the setting sun.

The most difficult part of all was yet to come. We knew of the Black Pyramid by descriptions from the earlier ascents but nothing prepared us for its sustained and improbable passages. The Black Pyramid is a distinctive area of dark, formidably steep rock, hundreds of feet high forming a rough triangle beneath a wall of ice. The rock was compact, with few foot-holds or cracks for pitons. This was one area where we took care to secure in place a life-line of rope for our descent. We did not have sufficient of our own rope to stretch all the way, so where the rock eased off into a slope of snow which ran up to the ice cliff we retrieved some remnants of ancient rope to use as a guideline.

Dick led the way up the wall of ice. I was pleased it was his turn in front, as the ice was hard and splintered at each blow of the axe. More remains of rope showed evidence of others who had passed this way but how the pioneers of the first attempt had climbed ice such as this I could not imagine. Dick went stolidly on. He had the ability to remain undaunted by any qualms about starting up such a repulsive section of ice, but he was exhausted by the time he reached the top.

There was an easy snow slope above and I went up it to scout around for our next camping site. Pete went off to the left and we had a heated disagreement about which way to go. The leftwards route proved best.

That camp-site, our fourth on the ridge, was the best so far. We had reached a shoulder of the mountain which went on upwards in an undulating incline of snow. We climbed up from the left edge of the ice cliff for another 300 feet to a level shelf, huge by comparison with any camping place we had so far used.

We had reached 24,700 feet. The effect of such sustained efforts at altitude was beginning to make itself felt, but all three of us were in good shape. For Dick it was the highest he had ever been. From this camp-site we could look over the edge of the ridge, only 20 feet away, at the precipice dropping sheer away down the South Face for 9,000 feet to the Godwin Austen glacier far below, and our Base Camp, invisible from this distance. Somewhere in this region two of the great tragedies in K2's history had taken place. In 1939 three Sherpas going up to rescue a sick American, Dudley Wolfe, disappeared. Bad weather closed in, preventing any other members of the expedition from returning to the mountain so that no one ever knew what had happened to the three Sherpas and the sick man. The second tragedy occurred in 1953 when another American, Art Gilkey, was taken ill from thrombophlebitis induced by inactivity due to the prolonged storms. The other members of the team attempted to lower him all the way down the mountain but, whilst the active members were recovering from a fall which had almost killed them all, the sick man disappeared from the side of the mountain. He had been wrapped in a crude hammock made from tent material and sleeping bag and was secured by ropes to the ice slope down which he was being lowered. On returning to continue the rescue his exhausted friends found the slope bare. The likely explanation was that an avalanche had swept him away but there was the lingering thought that he may have cut himself loose to relieve the others of a responsibility which would almost certainly have brought tragedy anyway.

The summit seemed within our reach, only one or at most two more camps, two or three more days and we could be on top. No illness or headaches had slowed our progress and there was every reason to hope that we could make it, providing the weather held out.

The next day, 10 July, the weather was magnificent. The sun shone in a clear blue sky, the snow under foot was mostly firm, and though the altitude made every step exhausting, forcing ourselves on was a discipline we had long since attuned ourselves to.

Before we left that spot on the shoulder we had sorted out only the bare essentials to take up with us. In a hollow in the snow we left the spare tent, extra food, a pan, spare gaz cylinders and any items of clothing we had found unnecessary. With the summit now in reach we intended to travel as light as possible.

The gentle incline of the slope steepened into a wall of hard snow topped by a cornice. We made for what looked to be a line of rope emerging from the snow. We were thankful for the direction shown by what we thought to be a relic from the past, but it was no relic, it was a shadow cast by the sun in a surface groove. We climbed on up never-theless, me forcing a way past the overhanging cornice and Pete taking over to lead an unexpected wall of ice.

I hauled my way up the rope which he had led out and saw him striding upwards where the cliff fell back into a snow slope, into the sun and stopping to shout that he had reached the shoulder.

We came onto the end of a huge promontory jutting out from below the final 2,000-foot summit pyramid. The crest of the promontory was a broad, rounded plateau with hundreds of square feet of room in which to camp. The promontory rose gently towards a rocky escarp-ment which cut across beneath the summit, forming a narrow couloir of snow where it met the distinctive and enormous buttress of ice, the last barrier before the summit slopes.

Our fifth camp-site was at 25,400 feet, on the level plateau at the end of the promontory. The summit of Broad Peak was now only slightly higher than where we were, and most other peaks were much lower. I felt satisfaction at seeing the surrounding peaks dropping away below as we neared this mighty summit. We scrutinised and memorised details of the summit pyramid for the next day, trying to assess the remaining difficulties and the time we would need to over-come them.

But next day we were trapped in our tent once again by heavy snow-fall and lashing winds. We lay dejected, with no means of passing the time except by daydreaming or cooking a meal. Our food was running short and after ten days on the mountain we ourselves were low in physical reserves. The illness which had afflicted Art Gilkey, arising from similar inactivity, preyed on our minds, and we discussed the pros and cons of continuing or going back down.

Over the radio, Major Sarwat was full of encouragement. He had come to have real faith in our ability after his early doubts about the likelihood of success for so unconventional a team. He exhorted us on as if he were a coach and we were his team of players. Reception on the little radio was poor but we could tell he was enthusiastic for us, mix-ing news of the weather with firm suggestions to press on.

By late afternoon the snow was deep outside and the weather showed no signs of let-up. I proposed that if the next day brought no improvement we should go down, recoup our strength and come back up with more supplies. Pete was against this idea and Dick was undecided. There were merits for both points of view. The summit was almost within our grasp and to go down now would set it back once again a long way from us. If the weather did clear, even if we had little food left there was a chance that we might be able to bring the expedition to a conclusion in one long, hard day of climbing, and thus avoid the uncertainty that a retreat all the way to Base Camp would entail. On the other hand there was the greater strength we would have in coming back up a route we now knew well after some rest and good food at Base Camp. With all the difficult passages prepared and little for us to carry except food, we could expect to regain our high point in perhaps four days. It is always hard to make a decision in such a situation, not knowing which will be best to achieve the desired outcome and not wanting to lose a position won against many odds. Though in reaching decisions we each propounded a more positive opinion than we actually felt as part of the process of thrashing out all possible angles on the decisions to be made, there was no conflict between us. Living in such close proximity to other people, when conditions are far from perfect, inevitably produces an abrasiveness of temper and curtness of manner, but we were all three experienced enough to recognise the tensions produced by the strain of the situation.

In the event, the decision seemed to be made for us. On the 5:00 pm radio call the Major informed us, with audible satisfaction, that he had picked up a detailed weather forecast. This had been transmitted for the sake of a Japanese expedition on Masherbrum, a mountain which we could see clearly in fine weather. The forecast, unusually specific in contrast to the norm, was for cloudy weather the next day, 12 July, with no wind or snow. The 13th was to be fine all day.

So the decision was clear. We would go up, using the day of cloud to reach a point as high as possible where we could camp in an advantageous position for the summit bid on the 13th. I slept with mixed feelings of excitement and reluctance at the test ahead. It was the nervousness of knowing that we were on the threshold of achieving something long desired and struggled for, but with apprehension about the test of strength, stamina and skill which the reaching of that goal would entail.

There was cloud next morning, thick and swirling up from a murky void which concealed the valleys below. We radioed down that we were setting off to make a sixth camp that day with hopes of continuing next day to the top. The wind was strong, blowing flurries of snow into our faces as we walked along the broad crest of the ridge. The forecast had said no wind but it did not strike us as unusual that high on the mountain currents of air should form localised turbulence. There seemed to be some snow falling as well as being blown from the surface underfoot, but even that was not a cause for concern in that such dense cloud could be expected to deposit a little of its moisture.

The ridge rose up gradually as we approached a wide couloir separating us from the main mass of the summit pyramid. The broad crest of the ridge sharpened into steep slopes and we picked our way carefully along one side, aiming for any rock which projected and offered a sense of security in the open expanse of snow. The crest of the ridge was to our right and to our left the mountainside dropped steeply away into a seemingly bottomless abyss of cloud.

We were roped together and moved simultaneously until we reached the couloir. The great channel was 400 or 500 feet wide and had runners scoured down it by the passage of avalanches. In the cloud above us we could sometimes glimpse the huge cliff of ice which guarded access to the summit slopes and which we guessed, occasionally sent avalanches thundering down the couloir. The snow in the couloir was deep and instilled fear that it might give way at every step and that we would go tumbling down to the bottom of the couloir and be flung out into the abyss.

We aimed for an enormous boulder in the centre of the couloir which had clearly withstood the force of many avalanches. That was a halfway point, a breathing place from which to tackle the second part of the frightening gully. There was no technical difficulty in the crossing, the angle was gentle enough for us to walk upright, only using an ice axe for balance against the slope or to lean on in rest when fatigue forced a halt. Every step, however, was dogged by a presentiment of catastrophe, as if, out of the mists above, a white wave of death would engulf us. The altitude enforced its own pace of movement, but we urged ourselves on to reach the rocks at the far side with as few halts as possible. Only when we gained those rocks and climbed up out of that terrifying gully could we allow ourselves the frequent rests and slowness of movement which our oxygen-starved bodies were demanding.

I do not remember at what point in the day it became evident that there was a steady snowfall rather than an intermittent flurry of wind-blown surface snow mingling with light flakes from the cloud. It was early afternoon before we reached the safety of the rocks beyond the couloir and we certainly knew then that we were in another storm but we still had faith in the broader outline of the forecast and expected the next day to be fine. We carried on along a sharp, rocky ridge beginning to look for a place to put up the tent for the night. The altimeter told us that we had risen above 26,000 feet and, as on Kangchenjunga, we hoped to be able to climb those last 2,000 feet to the summit in one day.

It was another 500 feet before we did stop for the night. The rock ridge had few places where it would be possible to erect the tent and always we pressed on, enticed further by the illusion of a better ledge a little higher. The fear of an avalanche in the night kept us to the rocks well away from the snow couloir where we could have dug out a platform, and well away from the fall-line of any blocks of ice from the cliff above.

Pete seemed indefatigable. He led on in increasingly deep snow and Dick and I trailed behind, following his tracks but still not able to match his pace. Dick was experiencing the exhaustion of altitudes he had never before been to and that exhaustion worried him. The afternoon wore on and Pete still forged a path through snow as deep as his thighs. Time and again the promise of a ledge proved to be false until Pete forced his way up a shallow gully beside a rock and announced that he had found a usable spot.

With many more rests before closing the gap between us, the three of us stood on top of a rocky prow which stood out from the slope. All around more rocks protruded from the surface of the snow and 100 feet above us stood a great wall of rock. The snow around us was anchored by the presence of so many rocks and the slope between the small prow of rock on which we stood and the great wall above was short enough to reassure us that no dangerous build-up of snow could form there. We believed the prow of rock to be safe for the night, but it needed two hours of work before we had chopped away enough ice to erect the tent. We tied the corners of the tent to aluminium stakes driven into the snow and hammered a couple of pitons into the rock as attachment points to give security to our precarious perch. We could ill afford the effort of cutting out the ice and it was night before we settled inside.

The ledge was barely wide enough for the tent and when all three of us tried to lie down inside, Dick, who was on the side of the tent nearest the edge, had to pad out the floor of the tent beneath him with the rucksacks. Half of his place in the tent was poised over nothing, but the alloy stays in the rucksacks formed a platform over that drop.

Radio reception was very poor. If the Major could hear us, we could hear nothing from him. Our location was probably as close to Base Camp as it had been at any time, and certainly in line of sight if the Major stepped out from camp a few hundred yards, but our proximity to the rock probably affected reception.

We were perched a mere 1,500 feet below the summit and, had it been a clear day, they would have been able to see us through the powerful telephoto lens from Base. The prow of rock on which we were camped was 500 feet up from the couloir we had so fearfully crossed. This couloir ran down for 2,000 feet before ending abruptly in the vast precipice of the South Face.

Across the slope from where we camped was the ice cliff which we would have to by-pass the next day. The rock wall above us spanned the rest of the slope, meeting the ice cliff at a narrow gully, the route past the cliff. That was the last remaining problem for us, and beyond we envisaged the slope easing off into the summit itself.

We hardly had energy left to make as many drinks as we needed; waves of sleep swept over me and I noticed that Pete and Dick too kept drifting off. Inside the tent, Dick was lying closest to the edge of the ledge, Pete was in the middle position and I was on the side closest to the ice and rock of the mountain itself, which we had exposed in chopping out the ledge. The tent was too narrow for us to lie all three shoulder to shoulder. Pete and Dick had their heads at the end of the tent nearest the tunnel entrance and I lay with my head at the opposite end. It felt airless inside the tent, lying with my head furthest from the door, and I fiddled with the vent, trying to let air in without an accompanying flurry of snow.

Outside, the snow was still falling thickly, the tent sagged a little under its weight and I could feel the pressure of snow building up between the tent and the wall of the mountain. I pressed against the side of the tent in an effort to close any gap and make the snow slide over the fabric and we talked about the safety of our situation with some apprehension about the persistent storm.

The snowfall was heavier than it had been all day and if it kept up we might find we could not make any progress next day, even if the day were clear, and retreat itself could be suicidal. We were stuck for the moment where we were, we needed rest and could not do much in the darkness anyway. We could not even find the energy to melt snow enough for more than one drink, in spite of all the knowledge we shared about the rapid deterioration in physical performance at altitude without plentiful food and liquid. We each went off to sleep without taking the customary sleeping pill lest we needed all our wits for any emergency which might arise from this storm.

I awoke to an instant awareness of the imminence of a sordid death. All was black, the tent was collapsed on top of us. A heavy avalanche of snow was pouring over the tent. I was lying face down, cloaked by the fabric of the tent, my body and limbs moulded and held in place by the weight of the snow, solid as concrete. I tried to rise, only my head and shoulders could move, but the snow crashed down on the back of my neck and my face was beaten inexorably closer to the ground. It was a brutal and implacable force of nature with no malice, which, impersonal and unfeeling, was bringing extinction. I felt awe at the power at work. There was no thought process, I was simply aware, knowledge without deduction, of all the implications of what was happening. I shouted to Pete and Dick by name; there was no reply. My arms were pinned down and I could feel, with my elbow, Pete's feet next to me, also pinned down. They were inert. Of Dick I knew nothing, could hear no sound. I presumed that they had caught the full force of the avalanche, had been struck by blocks of ice or rock, and were unconscious, if not dead already, and I knew I would not be long in dying too. The blows on my head from the avalanche went on and on, at any moment I expected the tent to be torn free and sent tumbling and cart wheeling for 10,000 feet with us inside, thudding into each other, resenting the blows from the others' flailing arms and legs, not the slow-motion impression of death as represented in films, a scruffy end, but not suffering for long before the impacts and collisions of the fall brought oblivion.

I felt no fear, only regret that our death should be so paltry and that we were to be extinguished without trace, because no one would ever know what had happened and there would forever be questions and guesses about our disappearance on the mountain, though our bodies would land only hours away from our Base Camp.

The blackness seemed to be inside as well as outside my head. Fire points formed jagged trails and then the blackness took me.

The snow had stopped falling when I came round. I realised that the tent was still in place—the snow anchors must have held it—my whole body was held fast by the weight of snow and only my head could move a little in a pocket of air. The air was stale, my breathing shallow from the crushing weight on my chest, and a slight panic that

I would die now from suffocation began to form inside me. I could see nothing in the dark but I knew that in the breast pocket of my windsuit I had a penknife with which I could cut an air-hole in the tent. My arms were pinned beneath my chest but one hand was near the pocket. My groping fingers failed to find the knife at first, and my breathing came faster, the panic growing. Then I had the knife and, one-handed, tried to open the blade, but fumbled it and the panic all but overwhelmed me. I opened the blade at the next attempt and twisted my arm awkwardly so that my hand could force the knife into the fabric of the tent, inches from my face. My arm movement was restricted and the slit was only three inches long, but cold air came in and I felt relief that I could at least breathe. With Pete and Dick both gone I had to keep myself alive first before I could decide on my next move. Whether I could emerge from under the deadly weight of snow with only one arm partly free I did not know. Whether there would be any life left in Pete and Dick if I could ever get to their bodies I had little hope.

Breathing came easier, then I heard voices and I realised that Pete's feet were no longer next to me. The weight of snow came off my back. I could raise myself and I had my mouth at the slit in the tent, sucking in the air and shouting to them, immensely relieved that the impossible had happened and they were still alive. I was eager for more air but refrained from cutting at the tent more, since if all three of us were alive we might need it as our only form of shelter.

The avalanche had struck us in the middle of the night. At its first impact the tent had been partly knocked off the ledge before the snow stakes and the weight of the falling snow held it in place. Dick was suspended, in the folds of the tent, off the edge of the prow of rock, only the tent fabric preventing him from plunging down 10,000 feet of mountain. Pete had been pushed to the edge of the ledge where there was less weight of snow on him. With his head close to the tent entrance he was able to pull himself out. The prow stood clear of the snow slope still and the entrance to the tent was clear. He pulled Dick out of the tent and back onto the ledge where both of them shouted for me for long minutes, hearing no reply. This must have coincided with my blacking out. They had begun digging for what they presumed would be my dead body under a deep, solid mass of snow, and perhaps the gradual easing of weight from my chest had allowed air to enter my lungs and consciousness to return.

I realised that I was no longer against the solid wall of the mountain. The tent was still hanging off the ledge and the pocket where Dick had hung was full of boots, stove, food and anything else which had been loose when the avalanche struck.

We conversed through the slit in the tent while Pete and Dick dug clear more snow. My sentences were fitful as I sucked greedily at the air in between words, until I could sit upright and open the tent door.

I passed out to them their gloves and torches. When I had gathered my breath I made ready to join them outside but Pete suggested I stay in the tent to gather up all the loose objects lest we lose anything vital. Each of us functioned automatically as if we had rehearsed for such an event. Few words were necessary.

The snowstorm of the previous evening was still continuing. Now that I was alive I began to feel cold and uncomfortably damp. Outside, Pete and Dick scraped away at the snow, clearing the ledge once again. I groped into the pocket which had held Dick and pulled onto the ledge inner boots, and boots, and realised only then that they were still outside in their stockinged feet. I pulled the whole tent back onto the ledge and was able to slide back against the wall of the mountain now that the snow had been cleared away. I leaned back, surrounded by chaos, wondering what to do next.

A dull, hissing thud started up again, and the heavy blows of falling snow hammered once more against my head. I could not believe that there was snow left to avalanche again but the snowfall was so relentless that a new avalanche had formed already. I pressed myself back against the wall to prevent snow forcing its way between me and the mountain and prising me off the ledge. I held tight to the tent with all its contents, lest boots and other vital clothing were lost. I wondered if Pete and Dick would still be outside when it stopped.

This second avalanche brought home to me how helpless we were, how tiny and insignificant our lives were on this mountain. There was no harmony with these forces of nature; we were specks in this colossal and uncaring universe. In my icy tomb I was terrified, fearing another death by suffocation, but I did not dare try to move from my position, embedded in the bank of snow over which the avalanche was pouring. Even if I had managed to move from the frozen mould the avalanche would have whipped me away once I broke through the smooth surface over which it was now sliding. I waited, unafraid, for an outcome which I could do no more to influence; unafraid of what death would mean but horrified by the suffocation by which it was arriving.

Finally the pounding stopped. I shouted to find out if the other two were there:

"Pete, Dick? You all right?"

"Yes."

They dug me free again. Pete had had the wisdom to tie himself with the rope to the pitons embedded in the rock. When the avalanche had struck he had grabbed Dick round the waist and held him all the while the snow was pouring down. We decided that the avalanches must be coming from the summit slopes above the great wall of rock 100 feet above us. I passed them their boots and we took it in turn to dress properly and gather individual gear together. We had been sleeping fully clothed, only boots and gloves had we taken off, but it took time for each of us to make ready. We packed our rucksacks and waited for dawn, hoping against all hope that we would be spared another avalanche, for we could not move from the prow in the dark without risking ourselves even more on the open slope.

At the first glimmer of light in a sky still a heavy grey with cloud and snow I led off down, trying to keep to the rocks to avoid triggering off an avalanche and taking all three of us in it. But it was impossible to follow the rocks. Deep snow covered everything and my crampons slipped and caught on unseen projections. I decided to plough straight on downwards through thigh-deep snow, just trusting that we would survive. Inside I had a feeling of hopeless desperation and, as if some almighty power were manipulating us, I wanted to plead that we needed a break, that we had suffered enough, that no more avalanches should be sent down on us.

The three of us were on one rope 150 feet long but I could barely see the other two. I could hear Pete shouting and knew that he would be critical of my going straight down the open slope of snow, thinking me mad to be running the risk of starting an avalanche. Equally I knew without doubt that it was impossible to try to follow the exposed rocks when many more rocks lay concealed beneath the intervening stretches of snow. I had slipped and fallen many times in trying to keep near the rocks and thought that was certain to lead to an accident. I went down the slope of snow knowing the risk I was taking, knowing that we would be lucky to survive at all, hoping that if the snow did give way beneath me, Pete and Dick might be able to hold me if they were on firmer ground in the trough I had made.

I recognised nothing from the ascent. The swirling cloud and falling snow obscured all but 20 feet in front and behind. I ploughed on in the knowledge that if an avalanche came from above the rock wall again we would be wiped out whether we were on rocks or snow.

I reached the top of the rocky ridge we had followed along the edge of the couloir and recognised where we were. I tried to go along the crest of the ridge but the snow was too deep and I kept losing my footing. Pete agreed that we did seem to be better off in the deep snow, worrying as it was. I carried on down the couloir, down through that zone of fear, trying to keep to the edge and minimise the risk of being caught in the open. We glimpsed in the middle a huge boulder remembered from our ascent only hours before, and we cut across, feeling naked and powerless in the path of any avalanche from all the vast space above. We reached the boulder and took a diagonal line to the far side of the gully. The snow broke away at every step and I knew we were running risks which we could never expect to escape from if anything went wrong.

The previous day I had broken trail up to the edge of the couloir but could still recognise nothing. Pete seemed to be in a daze, his normally powerful self broken as I had rarely seen him and accepting being led. Dick plodded on, equally weak, encouraging Pete.

It was well after dawn but there was no sun, only blizzard; I kept my sunglasses off to see better and my eyes were stung by the driving snow and hail. I wondered if I would go snow-blind, and if I did which medication my doctor had said I should use, eye drops or amethocaine.

I was slow but Pete and Dick did not seem to mind. I kept asking directions and was told to follow the line of rocks. Gradually the angle of the slope lessened and I ground to a halt, bewildered by the whiteness around me and utterly exhausted now that we were out of the worst danger.

Pete forged on, knee-deep in snow, revived from his former aimless state. Dick went next and I brought up the rear. Suddenly I was very weak and could hardly keep up with the other two. I trailed along, repeating to myself the fact that it was not far along this almost level plateau to spur myself to keep on moving. I kept glancing to left and right trying to recognise features which would tell me where we were. I thought the snow ridge to the left was familiar, and the oddly shaped rocks to the right. We were roughly in the right place, but the smallest distance seemed too far to travel. I was falling over snow, and tried to force my pace so as not to be too slow and a drag on the rope for the other two.

Pete waded through an extra deep patch of snow, Dick followed and I found I had collapsed in the snow inadvertently. I heard Pete's voice:

"I think this is the place where we camped."

I stayed sitting for a while, the snow was over my knees when I tried to walk, so I crawled over to join them.

It had taken us six hours to descend 900 feet. It was only nine o'clock in the morning but we were completely spent. We had brought down with us the tent which I had cut into and which had been further damaged by the avalanches, and to recoup some strength before continuing down we decided to put the tent up as best we could and carry on after a proper night of rest.

We had not strength enough even to level out the snow. We pitched the tent on a slight incline, hoping the weight of our bodies would flatten the snow sufficiently. The poles were bent and broken completely in one place. I bound an ice screw to the broken section, we drew the tattered tent over the misshapen framework and we had shelter. There were many vents and tears in the tent fabric but there were two layers of material and most of the holes were offset from each other. Little spirals of snowflakes came in but the main force of the storm was kept at bay. The wind battered the tent remorselessly but it stayed erect despite all the damage it had received.

Inside we lay on the sloping ground, wounded warriors resting from battle. Our weight did nothing to level out the snow beneath the tent floor, but we were too tired to stir again. We laid out our foam mats and pulled on our sleeping bags. Everything felt damp and we were chilled.

We needed food and drink but most of the food had been lost in the avalanche, as had the pan and spare gaz cylinders. We had only one cylinder of gaz on the stove and the pan lid in which to melt snow. Laboriously I melted handfuls of snow and poured the liquid into my water bottle. When it was full I heated the aluminium bottle on the stove and made a drink to share around.

I tried a radio call on the chance that the Major would be listening in but there was no reply. It was a gesture of hopelessness, wanting someone to turn to, someone else to take charge, someone with whom to share our catastrophe. We craved liquid but even the effort of melting snow on the pan lid was too much. I used my Swiss Army penknife to cut away the top of my water bottle and make it easier to push in lumps of snow. It made the melting of snow a little quicker but all three of us relapsed into a comatose state and if we started up from a doze, disturbed by the memories of avalanches and near oblivion, it was to stare dumbly about and to fall back doing nothing.

We found ourselves talking about our chances of coming back on the mountain until we realised how stupidly presumptuous such a notion was. Lying still, the pangs of hunger and fatigue forgotten in the dreamy state of rest after extreme exertion, we sometimes forgot the peril of our situation. We did not have all our wits about us, for when someone mentioned that we had not reached safety yet we all realised how much we had left to go through before we were off the mountain. The snow-fall had not stopped since the previous afternoon, we had thousands of feet of mountain to descend, many open expanses of snow which would now be far deeper and more likely to avalanche than when we had come up over them. There were all the difficult stretches of rock which would now be covered in snow and in the thick cloud we would have trouble finding the way. Getting down would be a nightmare. With only one cylinder of gaz, perhaps three hours' worth, and little food, we could not afford to stay where we were. If we waited until the storm abated we ran the risk of being too weak to get down at all.

I had no spirit left at all. I wanted to surrender. If there had been any escape, I would have taken it; if it had been the same as in the Alps, where rescue by helicopter is possible, I would have called one in, but we were way above the ceiling at which helicopters can fly anyway. I mentioned my thoughts to Dick and he was appalled. He said he would not dream of getting off the mountain by anything but his own efforts.

At 5:00 pm I made the scheduled radio call. It took Major Sarwat a long time to comprehend my message:

"Our tent was destroyed in an avalanche and we are back at Camp Five."

Through the crackle of interference I heard him saying:

"I get that you have reached Camp Six and are going for another try. Is that correct? Over."

I had to fight back the hysteria which was creeping into my voice. I could feel tears welling up in my eyes that we should be in such desperate straits and that there was no sympathy from below. The Major seemed pleased that we were sticking with the attempt to reach the top.

If the line had been clear I would have had no shame in saying: "Please take pity on us. We are only just alive. We are trying to get down," but I had to be blunt and clear; there was no means of subtle communication.

"The tent has been destroyed." I exaggerated a little to get the meaning across. "We are coming down." At the same time I did not want to cause alarm.

Jeff and Mike, the two Americans who were camped near our Base Camp, were with Major Sarwat. When he had finally understood that there had been an avalanche and we were on our way down, he told us that Jeff and Mike were leaving and wanted to say goodbye. There was nothing that they could do to help us, good climbers as they were. They had no knowledge of our route and they would have been equally at risk from new avalanches if they tried to reach us. I did feel, however, disappointment that they should be going. Even knowing that they were watching and waiting with us in spirit would have been a consolation. Obviously they did not know in what distress we were.

I understood from Major Sarwat something about them wanting to borrow our mail runners to be their porters. I consulted with Pete and Dick and they were equally aghast. I radioed down our refusal, feeling mean, but wanting the mail runners on hand for when we got down, if ever we did.

We all slept badly that night. I had pains in the back of my neck and realised only then that I had probably been concussed by the blows from the ice and snow on the back of my head rather than the suffocation.

It took a long time to get moving next morning. The storm still persisted. We packed our sleeping bags but abandoned the tent. I radioed down that we would like Gohar and Ali to come round to the foot of the ridge to meet us with food and a tent once we were off the mountain. If we were late getting off the mountain we could spend a night on the edge of the glacier and they could help us back to Base Camp with our loads. I promised to radio down every couple of hours to relay our progress and asked the Major not to let Gohar and Ali leave until we were sure we would reach the bottom of the Abruzzi Spur.

Pete led off over the crest of the ridge into a deep expanse of snow. He was making towards the ice wall which he had led the way up during our ascent. Dick and I waited, watching Pete making ungainly progress in snow which came up to his waist. He began expressing doubts about the feasibility of descending that way in all the fresh snow. Where the slope steepened he halted and finally shouted that he was coming back, to descend that way would certainly be lethal. He suggested we follow a route down some rocks. I looked about but did not understand which direction he meant. The cloud and snow limited visibility to a few yards.

He was a long time coming back, though he had only gone 100 feet on a gentle slope. The deep snow and absolute fatigue was affecting the movements of all three of us. When he arrived it was to snap at us for not moving.

"What's the matter? Don't you agree about the rocks?"

"No. I just haven't a clue where you mean."

Pete had noticed a line of rocks a long way to the left of the ice wall he had led and it was this he was proposing as a safer descent. "We should be able to get some anchors in the rocks," he said, "and in a few hundred feet we should be clear of the worst part."

He went off into the blizzard and after 300 feet launched off down some rocks which disappeared into the mist and snow below. Dick and I followed, all three of us on the one rope. I marvelled at Pete's forethought and memory of this line, trusting that his sense of direction was accurate, because I could not visualise which direction we were facing.

Sometimes the rocks were very steep and Pete shouted his need for tension on the rope as he floundered and groped for foot-holds and handholds in the snow. When he could, he took up a stance himself, fastening the rope to a piton driven into the rock till Dick and I joined him, slipping and sliding, with little control over the unseen slabs and projections.

My hands were numb with the cold and my gloves soaking with the constant contact with the snow. We normally wore thin gloves under thick mitts with a waterproof cover. My inner gloves made my hands colder with the dampness, so I discarded them, and used only the mitt which kept my fingers together, generating more warmth. As the steps downwards went on and on, as the insane floundering, wet, cold and seemingly hopeless, persisted hour after hour, I knew that we had been mad even to consider coming back up. I had had enough. Surely, I told myself, this was an honourable failure. Surely we had gone as far as could ever be expected. We had driven ourselves to the limit. I tried to make radio contact at the prearranged times but it was futile and the radio became packed with snow.

We could only see 20 or 30 feet at a time, and the descent seemed interminable. All the time my mind was full with the question of whether we were in the very place where Art Gilkey had been lost.

Eventually we came to the foot of a couloir alongside the rocks. Pete continued on in a diagonal line across a snow slope which I could barely distinguish in the mist. We tied two ropes together to give him extra scope whilst Dick and I still remained attached securely to the bottom of the rock ridge. The mist thickened and grew thinner by turns and after a while we could see that Pete was walking upright, facing outwards from the slope, and he was over the worst.

Together the three of us walked down the undulating slope looking for the small cache we had made, when we had left our fourth camp, of the spare tent, food and other superfluous gear. It was no longer superfluous. To descend 800 feet had taken us six hours. The afternoon was nearly over, there was no chance of getting off the mountain that day, and we badly needed to find the tent and food if we were to survive the night.

The white mist merged with the white snow so that it was difficult to distinguish one from the other, difficult to decide what was up, or down, or level. No shadows gave any shape to the slope. By sensation alone we knew we were on a shelf more even than the rest of the snow slope and we looked for any signs that this had been the place where we had once camped and had left the spare tent. The fresh, deep snow blanketed everything into a uniform whiteness.

We sat helplessly in the snow. There were hundreds of square feet to search even if it was the right place. Feebly we each poked at the snow with our ice axes, hoping to feel softness which could distinguish the buried tent from a rock or ice. Dick dug into a spot he was sure was the right location and uncovered a frozen turd, evidence at last that we were near, as we had not strayed far from the tent to relieve ourselves. We concentrated our search in that region and with mighty relief came upon the folded tent and the bag of food and spare gaz cylinders.

It was 3:00 pm. Inside the tent we were able to relax a little more, reprieved for another few hours from the prevailing certainty that every step we took invited death.

On the radio I told the Major that we would not be off the mountain that evening and hoped to make it next day. Jeff and Mike had not left after all, and the Major had a surprise for us. He said he was passing the radio to a friend of ours and we heard a voice familiar in its expressions:

"Hey, you guys, this is Georges. How goes it?"

It was Georges Bettembourg, who had been with us on Kangchenjunga, come to climb and ski down the neighbouring Broad Peak with a team of Frenchmen.

"'Ow are you? You 'ave it difficult. When will you be down?"

It was the same old Georges, bubbling with vitality, questions pouring out, not waiting for answers. I could imagine him bobbing up and down, running back and forth with the radio, impatient with the reception and trying to find a better location rather than concentrating on the conversation.

Pete was equally delighted and somehow Georges's arrival at our Base Camp gave us new heart. He was a friend who understood our predicament, but we told him there was nothing he could do for us. Pete spoke with him also and in spite of the feeling that we were in a condemned cell speaking on a telephone line to a free man we were able to exchange some of the banter and chatter we had enjoyed the previous year with him. The warmth of his company was a bonus to look forward to on our return to life.

There was food and fuel sufficient for our needs but we only had energy to melt a minimum of snow. We wanted to start early next day to try to descend all the remaining ground before dark, so we settled down early to sleep. We all took sleeping tablets, but I swallowed two to make sure that the drug deadened any discomfort and gave me the rest I craved.

I had a night of disturbing dreams. I was in the Vietnam war on a battlefield, standing beside a Colonel Kurtz. I had seen him in the film *Apocalypse Now.* The battlefield was a muddy mess of broken buildings and broken tents. Inside the fabric of the tents we could see the forms of people moving, and the Colonel took out his revolver and shot at pointblank range at the rounded shapes that were people's heads. The film had astounded me with the carefree manner in which the characters courted death. They were shown surfing off a beach whilst bullets poured out of the jungle, dropping napalm on villages to the sound of music from loudspeakers mounted in the helicopters, and sailing up the Mekong river into ambush as they danced to a song of the Rolling Stones, "Satisfaction", on a cassette deck. I woke with the same sensation of capricious flirtation with death, as if death was not final as we tended to think, as if death was not to be feared, otherwise why should people court it so playfully?

One last traverse across deep snow for 300 feet brought us to the top of the ice wall which Dick had led. Pete went first again as Dick belayed the rope. I sat and filmed Pete disappearing into the mist. I had recovered enough composure to use again the small movie camera we had with us.

The snow gave way at every step Pete made. He shouted impatiently, with annoyance engendered by the dangerous crossing, and I was glad of the excuse of filming not to be going first across the slope myself.

Pete abseiled down the ice cliff and as Dick followed him he dislodged some loose snow which caught Pete unawares. The snow knocked him from his footing and he fell 15 feet to be held by the frayed strands of the old rope we had knotted in place where we had thought it least important.

There remained 7,000 feet of descent, more difficult than the open snow slopes, but safer. The rock buttresses were too steep to hold much snow and we could hurry across the open gullies to the greater security of more rocks on the far side. We abseiled down some sections and in others the ropes we had fixed in place hastened our retreat. There was little energy left in any of us now but we had hopes of survival greater than at any time in the last three days.

I felt no wish that we had never started on the mountain in the first place, but now that we were reasonably hopeful of living I resented the long days of hardship that remained before we could relax. Even when our future had seemed bleak, there had been no space in my mind for consideration of anything other than how we could extract ourselves from our predicament. I knew then that I could not pretend to myself that I should have chosen some other way of life because I had had doubts before and had returned again and again to the mountains. Dreadful as our situation was, we had chosen to be in it.

I radioed down our position every hour, unable to say for certain whether we would make it down before dark. Gohar and Ali wanted to climb up to meet us but I ordered them not to. I lost time in making these radio calls, sometimes waiting for the call time behind a ridge which would shelter me from the wind while I spoke, and Pete and Dick drew ahead.

We were on easier ground now which was transformed by the new snow. Even on level stretches I could hardly walk upright. Where tattered remains of rope from the earlier expeditions hung in place I swung down on them, careless of their age, too weak to ignore them as we had done in ascent, and hoping to be allowed to escape from this mountain.

As we came lower, the cloud became less dense and the snow wetter. Sometimes the dark valley bottom was revealed and I was disheartened to see how far away it was and how far ahead Pete and Dick were.

Gohar and Ali were on their way round to us and late in the afternoon I saw their tiny figures on the ledge to which they had come with us when we had left all those days before.

It was dark before I reached them. By touch alone I felt my way down the wet rocks, guided by their torchlight. Pete and Dick were already there. The ordeal was almost over. I straightened up when I reached the platform for the last few yards but stumbled and was caught by Gohar who leapt forward. He and Ali pressed close, wrapping their arms around me and squeezing tight their welcome. They held me for a long while and I wept with relief, surrendering myself unashamedly to the care of these strong, capable men whom we had hired to work but whose concern and affection for us was beyond what money could buy.

They would not let us carry anything ourselves. We had to descend a few hundred feet to the glacier where they had tents and food. The rock under foot was wet and in places icy, but we were alive. Gohar and Ali were solicitous for our every move and shepherded us, as they would their children, down to the place where we would spend the night. They had waited for us for hours, in the cold, in thin clothing on that ledge, forbidden to come higher but reluctant to go back to the tents where they had left their warmer clothing.

At the edge of the glacier we three settled into one tent while Gohar and Ali cooked and served us from a second tent. We were thoroughly damp but we slept in the comfort of knowing we were safe, and that our responsibility was over. We did not even need to carry anything back to Base Camp.

Gohar brought us tea in the morning and Ali presented us with a tiny flower he had picked from the desolate moraine. The ordeal was over.

Our steps were weak and faltering, even on the level part of the glacier. Gohar and Ali carried monstrous loads, refusing to let us take anything from them. For Ali this was the first expedition he had been on and he was unfamiliar with mountaineering techniques, but he was proud to be needed and insistent on doing more than we would ever have asked him.

The weather was clear for the first time in an age as we made our way to Base Camp. There were clusters of people outside our tents and as we came up off the ice they were looking towards us. I felt uneasy at meeting people who would ask about and revive the pain of our ordeal and then Georges was running towards us, his face wide in a smile, and my eyes were brimming with tears. I stumbled into camp blinded by the mist on my sunglasses, glad that their mirror-like reflections would save me explaining the tears, and Major Sarwat was shaking our hands, pleased that his boys were back.

from The Shining Mountain
by Peter Boardman

Peter Boardman (b. 1950; d. 1982) teamed with Joe Tasker on myth-shattering climbs in the late '70s. Their 1975 ascent of Changabang's West Face helped prove that a two-climber expedition could ascend a stunningly difficult route at altitude, and helped usher out the age of enormous, siege-style expeditions to big mountains. Here, the pair confronts extreme climbing difficulties as they approach the summit.

Outside the night roared. Winds were breaking around the great white rock of Changabang, and then retreating, drawing in their breath with anger, gathering their frustrated powers beyond the mountain, to return again through the darkness. And the mountain rolled on. Only dreams of the summit helped us cling to its side

It was three in the morning, and pitch black. "It sounds bloody awful out there," said Joe.

It always did from inside the tent—the crackling walls seemed to be shaking with the constant threat of imminent disaster and were turning the tent into a sound box. Joe was still lying on the outside, and only the bulging nylon of the walls was holding him in place. When the wind gusted violently, the side of the tent tried to roll him over. Fortunately, I had chipped the ice ready for melting for breakfast the night before, and soon had a pan on the stove. The flame of the stove reasserted our defiant right to be there. The tent walls moved the air inside, and the flame swayed slightly from side to side, as if it were continually slipping and righting itself—shaken but always recovering its balance.

We were ready to move at half past six. We had very little equipment, just a climbing rope, a sleeping bag and a bivouac sack each, and a stove, a pan and a little food.

"It's going to be a long cold haul back up there," I said. "Do you want to go first and sort out the rope just below the high point? Then you can get belayed ready for me to lead the top pitch. The Big Groove jumar might get you buzzing."

Joe agreed and I was thankful. I did not want to be the first to jumar the Big Groove, and wanted him to find out what it was like.

The wind was gusting up to 50 miles per hour, and it was agonisingly cold. Every 15 minutes I had to stop in my jumars, undo the zip on the front of my oversuit and down suit and thrust my hands deep under my armpits, gripping my fingers firmly under my arms. "If this goes on any longer I soon won't be able to warm them back up again," I thought. It demanded a disciplined effort to recognise when my fingers were reaching the danger zone, because many of the ends were numb already.

Joe had forgotten to tighten the rope below the high point—it had been a misunderstanding. Still, it did not matter. We had an old hawser laid rope which we thought would reach the Ramp, and probably would not need any more. I took off my sack and left it with Joe, and set off up the pitch. A day's climbing was ahead and we had no idea where we would be at nightfall. A day to hold in the front of my mind, to pace myself through. But the immediate problem was the Groove.

There was a lot of ice on the rock but I wanted to avoid using crampons. First I had to reach the foot of the Groove by crossing its right-hand wall from Joe's stance. There were some good incut holds for my fingers, and soon I was 15 feet above his head. However, my fingers had lost all sensation again; I clipped an etrier into a spike runner, stuck both feet in it and tried to warm them up. I knew I could keep on climbing with numb fingers, but that would do permanent damage, and we had a few days to keep going yet. If Joe resented having to wait in the cold during my re-warming antics, he never complained. However, this was the first time we had been forced to do desperate climbing out of the sun—it was a good excuse.

A flake of rock curved into the Groove and I hand-traversed across this, finding little flaky holds on the granite beneath to support my feet. Soon I was poised next to the Groove, uncertain whether my legs would stretch to a small foothold on the other side if I launched myself across it. I took a deep breath and, feeling as if I were stepping from a secure quayside into an untethered rowing boat, lunged across. My foot missed the hold but, with my hands, I steadied myself against the left-hand side of the Groove, and eased myself carefully into a bridging position. After 20 feet the Groove moved from the vertical to over-hanging. The right-hand wall had become blank and I could no longer bridge across. I placed a nut in the crack and clipped into it, gasping for oxygen. I twisted my head back and looked around.

It was the most amazing, exhilarating situation I had ever been in. I looked down and across at Joe, who was hanging on the edge of space. Directly below me almost our entire route fell sheer away. Over 1,000 feet below was Camp Two, and yet the Upper Tower was so fore-shortened beneath me, and the air so clear, it felt close enough still to be our home. Beyond the icefield, the undulations and peaks on the ridge between Rhamani and the Bagini Glacier were flattened by the perspective of my height. The ridge drew a vertical line across the earth beneath my feet between light and shade, white and brown, known and unknown, explored and forbidden. The black spot of Camp One on the ridge was the only sign of our passing in that wilderness. The rock of the Groove seemed poised on the edge of the mountain. I was directly above that tent nearly 4,000 feet below. For a moment I was speeding through the skies above the wrinkled world.

Above me, a great arc of colours stood across the sky in a rainbow around the pool of white light of the hidden sun. The ice crystals in the air of the upper atmosphere were forming a halo around the sun, the classic herald of an approaching front. I wondered if Joe had read the signs as well, and when the storm would arrive; I hoped it would not be a big one.

The big block crowning the Groove was suspended above my head. I leant out on the nut I was hanging from and pushed it. It did not tremble, so l moved up onto another nut higher in the Groove, pulled a leg clear and kicked it. I did not want to dislodge it in case it chopped the ropes or hit Joe. It probably weighed half a ton. Since there were no signs of it moving, I decided it would be safer to try and squirm behind rather than risk levering it away by pulling around its outside.

As soon as I had wriggled my shoulders through the hole my feet swung out into space. After a lot of undignified wriggling and heaving, I suddenly popped out onto some snow. From above, the block seemed to be balanced on a perch that defied gravity, and I quickly moved my weight off it. I looked upwards and saw snow, the easiest angled snow I had seen for 4,000 feet. I had popped through the Keyhole that, at last, seemed to have opened the door to the climb—surely nothing could stop us now?

"I'm on the Ramp," I yelled into the wind.

Within seconds the sun moved onto me, to help match an outer with inner warmth. I tied off one of the ropes for Joe to jumar up, and started hauling up my sack. As Joe neared me, he had to take his own sack off and attach it to mine, so that he could squeeze the sacks and himself separately through the Keyhole. He was pleased to join me in the sunshine. . . .

The sun was weak and watery, but now we had movement to warm our limbs. We shed most of our hardware and took with us two ropes and a handful of pegs, slings and karabiners. We were still adhering to the pattern of leading two pitches each at a time, and I quickly set off, kicking steps up the snow above us, plunging the spikes of my axe and hammer with a steady rhythm. It was a joy to be able to move so freely, to begin to gain height with such ease. Dumping most of the hardware had made a big difference.

Another buttress of rocks towered above us, rearing its head between us and the summit slopes. The snow I was climbing was powdery and unstable and I decided to aim for these rocks to gain the security of a rock belay. To reach their nearest point, I had to climb diagonally across the slope. I touched the rock at the same moment the rope stopped coming to me from Joe. It had just been long enough.

Joe soon joined me. We had left the jumars behind and were now climbing in the Alpine style with which we were familiar, moving as a fluid integrated unit, our sacks geared for survival. We had cast off from the fixed ropes and the rope between us had been demoted from master to servant; for a while, at least, the mountain would be our total support, and we were reprieved from the hanging, fragile line. The leader and the second could share the climbing movement, no longer were we jumaring past the verticality of each other's achievement. The movement had become all-important. The afternoon was ticking past—we were committed to the summit and our speed would be our only defence.

"This must be the Ramp," I said, "and so we ought to keep on traversing right. It should curve up through this buttress onto the summit snowfield."

Joe, however, thought we should go straight up, following a more direct gully line through the rock buttress. "It looks all right, it'll be much shorter, and it'll be easier to abseil down," he said. Also, he didn't like the state of the snow, and considered that a lot of traversing without the assurance of there being good rock belays would be more dangerous. I was worried that the gully might be too difficult, and that we would waste too much time on it. But it was Joe's lead and so it was his decision to make. After taking a few slings from around my neck he moved off and, after hugging the foot of the rock, led a difficult diagonal pitch over mixed ground up into the gully.

The upper section of the gully was out of sight from us, hidden by an ice slope 50 feet wide, that bulged at 80 feet. Joe pulled over a short rockstep and climbed steadily on the ice up to and over the bulge. Many ice fragments started falling down and the rope stopped moving out so evenly. The texture of the ice had changed from being white, aerated and firm to black, hard, unyielding water ice. Joe climbed for 30 feet up this 60-degree, steely surface towards the left-hand side of the gully at a point where the gully walls closed in. As he climbed he tried to protect himself by hammering in ice pegs. The ice was so hard that it splintered after the ice pegs had entered more than a couple of inches, and he had to tie them off. They offered him little more than psychological protection. His axe and hammer picks and crampon points were blunt after all the previous climbing and demanded heavy swings before they penetrated enough to offer any support. It was mentally and physically an exhausting pitch, and by the time Joe hammered in a rock peg, he had cramp in his forearms and calf muscles. He managed to nick a small foothold in the ice to stand on, and pulled the rope in.

"I found that quite hard," said Joe when I eventually reached him.

There was not much room, and I found I became spread-eagled around him, with one foot on the ice and one foot on the gully wall. I had enjoyed the pitch immensely. It had been the first time on the route I had been able to relish hard technical climbing under the safety of a top rope.

"Excuse me, " I said, since I was half hanging from his harness in my attempts to pass him.

"It's about time you had a wash," said Joe.

I returned to the original subject. "Yes, that last bit was rather tricky. Where do we go now—over there on the right?"

Joe agreed, he had been weighing up the next section whilst I had been climbing. On the right at the back of the gully was a line of apparent weaknesses in the broken ground, where the rock and the ice met. It was impossible to judge its angle and difficulty from where we were.

Trying to appear as confident and forceful as possible, I took a few deep breaths and vigorously front-pointed for 15 feet across the gully until I could brace a foot across a spike and scrape my other crampon against the ice until I was in balance.

For me, it was a perfect pitch. Every move was intricate, technical and yet I could recapture my balance after every two or three movements. Every technique I had ever used was tested and applied, half consciously—bridging, jamming, chimneying, lay-backing, mantle-shelfing, finger pulls, pressure holds all followed in a myriad of combinations. The struggling rope acrobatics of the Upper Tower were forgotten, for this was mixed rock and ice-climbing at its finest. I felt in perfect control and knew the thrill of seeing the ropes from my waist curl down through empty space. I was as light as the air around me, as if I were dancing on tip-toes, relaxed, measuring every movement and seeking a complete economy of effort. Speak with your eyes, speak with your hands, let it all flow from your heart. True communication, true communion, is silent. Chekhov once said that when a man spends the least possible movement over some definite action, that is grace. This was my lonely quest, until the jerk of the rope reminded me that I must stop and secure myself—and that I had a companion. Looking back at Joe, I realised how late it had grown. The gully had turned into a golden amphitheatre, poised on the edge of darkness.

It was an awkward pitch for Joe to follow:

> "The rope was pulling me rightwards; I had to climb into
> the back of the gully but was pulled off balance each time
> by the rope. I shouted to Pete but he did not seem to hear
> and I could not pull any slack down. With a fervent prayer
> that he had a good belay, I swung on the rope across the gully
> and grabbed the rock on the other side."

Our awareness of each other, and our strength, flowed between us in waves. Now, when Joe arrived, I realised with an almost physical sense of shock that he was tired. For a few moments the mask of silence between us fell aside. Nearly 300 feet above us, the gully seemed to finish in a crest against the summit slopes. There were no ledges where we could spend the night around the narrow snow slope, broken by rock-steps, above us.

"I'll take us to the crest if you like," I said.

"Yeah, I'm a bit tired," said Joe.

I was filled with urgency, and determined to stay in the sun until I reached the crest. It was an invented game, to pluck us from the grasp of darkness. It gave me a surge of strength, keyed up as I was by the rhythm of the action. The gully was sheltered and, as I churned upwards with my feet, the powder snow poured straight down. The air was becoming colder but the light was warm and red. The sun was pushing me upwards as if I were soaring on particles of solar light.

Ten feet beneath the crest, I plunged a deadman into the snow and pulled the rope in, but Joe was already moving. I saw his red helmet bob over a rock step, lassooed by the evening light. For the first time since I had followed Joe's pitch up the gully, I could look around me. But night was quickly closing its doors and only the sun held my gaze. It was a glorious sunset that spread its calm into me and abstracted me from the time and space below us. Numb toes and racing heart were forgotten. But these were moments I could not savour. The advent of Joe, darkness and cold stopped our upwards motion. We had to bivouac.

The crest of snow where the gully met the summit icefield was on the edge of the mountain. We reckoned we were at 22,000 feet—with about 500 feet to gain to reach the summit. As soon as we moved onto the crest, the whole atmosphere of the evening changed, for we moved from the shelter of the gully into the wind. The wind was blowing agitatedly across the crest, as it accelerated around the top of the mountain. The temperature was plummeting as the sun disappeared.

"We'll have to stop here," I said, "we might be able to dig in." I felt unusually assertive, as if it was my job this time to organise the bivouac. I fixed up a belay line to some nuts and a piton I had placed in a rock that poked out of the snow, and we both tied onto it. I traced out the area of snow that we ought to excavate, with the pick of my axe, and Joe started digging at one end and I at the other. It was becoming colder by the minute, and soon we were digging with the feverish haste of gold-crazed prospectors, using feet, hands and axe, and throwing up clouds of snow into the wind.

Rock was disappointingly near the surface, and our hopes of a snowhole faded. Eventually we managed to gouge a tiny platform. We were now dangerously cold and it was vital to warm ourselves up. We had brought two small bivouac bags with us in case we had been unable to find a ledge and had to bivouac separately. This meant we had no shelter large enough to cook inside, out of the wind. There would be no evening drink or meal.

"It's your turn to sleep on the outside," said Joe.

"Are you keeping your boots on inside your pit?" I asked him. Yes, he was. We only had our two-pound, lightweight sleeping bags with us, and would need as much warmth as possible.

With his habitual bivouacking speed and catlike search for comfort, Joe was soon ensconced in his green cocoon.

> "Our values had sunk ever further. Tonight, bliss was cessation of activity, a place out of wind and warm sleep."

I was struggling with my sleeping bag, feeling angry at my own comparative ineptitude. I felt very insecure, as if I were only preventing myself rolling off the shelf by keeping my muscles tense. I was lying on my side, facing into the slope which was not quite long enough for me. My feet were poking out over the crest and the wind was tearing at them so fiercely, it felt as if there were no layers protecting them.

Joe seemed to gain a few inches of the ledge every hour. An irrational, miserable little corner of my mind started resenting him. "I bet he's really warm. I bet he's fast asleep. Why does he always seem more comfortable than me? Why does he need so much room?" Every time I dozed off and relaxed, my back and leg muscles would jerk back awake as gravity started to topple me off the ledge. There is a bivouac story of a climber who stayed awake all night so as not to wake his sleeping leader who had slumped against him. Well, that was not me—and I had had enough.

"Hey, Joe, you're pushing me off!"

"Oh, sorry." He sounded wide awake, and immediately made some room for me.

I must have fallen asleep. I pushed the tiny hole left where the draw cord had been drawn tight at the top of the bivouac bag, round to my eyes. It was still dark. It was even colder, and the wind felt as if it were blowing through me like a sieve. Then I realised. My feet. I could not feel my feet. I fought the overwhelming desire to flop back to sleep again and struggled into the fetal position and started taking my boots off: One foot, and then the other; I tried to warm them alternately by pushing both hands down the sock and rubbing and holding the base of the foot and then the toes. It took two hours to bring the feeling back into them.

Dawn meant nothing to us and we were not ready to accept it. I was wincing uncontrollably with the cold.

"Shall we wait for the sun?" I bawled into my bivouac bag, hoping that the sound would manage to escape somehow through the hole above me.

"Yeah," came the strains of a reply. "We should be on the top in an hour or so from here."

I was too cold to think. Two hours later, however, the bivouac king was bored.

"I'm making a brew," he announced, the trade union job differential forgotten. An hour later, a lukewarm mugful of something nondescript was thrust through the gap and I downed it in a couple of gulps.

"The sun's out you know," came the second announcement. And so it was, but all its power was filtered by a high veil of cloud, and it was not warming the day up as we had hoped. I counted up to ten, steeled myself and started getting up.

"Could you tie my bootlaces, Joe?" I knew if I tried to do it my fingers would never recover.

Joe stooped down without a word and tightened them up for me. I felt like a pathetic little child—but Joe did not take the opportunity to throw a gibe. "He must have had a lot of practice doing this for all his little brothers and sisters," I thought.

"We'll leave all the gear here, shall we?" said Joe.

So we were not going to descend the other side. "We'd better take a rope and a couple of deadmen," I said. And we were ready.

It was as if I had done all this before, in a dream, but now I was in the dream itself. We quickly climbed through a short rock step above the bivouac site and started moving together up the 50-degree snowfield. Joe was in the lead.

"I wanted to get it over with. The romance for me was gone . . . the fatigue of altitude and exertion were familiar and not disconcerting. I never looked back to see how Pete was doing whether he was moving faster or slower. I could feel the rope tug at my waist and I would wait, but did not know if it was Pete on the other end or whether it was just dragging in the snow . . . The "Horns" of Changabang were now below us and faintly, in the depths of my consciousness, was the awesome thought that at long last we were clawing our way up a slope, poised breathtakingly above the precipice of the West Wall, 5,000 feet above the glacier. A few points of metal on our boots, a couple of metal tools in our hands and a rope tying us together, were all that were holding us in place."

The light, like an over-exposed photograph, now had no warmth, no colour, no perspective and the snow could have been of any angle—except my gasping breath and heavy feet told me of its height. The wind bowed my head. My eyes were lowered to the moving ground. Wind-buffeted powder snow scurried past in an endless stream. The standstill feeling had returned, which I had felt so many times before when climbing on snow. I was inside a shell that moved in slow motion, with a steady mechanical high-lifted step.

I was blinkered in mind and vision. Clouds were surrounding us. This was Changabang, soon I would be able to see its other side. Would I be able to see Nanda Devi and the Sanctuary of my childhood dreams? It seemed simplest to stay in a single, intense thought, to feel the prospect of a wider horizon draw me like a magnet towards the summit ridge. The memories of a month's struggle on the West Wall lay beneath my feet and the summit was the distillation of all my hopes.

Joe was sitting on my horizon line. He had reached the ridge and was pulling in the loops of rope between us. For the final 50 feet there was a wind-carved crust of hard snow on top of the powder which collapsed under my weight. I steadied my impatience and kicked through it carefully. Joe was as relieved as I was excited at the view. "Don't worry, you can see it," he said as I arrived. It was as if he would have felt responsible if I could not but, so reliable, had managed to arrange a convenient break in the clouds. And there it was, Nanda Devi, the bliss-giving goddess.

Clouds plumed horizontally from its summit above its shadowed North-Eastern Walls. These 8,000-foot walls formed a vast, forbidding amphitheatre of swirling mist. To the west, however, the sun picked out a silver track along the Northern Ridge that threaded its way to the main summit. And the summit was clear. Below the spaciousness between our spire and the twin-peaked mass of Nanda Devi, stretched the upper arms of the promised land. Long orderly brown moraines lined the sides of the glaciers, as if fashioned by giant hands. It was the 15th October and winter would soon cover all that wilderness. No man slept there.

The summit, the highest point on the whole of the ridge, was 30 feet away.

"You might as well move across," said Joe. The top was only a few feet higher than the point where we had reached the ridge.

I thought we would at least shake hands, but Joe did not make any gestures. I wondered if he felt he had just done another climb and that life would just go on until he did his next one. Perhaps wiser than I, he had already started focusing his concentration on the problems we were to face in the descent—perhaps to touch each other would have broken the spell of our separateness. I took some photographs of him sitting on the ridge, with Nanda Devi in the background. His beard and mouth were encrusted in ice and his mirror sunglasses hid any feeling in his eyes. In the mirrors I could see my own reflection. How could I ever know to what depth he was retreating? His few words seemed so inadequate. I could not know if practicality did rule him, or if he was concealing his emotion. Was it that we had different attitudes to expression? Or were we really living at different levels?

It was difficult to judge the size of the cornice and we belayed each other and peered alternately over the edge and down the upper ice slopes of the South Face. We could see about 200 feet, and then the Face cut away into the unknown.

"There don't seem to be any tracks anywhere," I said, "perhaps the lads haven't done the South Face."

I was glad there were no tracks, for they would have taken the edge off our isolation. To the north-east, we could see Kalanka Col, with Kalanka rising from it. Beyond that more white mountains, and I photographed them, determining to discover their names later. But they were tame to our eyes, after the vertical world we had left beneath us. I wished we had decided to descend the other side, to bring a new dimension to our experience of the mountain.

I sat in the snow and changed the film in my camera. But now Nanda Devi and Kalanka were obscured by cloud. "Have you seen over there?" asked Joe.

The storm cloud which had been darkening the northern sky over Tibet all day, had suddenly grown and was moving towards us. The coming of the storm had been announced by signs in the sky, 24 hours before. Now it had arrived.

I did not want to leave and hated the prospect of descending the West Wall. The sight of the other side had liberated my spirit. The isolation of our situation, and the size of the wilderness beneath us, intensified our strength. For a moment I felt omniscient above the world. But this feeling of invincibility was an illusion of pride, for we had yet to descend. It was two in the afternoon and we had been on the summit for half an hour when the first snow flakes began to fall.

from The Snow Leopard
by Peter Matthiessen

Peter Matthiessen (b. 1927) is a novelist, naturalist and explorer. He is not a mountaineer, but The Snow Leopard *describes an epic of sorts. In 1973, Matthiessen traveled to Nepal to study the Himalayan blue sheep and search for the rare snow leopard; for Matthiessen, a Zen Buddhist, the trip was a quest for enlightenment. After an encounter with the revered Lama of Shey on the Crystal Mountain, he must return to the lowlands.*

November 21

The camp is less than a thousand feet below the Namdo Pass, and so this morning there is biting cold, with no warmth in the frozen sun when it appears over the eastern rim. This canyon plunges eventually into a maelstrom of narrow, dark ravines that must emerge into that eastern arm of Phoksumdo that we saw on October 25, for there is the aura of a void between one spine of summits and the next where the turquoise lake of the great demoness lies hidden.

Despite the cold, Tende and Chiring Lamo sit near naked on a sheepskin by their daybreak fire, the child's head laid amongst the beads and amulets and cold silver on Tende's round brown breasts. But Dawa is sick this morning; through Tukten, he tells me that even before leaving Shey, he suffered from dysentery and internal bleeding. That last is worrisome; it might well lead to worse. Perhaps he should rest, but we cannot stay in this wild place between high passes. And of course it is only luck that he came out with us; had it not been for Gyaltsen's fear of Tukten, Dawa might have remained behind and died there, without ever speaking up, less out of fortitude than in that peasant apathy and fatalism that is so often taken for stupidity.

I give him something for his dysentery; it may kill him. In his weakened state, Dawa longs to be taken care of; it pleases him to be reminded that he must wear a snow mask, so as not to complicate his sickness with snow blindness. He stands before me in knee britches, big head hanging, like a huge disobedient child.

The yak route descends into night shadows, crossing the ice rivers of this canyon and emerging again on sunny mountainside. Here where sun and shadow meet, a flock of Himalayan snow cock sails away down the steep mountain. To the north and west, across the canyons, the thorn-scrub slopes are cut by cliffs, and soon blue sheep come into view, two far pale bands, one of nine, and the other of 26. I search in vain for sign of the snow leopard.

Down in the shelter of a gully, a yak caravan is preparing to set out; two men strap last loads on the balky animals. Before long, there appears another caravan, this one bound north; having discharged its salt and wool, it is headed home with a cargo of grain, lumber, and variegated goods, its yaks rewarded for their toil with big red tassels on their packs and small orange ones decking out their ears. The dark shapes of the nomads glint with beads and earrings, amulets, and silver daggers; here are the Ch'ang Tartars of 2,000 years ago. With their harsh cries and piercing whistles, naked beneath filthy skins of animals, these wild men bawling at rough beasts are fit inhabitants of such dark gorges; one can scarcely imagine them anywhere else. The Redfaced Devils are inquisitive, and look me over before speaking out in the converse of the pilgrim.

Where do you come from?

Shey Gompa.

Ah. Where are you going?

To the Bheri.

Ah.

And as the wary dogs skirt past, we nod, grimace, and resume our paths to separate destinies and graves.

Winding around beneath towers of rock that fall away into abyss after abyss, the path wanders randomly in all directions. In the cold shine of its ice, this waste between high passes is a realm of blind obliterating nature. The labyrinth is beautiful, yet my heart is touched by dread. I hurry on. At last the ledge trail straightens, headed south, and I reach the foot of the last climb to the pass just before noon. On a knoll, there is a prayer wall and a stock corral for those who come too late in the day to start the climb. Plainly, we shall not reach Murwa before nightfall, despite Karma's assurances to the contrary; we shall have to press hard just to cross the pass and descend far enough below the snows to find brushwood to keep warm. Lacking mountain lungs, I am slow in the steep places, and I start the climb at once, without waiting for the others to come up.

Looking back every little while as I ascend, I see that Karma, arriving at the prayer wall, sets out a sheepskin and lies down, while Tende, Dawa, and Tukten perch on rocks. No doubt Karma will build a fire here and delay everyone with a lengthy meal, thus assuring himself and his wife and child the miserable task, at the end of a long day, of setting up camp in cold and dark, for he is as lightheaded as he is lighthearted, and gives the day's end no more thought than anything else. Every piece of information that this smiling man has offered has been wrong: the climb to this pass, it is plain to see, is not only steeper but longer than the last one.

In the cold wind, the track is icy even at midday, yet one cannot wander to the side without plunging through the crust. The regular slow step that works best on steep mountainside is difficult; I slip and clamber. Far above, a train of yaks makes dark curves on the shining ice; soon a second herd overtakes me, the twine-soled herders strolling up the icy incline with hands clasped behind their backs, grunting and whistling at the heaving animals. Then black goats come clicking up the ice glaze, straight, straight up to the noon sky; the goat horns turn silver on the blue as, in the vertigo and brilliance of high sun, the white peak spins. The goatherd, clad from head to boots in blood-red wool, throws balls of snow to keep his beasts in line; crossing the sun, the balls dissolve in a pale fire.

Eventually the track arrives at the snowfields beneath the summit rim; I am exhausted. Across the whiteness sails a lammergeier, trailing its shadow on the snow, and the wing shadow draws me taut and sends me on. For two more hours I trudge and pant and climb and slip and climb and gasp, dull as any brute, while high above, the prayer flags fly on the weltering sun, which turns the cold rocks igneous and the hard sky to white light. Flag shadows dance upon the white walls of the drifts as I enter the shadow of the peak, in an ice tunnel, toiling and heaving, eyes fixed stupidly upon the snow. Then I am in the sun once more, on the last of the high passes, removing my woolen cap to let the wind clear my head; I sink to my knees, exhilarated, spent, on a narrow spine between two worlds.

To the south and west, glowing in snow light and late sun, the great white Kanjirobas rise in haze, like mystical peaks that might vanish at each moment. The caravans are gone into the underworld. Far behind me and below, in the wastes where I have come from, my companions are black specks upon the snow. Still breathing hard, I listen to the wind in my own breath, the ringing silence, the snow fire and soaring rocks, the relentless tappeting of prayer flags, worn diaphanous, that cast wind pictures to the northern blue.

I have the universe all to myself. The universe has me all to itself.

Time resumes, there comes a change in mood. Under the pack, my back is sweating, and the hard wind chills me. Before I am rested, the cold drives me off the peak into a tortuous descent down sharp rock tumulus, hidden by greasy corn snow and glare ice, and my weak legs slip between the rocks as the pack's weight pitches me forward. A thousand feet down, this rockfall changes to a steep snow-patched trail along an icy stream. Toward dusk, in the painful going, I am overtaken by Tukten in his scanty clothes and sneakers. Tukten's indifference to cold and hardship is neither callous nor ascetic: what it seems to be is calm acceptance of everything that comes, and this is the source of that inner quiet that makes his nondescript presence so impressive. He agrees that Murwa is out of the question, and goes on down, still quick and light, to find fuel and a level place to camp.

The steep ravine descending from the pass comes out at last on sandy mountainside that drops into the upper canyon of the Murwa River. Dusk has fallen, and I keep my distance from two herders' fires for fear of the big dogs. Farther on, as darkness comes, I call out, "Tukten, *Tuk-ten,*" but there is no answer. Then, below, I see him making a fire; the inspired man has found a stone shed by a waterfall.

Dawa turns up an hour later, and lies down in the shed without his supper. Every little while we call to Karma and his family, but another hour passes, the stars shine, and no one comes. This morning a yawning Karma had excused his reluctance to get up by saying we would arrive at Murwa in midafternoon. Doubtless it was this feckless minstrel who told Jang-bu, who told me, that "one hard day, one easy one" would take us from Saldang to Murwa: two hard days and one easy one are now behind us, and still we are not there. In his airy way, Jang-bu concluded that we could cross both passes in a single day, since neither one, so he was told, was as high or as arduous as the Shey Pass, not to speak of the Kang La. Being ignorant, I didn't argue, though I had to wonder why, if this were true, the wool traders, coming from Saldang, had chosen the Shey Pass-Kang La route over the other. Tonight I know. Because the icy north face of Kang La is too steep for yaks, the traveler must break his own trail in the snow; otherwise that route is much less strenuous than the Shey-Murwa route, in which three passes must be crossed. And the descent from the third pass up there, in snow conditions, is as wearing as the climb. I hate to think of Chiring Lamo in the ice and starlight, swaying along near-precipices on Tende's small and tired shoulders; these ledge trails should not be traveled in the night, without a moon.

However, I am too tired to act, or even think. I am already in my sleeping bag when this innocent family appears out of the darkness; hearing Tukten's voice, I end these notes and go to sleep.

November 22

Last night I was asleep by eight and slept soundly until four, when I awoke in a deep glow of well-being; I am over the high passes before winter, I am going home. Unaccountably, the joy expresses itself in a surge of gratitude to family and friends, who were so generous in those days of D's dying—so many sad and happy memories at once that lying there in the black cold I grow quite warm.

In D's last hour, Eido Roshi came; he had shaved his head. I held D's right hand, and the Roshi took her left, and we chanted over and over again our Buddhist vows. A little past midnight, effortlessly, D died.

I left the hospital just before daybreak. It was snowing. Walking through the silent streets, I remembered D's beloved Zen expression: "No snowflake ever falls in the wrong place." Even in this grim winter dawn, everything was as it should be, the snowflakes were falling without effort, all was calm and clear. In her book, she says:

> The flower fulfills its immanence, intelligence implicit in its unfolding. There is a discipline.
>
> The flower grows without mistakes.
>
> A man must grow himself, until he understands the intelligence of the flower.
>
> To proceed as though you know nothing, not even your age, nor sex, nor how you look. To proceed as though you were made of gossamer . . . a mist that passes through and is passed through and retains its form. A mist that loses its form and still is. A mist that finally dissolves particles scattered in the sun.

Tukten brings tea and porridge to my tent, and is routing out the others as I set off down the valley. Dawa is staggering, but he is no malingerer; if he collapses, it is very serious, as there is no doctor in these mountains, and we cannot just abandon him in Murwa. In the hope that he can be helped along to Jumla, we have spread his load amongst ourselves, and Karma has agreed to go as porter as far south and west as Tibrikot, on the Bheri River. Fortunately, our supplies are much diminished, and I discard something every day: it suits my spirits to arrive at Jumla on the wind.

The upper Murwa is a broad canyon of juniper and lone black-lichened granites, scattered like monuments in a natural pasture that descends in gigantic steps; the river itself has cut a gorge along the east wall of the canyon.

It is still dark, the sun is far away. To the south, in a wedge of light where the canyon sides converge, the dawn is touching the pink pinnacles of the Kanjirobas. From high across the canyon comes the tinkle of yak bells, and a ghostly smoke arises from the granites: behind a windbreak of heaped sacks, two herders hunch like stone men at their fire, and behind these figures, OM MANI PADME HUM is carved in immense characters on a huge boulder.

ཨོཾ་མ་ཎི་པ་དྨེ་ཧཱུྃ

Thinking of a friend's note, received before leaving home, I smile: "I can hardly imagine all the strange and wonderful sights that you will see." At sunset yesterday afternoon, far overhead, a rock turret cast a huge semblance of my silhouette on the high walls. This morning, I find a great round rock split clean as an apple, and in the split as on an altar a stone orb has come to rest, placed so strikingly by elements and cataclysms that its perfection stops me in my tracks, in awe of the wild, murderous, and splendid power of the world.

I cross a bridge where the torrent swings from the east wall to the west, digging ever deeper into stone to form its gorge, and continue down the mountain in long bounds, carried on waves of gratitude and mirth. My life and work, my children, loves and friendships, past and present—all seem marvelous, full of marvels.

On a bluff above the river cliffs stands the yak herd first seen yesterday on the snow slopes of the pass, and below this place I see a forest, see each birch and fir. And still the path steeply descends even as the canyon opens out, and the cedar and fir of tree line turn to spruce and pine, until at last Murwa itself comes into view, deep down in morning shadows of the mountain.

At Murwa, crows replace the ravens, for it is 4,000 feet lower than Shey. It is as picturesque as I remember it, a grouping of orderly farms behind stone walls set in patterns on an open slope, under the great wall to the northwest that dams Phoksumdo Lake; the slope ends abruptly at the river cliffs where the Murwa torrent strikes the waterfalls below Phoksumdo.

Because Dawa is sick and we are all sore and tired after crossing three high passes in four days, the rest of this day will be spent at Murwa, where camp is set up below the spruce forest, by an abandoned farm. In a stock corral nearby are the bright strange tents of a Japanese mountain-climbing expedition, returning from a climb of Kanjiroba. The red tents bring on confused feelings—the re-entry into the 20th century comes too fast. Still, it is good that the Japanese are here, for the expedition leader is a doctor. But for this improbable encounter, Dawa would have had no help before reaching Jumla. He does not realize how lucky he is, but Tukten does. "Nepali doctors," Tukten says, with a shrug and a sad smile; all the good Nepali doctors leave the country. Our kind benefactor gives Dawa a good going-over, and doses him with bright blue pills that Dawa, miserable though he is, will have to be prodded to ingest four times a day. The doctor thinks he has dysentery, highly contagious, and has pressed preventive dosages on all the rest of us, refusing any payment for his generosity. How we have avoided Dawa's dread disease until this moment is a mystery, since camp procedure is casual, to say the least. I have long since avoided looking at the way our food is handled, and the hands that handle it, since my own would be no better; ironically, until his morale disintegrated, Dawa was much the cleanest of the sherpas, and the only one I ever saw to bathe.

From the maps of the mountaineering expedition, and from Anu, its head sherpa (a neighbor and friend of Tukten, from Solu Khumbu, near Namche Bazaar), I learn that the peak of Kanjiroba with the precipitous glacier face like a huge ice waterfall—the one I admired from Cave Camp and again from the summit of Somdo mountain, behind Shey—is called Kang Jeralba, the Snows of Jeralba, which is another way of saying Kanjiroba; the true Kanjiroba is farther west, up the Phoksumdo River. Although theirs is the second climb of Kanjiroba, which is more than 23,000 feet high, the route of ascent was a new one, and therefore they may claim that they have conquered it.

As to names and locations of the passes we have crossed, the map is vague. Where the "Namdo Pass" should be is a pass called Lang-mu Shey, or "Long Pass in Shey Region"—a good description of the pass between Shey and Saldang. Yesterday's pass is located correctly and is known as Bugu La; it is 16,575 feet in altitude. According to Anu Sherpa, "Bugu" refers to a struggle that took place between a mountain god—Nurpu, perhaps?—and a demon who wished to kill him: at Murwa, the god vanquished the demon, who perished in this torrent beneath the falls.

I am grateful to the mountaineers, but the bright tents and foreign faces, like the mail at Shey, are an intrusion, and the high spirits of the upper Murwa die away. Sunlight will not come until late morning and will be gone not long thereafter: the world is dark. Two hours ago, it might have struck me as quite wonderful that the sun will never touch this tent, where its worshiper awaits its warmth, to wash; now I allow this to become a source of anger, and such foolishness annoys me all the more—have I learned *nothing*? Imperturbable, Tukten observes me; I glare coldly. That crazy joy, that transport, which made me feel as I ran down the mountain that I might jump out of my skin, leap free of gravity, as I do so often these days in my dreams—was that no more than pure relief at crossing the last high pass? If so, how sad it seems to celebrate the end of precious days at Crystal Mountain. Perhaps I left too soon; perhaps a great chance has been wasted; had I stayed at Shey until December, the snow leopard might have shown itself at last. These doubts fill me with despair. In worrying about the future, I despoil the present; in my escape, I leave a true freedom behind.

To an evergreen grove on the cliffs above the Suli Gad, below the village, I take this notebook and a few chapatis, desperate to get away from humankind. Not that I have talked much in this silent time, for in my party, only Tukten speaks a little English, and we have long since exhausted our few subjects; Tukten and I communicate much better without speaking. One of these Japanese has some English, too, but neither of us wishes to take advantage of it; the mountaineers must be as sorry as myself to meet a foreigner in such strange country.

The ponderous water rush, the peaks, the concord of brown habitations of worn stone are very soothing: I sit on sunny lichens, hidden from the wind, feeling much better. Above the falls, the rampart that contains Lake-by-the-Forest fills the sky. Up there, a month ago, a young girl gave me cheese from a wood flagon, and men on silvered saddles, cantering by, called out that the snow was much too deep to cross Kang La.

In early afternoon, the sun is pierced by the snow pinnacle to westward, and I rise, stiff and old, and return to camp. It is very cold. The fields are stubble, and the people stand huddled on the path, waiting for winter. A cold wind blows up dust in whirlwinds, so violent and choking that I move my tent into an empty shed beneath the abandoned farm. Then down off Bugu La come strangers from the north: they invade the house and drive their *dzo* into a stall behind my tent, uprooting the tent stays in the process. Resurrecting the tent, I lie awake most of the night, wondering what sort of cud this beast is chewing.

The Murwa people are denouncing what they call "the tiger," which last night killed a young yak above the village. Tomorrow I leave the snow peaks and descend the Suli Gad, and the last hope of seeing the snow leopard will be gone.

November 23

I wake refreshed and lie awhile, listening to the great rush of the falls. Dawa is better already, I can hear him singing. At daybreak, as I leave our camp, Karma gives me a spruce stave that he cut yesterday as a surprise present: his joy in his own generosity is so infectious that I laugh aloud. Tende is warming Chiring Lamo's bottom over the fire, and Tukten is cooking the neck of the yak—killed by the snow leopard—which he acquired from the new friends he has made here. Tukten is cook on this expedition as well as everything else, and on this outward journey will be paid as a head sherpa, provided he does not mention this to Dawa.

At the Murwa stupa I place upon the wall my shards of prayer stone, on an impulse not to carry them away from Dolpo. Officially, the whole Suli Gad Valley lies in Dolpo, just as Dolpo, geopolitically, lies in Nepal. But it is here at the head of the river, under the snow peaks and the waterfall that thunders down out of the magic lake, that I shall pass from one world to another.

Already this place seems far away, although I am still here. In Rohagaon, the next village to the south, there are no prayer walls, and Masta takes the place of Nurpu; below Rohagaon lie the villages of the Bheri Valley, and the first scent of Hindu attars from the plains of the great Ganga that bears away all whisper of Sh'ang-Sh'ung into the sea.

In the winter canyon of the Suli, all has changed. Where banks of berries shone before, lone small red leaves still cling to the withered bushes; the green lichens on the stones have turned to gold. The moon bear's nest has been ripped down, perhaps for fuel, and the falling leaves have left exposed the ravaged canyon sides charred by man's fires.

In the autumnal melancholy I remember France, in the years that I lived there, still in love with my first wife. One day in Paris, I met Deborah Love, whom I was to marry ten years later. And now, in different ways, those life-filled creatures are both gone. I hurry with the river.

All my life, I have hurried down between these walls, the sun crossing high over my head, voice swept away in the din of this green flood. The river, and life going, the excruciating sun: why do I hurry?

The sun reveals itself, pouring out of a ravine. In an icy stream, I wash away the Murwa dust, and brush my teeth, and deck my cap with a rock dove feather found along the trail. Below, the Suli Gorge is deep and dark again; at this time of the year, there must be parts of it that never see the sun.

Toward noon, the trail climbs up out of the gorge onto the mountainside. In October, when I stared behind me at the snow peaks, this prospect struck me as one of the loveliest in all my lifetime, and I had thought to enjoy it even more on the return journey, in a slow descent into the valleys. Instead I feel driven, and my pace is urgent. Even the narrow trails no longer slow me, I am hardened to all but the worst of them. The season is turning rapidly from near winter to late autumn, and down the mountainside, fresh green bamboo appears along the river.

On a grassy lookout high over the green torrent, I eat one of Tukten's blackish "breads," then keep on going. Probably it would be best to wait for Tukten; I cannot. I keep on going, high on all the oxygen of lower altitudes, up and down and up and down the stony path that drops to the river and climbs up the steep canyon sides and drops again. The wind cave is passed, and the upside-down falls, but the stone demon—doubtless he who lost the epic struggle with the mountain god at Bugu La and was cast down into the Suli Gad ravines—is lost in the shifting lights of the swift river. I thought I remembered just the place, but the stone is gone.

The valley woods shelter herdsmen and their fires, and near the hut, a big corral has been set up for yaks, dogs, goats, and human beings in rough skins and pigtails. In the chill air, the dark-skinned northerners sit stripped to the waist, amidst semicircles of striped wool sacks that mark out each encampment. One gesticulates; he knows me, for he points and cries, "Shey Gompa!" I am told to stay, and so I do for an hour or more, skirting the half-wild wolf-eyed dogs as I stroll in curiosity about the camp. It is early afternoon, the sun here is already gone, and since Tukten and the others are so late, it seems sensible to remain here with the herdsmen. But I am too restless, I cannot wait here in this gorge when sun still shines on the trail along the mountain; abruptly I rise and, watched by impassive Tartar faces, set out without goodbyes toward the south.

At the only brook on this dry mountainside is a small meadow where it is level enough to pitch a tent; surely Tukten will catch up with me before I reach this place, in midafternoon. But he does not, and anyway, the meadow swarms with men and beasts; I drink cold water from the brook and hurry on. Now I am certain that Tukten is not coming, and disturbed about what might have happened—was Dawa too sick to travel after all? Did Chiring Lamo fall into the fire? Has Tukten borne out all the warnings of his doubtful character, and made off to India with my gear? I carry my notes, binoculars, and sleeping bag, with a change of clothes; he is welcome to the rest.

Still, it grows late, and I have neither food nor fuel, and there is no flat place for a fire, except this narrow path along steep mountainside, exposed to wind. I must go to Rohagaon although I cannot reach it before dark. Yesterday, in the spirit of discarding, I threw away my cache of marijuana; today I want it for the first time since I gathered it at Yamarkhar, for I am worn out after ten hours on the steep sides of the Suli Gad, and have no heart for Rohagaon's denizens and dogs. And this thought of *Cannabis* has scarcely occurred when a small withered specimen turns up, just off the trail. I chew up a mouthful on the spot, and thus fortified, march ahead. An hour later, when the cairn to Masta looms on the corner of the mountain, I am all set for this dog-ridden hole, thumping the path with my new spruce stave, not to be trifled with by man or beast.

The dogs are still chained, as it turns out, but the school hut where I hoped to stay is already occupied by a wool trader who displays small enthusiasm for my company. On the roofs above, the somber townsmen gather. The children of Rohagaon now fall silent, and the dogs: all look down from the walls above, as if on the point of carrying out some dreadful judgment. Who is this tall, outlandish figure, come in out of the darkness without porters? For in the dark, they do not know me from the month before. *"Aloo, aloo!"* I cry, making weird hunger signals, as if this might identify me with mankind, and after a while they understand that I am trying to say, "Potatoes!" There are no *aloo*, it appears, only small *anda* laid by the gaunt chickens, which a filthy man of suppurating eye cooks for me in a skillet that his woman has wiped first on her black rags. I think of the kind Japanese doctor and his earnest warnings about boiling all food and drink, no matter what, and hope that by now I have absorbed sufficient germs to fight off everything. Another inhabitant, luring me to his low chamber, persuades me to buy a brass cup of his alcohol, which looks and smells like a pink gasoline; this stuff, I think, might disinfect the eggs. My host is teacher at the school: he calls me "my dear brother"—a Hindu habit he has picked up in the lowlands—and tries out other English, too, which I praise lavishly in a successful effort to usurp his bed. Safe from the dogs and the night cold, my belly placated by *anda, Cannabis,* and pink lightning, I lie back in near-spiritual bliss: why in hell do I work so hard at meditation? Someone once said that God offers man the choice between repose and truth: he cannot have both. I have scarcely decided on a lifetime of repose when the dogs set up a terrific row, and everyone rushes forth into the night.

The faithful Tukten has arrived in the pitch-dark, along trails that I don't care for much even in daylight. Dawa and the rest, says he, will no doubt turn up shortly, as indeed they do, with Chiring Lamo crying. While arranging for roof, firewood, and water, Tukten makes a place for me at the family hearth of Infected Eye, where I witness cooking rites so simple and certain in their movements that I sit marveling upon my goat skin, scarcely breathing. The cooking is done by the woman in black rags while Infected Eye lies glowering against the wall; the slow deft handling of burning twigs as *tsampa* and dried pumpkin squash are cooked on a brazier, the breadmaking, the murmuring, the love and food extended to the children without waste words or motion, the tenderness toward the sick husband—all has the pace and dignity of sacrament. Earlier, to impress his fellow villagers, Infected Eye had shouted senselessly at his woman, hurling my rupee note into her face; here by his hearth, where no one can be fooled, he is soft-spoken, humble, full of pain, and this good woman and his children tuck him up against the earthen wall in blankets, laying the infant in beside him. Under the black rags, filth, and brassy earrings of the valleys, she is young: I had thought her a crone. Now she eats the children's leavings—and that only—and sighs and yawns and spreads herself a mat beside her husband. Remarkably, all this takes place as if my own big unfamiliar presence were not there, though I sit here like a Buddha by the hearth. For some time, I have been utterly still, and the children look right through me; it is very strange. Perhaps I have grown invisible at last.

November 24

In the entrance of the dwelling of Infected Eye, I slept last night on a soft bed of dust a half-inch deep. The mad dog of Rohagaon, chained outside, barked all night in vain, for I was too tired to be bothered by his uproar. Only in the early night, when he first woke me, did I go out and threaten him with my stick. This incensed him to the gargling point; he fairly tore his chain out of the wall. Carried away by drunkenness and mirth, I pissed on him, thereby wreaking my revenge for that nightmarish October night as well as this one. And on the wings of this cowardly act, perpetrated by the light of a darkling moon, I went in the greatest peace and satisfaction to my rest.

At dawn, the family's sighed complaints came through the earthen wall, and then the father hobbled out into the light to hawk and piss and spit into the daybreak. Soon his woman went off around the mountain to fetch water, and perhaps squat at the path edge, gazing south at the dawn snow peaks on the far side of the Bheri, and letting who knows what manner of lorn thought pass through her head.

Even before sunrise, the air feels warmer; I can scarcely see my breath in the mountain air. A flight of rock doves, leaving its roost in a ravine below Rohagaon opens out in the morning sun over the valley in a burst of blue-silver wings.

I pass the rock where the Tamangs cracked small walnuts, then the wild walnut wood, now stark and bare. The yellow is gone and the rich humus smell; and the brook that trickles through the wood, muted a month ago by heavy leaf fall, is now insistent, hastening away down the steep mountain to the Suli. There is only a silent company of gray trunks, dulled mosses, stumps, and straying leaves, and the whispering

small birds of winter. But farther down the valley, the abandoned village, so empty-eyed and still in early autumn, has been brought to life
by voices of man, dog, and rooster, for its slopes are winter pasture now
for the yak herds from the north.

From the village, a southward path quits the main trail, descending
through rocks and shining olives to a bridge on the green river. The portals
of the bridge are carved in grotesque figures, yellow and red. Awaiting the
others, I stand on the hot planks in the noon sun, overtaken by a vague
despair. In this river runs the Kang La stream, by way of Phoksumdo River
and the lake, and also the torrent down from Bugu La, and the branch that
falls from the B'on village at Pung-mo; the Suli carries turquoise from
Phoksumdo, and crystals of diamond blue down from Kang La.

Another hour passes; no one comes. Beside myself, I go on across
the bridge and climb the bluff. A half mile below, the jade water of the
snow peaks disappears into the gray roil of the Bheri River, which will
bear it southward into lowland muds.

The track follows the Bheri westward in a long, gradual climb to the
horizon, arriving at a village in a forest. In the cedars of Roman, a fitful wind whips the mean rags on the shrines, and phallic spouts jut
from red effigies at the village fountains, and west of the village stand
wild cairns and tall red poles. From fields below, a troupe of curltailed
monkey demons gazes upward, heads afire in the dying light. Then the
sun is gone behind the mountains.

I have a headache, and feel very strange. The whole day has been
muddied by a raging in my head caused by the tardiness of my companions, who were two hours behind me at the bridge—an echo of
that grotesque rage at Murwa, where for want of unfrozen air in which
to bathe, I vilified the sun that dodged my tent. I seem to have lost all
resilience, not to mention sense of humor—can this be dread of the
return to lowland life?

Walking along the Bheri hills this afternoon, I remembered how
careful one must be not to talk too much, or move abruptly, after a
silent week of Zen retreat, and also the precarious coming down from
highs on the hallucinogens; it is crucial to emerge gradually from such a

chrysalis, drying new wings in the sun's quiet, like a butterfly, to avoid a sudden tearing of the spirit. Certainly this has been a silent time, and a hallucinatory inner journey, too, and now there is this sudden loss of altitude. Whatever the reason, I am coming down too fast—too fast for what? And if I am coming down too fast, why do I hurry? Far from celebrating my great journey, I feel mutilated, murderous: I am in a fury of dark energies, with no control at all on my short temper.

Thus, when a Hindu of Roman, knocking small children aside, pushes his scabby head into my tent and glares about in stupid incredulity, yelling inchoate questions at my face out of a bad mouth with a rotting lip, I lunge at him and shove him bodily out of my sight, lashing the tent flap and yelling incomprehensibly myself: I do not have the medicine he needs, and anyway there is no cure for him, no cure for me. How can he know, poor stinking bastard, that it is not his offensiveness that offends me, the pus and the bad breath of him—no, it is his very flesh, no different from my own. In his damnable need, he returns me to our common plight, this pit of longing into which, having failed in my poor leap, I sink again.

"Expect nothing," Eido Roshi had warned me on the day I left. And I had meant to go lightly into the light and silence of the Himalaya, without ambition of attainment. Now I am spent. The path I followed breathlessly has faded among stones; in spiritual ambition, I have neglected my children and done myself harm, and there is no way back. Nor has anything changed; I am still beset by the same old lusts and ego and emotions, the endless nagging details and irritations—that aching gap between what I know and what I am. I have lost the flow of things and gone awry, sticking out from the unwinding spiral of my life like a bent spring. For all the exhilaration, splendor, and "success" of the journey to the Crystal Mountain, a great chance has been missed and I have failed. I will perform the motions of parenthood, my work, my friendships, my Zen practice, but all hopes, acts, and travels have been blighted. I look forward to nothing.

from Minus 148°: The Winter Ascent
of Mt. McKinley
by Art Davidson

*Things have changed since 1967, when Alaskan
climber Art Davidson (b. 1943) and his seven
companions attempted a winter ascent of North
America's highest mountain. Today, most
climbers know the 20,320-foot peak by its traditional name, Denali—the High One—and
more than 1,000 climbers ascend it each year.
Back then, ascents of McKinley were still a rar-
ity—and no one climbed it in the winter. In this
excerpt, Davidson and two partners descending
the peak find out why.*

March 1

The wind woke us. The wildly whipping parachute billowed and
snapped with reports like those of a bullwhip or rifle. The wind
blasted against the rocks we were nestled among with a deafening eruption of noise; crosscurrents in the storm fluctuated its
pitch to a groan or a prolonged whine. A dull, aching pressure along
my backside was the cold, pressed into me by the wind.

I twisted in my sleeping bag to grope for the loose section of parachute thrashing me from behind. The moment I caught it my hands
were pierced with cold; groggy with sleep, I'd forgotten that the
nylon, like everything else outside our sleeping bags, was about
minus 40 degrees. The cold sank into my fingers while the parachute, jerking and cracking erratically, resisted my attempts to
anchor it. As soon as I managed to gather the slack material under
me, the weight of my body holding it down, I shot one hand under an
armpit and the other into my crotch for warmth. I was out of breath
from the effort.

Drawn tighter, the parachute made less noise, and I was able to relax for a few moments. My fingers, aching inside from being deeply chilled, began to gradually rewarm with strong tingling sensations. I pressed the length of my body against Dave to be warmer on that side, and I felt Dave shift inside his bag, trying to press against me. I snuggled close to him and lay quietly for a long time, hoping I'd fall asleep again, as if not thinking about the wind and cold would make them disappear.

I couldn't sleep, and the wind only grew more vicious. I tried to ignore the cold along my backside, away from Dave, but when the first shiver ran through my body I turned to check the sleeping bag where it touched my back. To my horror it was no thicker than its shell, two pieces of nylon. The wind had pushed the down away. I could hardly believe it possible that the parachute, designed to resist wind, was letting the wind eat through it and into my sleeping bag.

The parachute began cracking again. "Oh, hell," I mumbled. The cracking meant a portion of the parachute had broken loose again. Feeling I didn't have the strength for another attempt at anchoring it, I curled up in my bag, shivering occasionally, waiting for something to happen; I didn't know what. After what seemed like several minutes but was probably only a matter of seconds, I heard Pirate trying to tie down the parachute.

"Art." Pirate's voice sounded far off and unfamiliar. "Help me hold it."

Hearing his voice made me realize that the three of us had been awake for more than an hour before anyone had spoken. Burrowed into my sleeping bag, I didn't want to budge from its security, false as it was, for even a moment. While I was deciding whether to help Pirate or prolong my rest, I felt Dave get to his hands and knees and begin wrestling with the parachute, which was now pounding his head and back as it billowed and cracked back in rapid succession. Yanking and cursing, Dave managed to pull part of it around him again, only to have it whip off as soon as he settled down into his bag.

"Look, we gotta get outa here!" Dave yelled.

"Where? We'd never make it down!" I said, grabbing onto the piece of parachute that Pirate was clinging to. "Maybe it's a morning wind that'll die down."

"Morning wind?" Dave looked at me with disbelief. "It's a bloody hurricane, you fool! I'm checking the other side of the rocks."

"Awwghaaaaa. . . ," Pirate growled, staring up into the wind.

Instead of getting completely out of his bag, Dave tied the drawstring at the top tight around his middle. With his legs still in the sleeping bag and his arms free, he lurched toward the crest ten feet away. I was horribly apprehensive. If he lost his grip on the rocks he could easily be blown off the mountain. On the other side we'd never hear him again if he called for help. How far was he going? Maybe he'd be hidden behind a rock where we wouldn't be able to find him if we needed his strength. Besides the logic of my fear, I recoiled emotionally against Dave's leaving because it seemed to break our trust; it violated a fundamental law of survival—stay together.

"Dave," I cried. "Wait! I think it's safer here."

"Stay if you want!" he hollered back. "This wind's bad, and I'm gettin' out of it!"

"Where are you going?" Dave didn't hear me. "It's exposed over there!" He had disappeared over the crest.

Since my mittens were too bulky to grip the parachute, I pulled thick wool socks onto my hands; my fingers were nearly numb already. I was astonished as I looked up to see Pirate holding the parachute with his bare hands. Just as I yelled at him to get something over them, one of my socks started to slip off. Pulling it back on, I shifted position, and the wind seized the wind parka I had been sitting on. Inside its main pocket was the tape recorder I had been using for the physiological testing, but at that moment I was much more concerned about the loss of the half dozen cookies I'd stashed in the pocket. One moment the parka had been next to me, then I saw it whirling through the air, 50, 100 feet up, sailing in the direction of McKinley's summit.

With Dave gone, his loose end of the parachute caught the wind, and this threatened to rip the entire piece of nylon from our grip. We gave up trying to wrap the parachute around us; the pull on our arms wrenched our whole bodies as we clung to it to keep it from escaping. The parachute was our only shelter.

"My hands are bad!" Pirate's voice was weak, almost a whimper. His face was drawn up into a hideous, painful grin. Ice caked his beard.

"Bring them in!" I yelled, though his head was only inches from mine. His fingers felt like chunks of ice against my stomach.

"They're stiff!"

"Move them!" I reached for a better grip on the parachute. It slipped. I lunged. Pirate caught it as it whipped past him. He winced in pain.

"Aw, the hell with it!" Pirate sighed. As he let loose, the parachute twisted through the air. It snagged on a rock. I saw it starting to rip, then it was gone.

For the first time I noticed the sky. It was a blue wall, smashing into the mountain. Thin pieces of cloud shredding—everything grew blurred. My eyes were watering and stinging from squinting into the wind. Compared to anything I had ever experienced, this wind was like another element. It was as if gravity had shifted and, instead of holding us down, was pulling us across the landscape.

Pirate began digging his hands in under my parka. The top of my bag had fallen open to the wind. As I pulled it shut, I fell against Pirate. We grabbed each other.

"Hold onto me!"

"Art, let's get into one bag."

"How? There's no room. . . . Give me your hands." I felt his icy fingers grabbing the skin around my middle. My bag had opened again, and to keep the wind from getting to me Pirate pushed himself over the opening. I just leaned against him, trying to catch my breath. Shivering, teeth chattering, my whole body was shaking with cold.

"Pirate, it's no good!" Wind was coming into my bag. We were both losing our warmth. "Each in his own bag . . . it's better."

"I can't feel my fingers!"

"Put 'em between your legs!"

"I don't want to lose my hands!"

I remembered Dave. If it was less windy on the other side of the rocks, he would have come back to tell us. If it was just as windy, I thought he would have returned to be with us. Something must have happened to him. But maybe he had found a sheltered corner. How could he abandon us?

"Pirate, let's try the other side!"

"Naw . . . the wind's everywhere!"

We huddled together, hunched upright in our sleeping bags, wedged tightly between two rocks. Whenever we relaxed the wind caught us, started us sliding along the ice which gradually sloped away, and forced us to push and fight our way back up into the rocks. Leaning against Pirate didn't make me any warmer, but it was comforting—I wasn't alone. We didn't talk. I could breath more easily with my head inside my bag. I wondered what the others were doing down in the cave. Shiro's cough, Gregg's foot, John's swollen ear—it was too frightening to think about.

Beneath me I felt the ice sliding. Slipping onto my side, I brought an arm out in time to grab Pirate's knee. I pulled myself back against the rocks. My arms trembled from exhaustion. Pirate stared blankly out of his bag. His head turned slowly toward me with a groggy nodding motion. Was he slipping into a stupor? I wondered whether I looked as awful.

"It's no use here," I sighed.

I could barely keep myself up against the rocks. There was nothing I could do for Pirate. Maybe Dave had found a safe spot. I had to check the other side of the rocks, but that would be deserting Pirate. Yet there was no way I could help. How could I just leave him? I had to do something for myself!

"I'm going over." He didn't move. "Pirate," I yelled, "I'm going after Dave!"

His head shook from side to side as he half mumbled, half shouted, something I couldn't understand. I grabbed at the rock above me and pulled myself up the slope. Another rock; its sharp cold cut through the wool socks. Another pull. I reached the crest. To my tremendous relief

I saw Dave crouched on the ice only about 15 feet away. His back was toward me.

"Dave!" He couldn't hear me. I worked a little closer to him. The wind threatened to throw me off the crest. Beyond lay bare glacier where I'd never catch anything to hold onto if I was blown from the rocks.

"Dave!" This time he turned and saw me. I was out of breath and must have been gasping as much as yelling. "Is it better where you are?"

"What? . . . It's the same. Go back!"

I didn't want to go back, and waiting here on the crest was impossible because it was completely exposed to the wind. Before I'd decided which way to go, a cross-current gust caught me. I grabbed for rocks. One came loose. I caught another one nearer Dave. Somehow the sock on my left hand had blown off. I shoved the bare hand into my sleeping bag. The other hand held onto a rock. The wind flung and tossed my body as though it were weightless.

My right hand ached with cold from gripping the rock, and my forearm began cramping from the strain. I couldn't go back into the wind, but neither could my right hand cling to the rock much longer. The only other rock I could reach was three feet to my left, near Dave. My numb right hand had become so dead that I couldn't feel the rock it held onto. My shivering body seemed on the verge of going into convulsions.

I tried to think. If I lost my grip, I'd be blown across the ice. My mind was racing. I had to grab for the rock near Dave with my left hand: it was bare, no mitten or sock. It would be frozen. I had to. Suddenly, my bare hand shot out to grab the rock. Slicing cold.

I saw Dave's face, the end of his nose raw, frostbitten. His mouth, distorted into an agonized mixture of compassion and anger, swore at me to get a glove on. I looked at my hand. It was white, frozen absolutely white.

I pulled my body onto the rock. Dave was only five or six feet away on the ledge he had chopped in the slightly sloping ice.

"Christ, Art." His voice cracked. "You froze your hands!"

I pushed off from the rock, letting the wind throw me against Dave.

He flung his arms around me. All I could do was lie across him, wheezing and shaking, trying to catch my breath.

"Man," he said, "we gotta dig in!". . .

Dave cradled Pirate's feet against his belly and massaged them gently until they began to rewarm.

"Dave," I said, "you know you saved us out there." My words sort of hung in the air. They sounded hollow, and Dave bit at his lip self-consciously. I didn't say more, but my eyes followed Dave with admiration and a kind of love as he tucked Pirate into his bag and then reached for the stove.

For more than an hour I had clung to the ledge on the ice, feeling the frostbite blisters swell on my hands and watching helplessly while Dave dug a cave in the ice. Just before he had completed it, Dave had collapsed from exhaustion; by then Pirate had pulled himself together, and despite his hands and feet, which were beginning to swell with frostbite blisters, he had somehow made it over the crest to finish hollowing out the cave. Dave had recovered enough strength to help me through the small hole in the ice which was the entrance to our new home.

Now inside our cave, Dave leaned on his elbows, and steadying the stove with one hand, he prepared some food with his free hand. In this cramped chamber under the ice cooking was more miserable than it had ever been in the last four weeks; Dave had quietly accepted the job because his were the only hands capable of working the stove. At least he had found some good food to fix—four pound-and-a-half cans of ham, bacon, and peas which had been cached by a previous expedition among the rocks we had bivouacked against. Since our pot had blown away, he heated the ham in its own can, then used the can to melt water in.

Flattened against the wall while Dave cooked in the middle, I realized how small our cave was. At the wide end there was barely enough room for our shoulders, and at the narrow end our feet in our sleeping bags were heaped on top of each other. Because of the rocks behind us, Dave and Pirate had been unable to make the cave long enough for us to stretch out completely. Over our feet the ceiling was about a foot and a half above the floor; toward the larger end there was just enough height to turn or lie on our sides with one shoulder touching the ice on the floor and the other touching the ice on the ceiling. We were quickly learning that our every movement bumped the next person. This cave certainly wasn't pleasant or comfortable by ordinary standards, but it kept us safe from the wind, and that was all that mattered, for the moment.

Dave looked for his journal and found it missing. We had lost too much to the wind—the use of four hands and two feet, an incalculable amount of body warmth, two packs with half our food in them, the parachute, my wind parka, and—perhaps our greatest loss—the foam pads which would have insulated us from the ice and helped to keep our bags dry. Yet we felt secure. We were supplied with enough gas to make water for another day, maybe two more days if we stretched it. With four lunches left, and three remaining cans of food, we needn't worry about starving.

That night ham and hot water were a feast, not filling, but delicious nonetheless; it was our first warm food since leaving the cave down at 17,200 feet more than 30 hours before. My hands had become so inflexible that Dave had to place each bite of ham—there were five of them—in my mouth, then tip the can to my lips to let me drink. Eating made us giddy with pleasure and almost got us feeling warm.

We were actually exultant, not from any sense of conquering the wind, but rather from the simple companionship of huddling together in our little cave while outside in the darkness the storm raged through Denali Pass and on across the Alaska Range.

We agreed that the wind coming out of the northwest was funneling through the pass at least 130 miles per hour. We remembered that a wind of such velocity, combined with the minus 30-, minus 40-degree air temperature outside our cave, created an equivalent wind-chill temperature somewhere off the end of the chart; the last figure on the chart was minus 148 degrees.

"148 degrees below zero."

It was frightening to say the least, but the worst was over, we thought. In the morning the wind should slack off; we would descend, greeting the others at 17,200 feet with the news that we had made the summit; we would get off the mountain and go home. We wanted to believe the climb was over, that in a couple of days everything would be warm and easy again. Yet the wind, howling and pounding the slope overhead, reminded us that we couldn't move until it died down. We talked of the cave as our refuge, but the suspicion that we were being held captive in the ice must have entered each of our minds as we fell asleep listening to the wind.

March 2

. . . Through the night I had slept restlessly, waking every time Dave's knees and shoulders pushed into me. Each time my mind started to clear, the thought that the wind might be down rushed up, but before I'd be fully awake the damnable roar would be running through my head. A shift of legs, or a roll to the other side—in any position the ice was too hard to be comfortable. Sleep made time pass, but the altitude caused a nervous wakefulness.

Staring at the ice, supposing the others were asleep, I looked forward to discussing a plan of action when they woke. Eventually their shifting to find a more comfortable position convinced me that they must already be awake. I asked, and they both said they had been lying silently for an hour or more. I realized there was nothing to say. It was horribly simple. We would have to wait here until the wind stopped, at least until it died down. One sleepless hour after another we listened for the first lull.

During the morning the wind remained constant. The fluctuations in its monotonous tone were so slight that it reminded me of the perpetual roar inside a conch shell—only much, much louder. Later in the day, extraordinary blasts of wind hit the surface of the ice overhead with enough force to actually shake the roof of our cave, causing loose ice crystals to fall from the ceiling.

There was no joking, no idle conversation, hardly any talk at all. We retreated into ourselves, silent, waiting, staring at the ice on the ceiling, staring at the ice on the sides of the cave, staring into the darkness inside our sleeping bags. I tried to think constructively, develop a plan or project for the next summer, but it was useless. The altitude was heckling my mind—the same restless lightheadedness that was keeping me awake also prevented me from concentrating. Wandering thoughts always returned to the sound of the wind, and to the dreary question repeated continually—"When will it stop?"

The only event during the day which aroused any interest at all was our one meal, stretching from late afternoon till after dark. Dave, manning the stove again, thawed and melted more than he actually cooked. Patiently, he dropped chunks of snow and ice into the can, watched them melt, added more snow and ice, and finally—with what Pirate and I agreed was a stroke of genius—he dumped in a package of gorp. When the grog became hot the chocolate bits melted into a fascinating brew, filled with cashews and raisins. Flavored partly with my considerable thirst, it was undoubtedly the best drink I had ever tasted. However, when I had gotten my portion down, a curious, mildly unpleasant aftertaste remained.

About an hour after the hot drink, Dave served the rest of the ham. He heated it over the stove only long enough for it to thaw. Warming it would have meant wasting fuel, which we would need in case the wind held us here another day. Dave placed two pieces of ham, each about the size of an apricot, in my mouth, followed them with several slices of cheese and salami, and finished with three pieces of hard candy.

After another hour Dave melted enough snow and ice to fill the can with water. When it was warm he emptied a tiny can of chopped pork into the water to make a thin soup. Before I drank my portion I felt the need to relieve myself. Going outside was unthinkable.

"Dave," I asked, "isn't there a spare can or a plastic bag we can use for a pee bottle?"

"Nope, Art," he answered. "All we've got is the cooking can."

"Then what did you use?"

"Well," Dave started uncertainly, "I thought you wouldn't eat or drink if I told you, but I used the cooking can."

Now I recognized the scent or flavor that had remained as an after-taste—urine. It didn't matter. I thought it should, but it just didn't.

After Dave poured the last of the soup into me, I prepared to use the can myself—inside my sleeping bag. This would be the first thing I had attempted to accomplish with my swollen fingers; it was a task that even under more normal conditions required considerable technique. An accident would not only be wretchedly unpleasant but disastrous as well, because the extra liquid in my bag would consolidate the down, thus ruining its insulation.

I listened anxiously as the can began to fill. The liquid level rapidly approached the rim, but in the nick of time I managed to maneuver out of what would have otherwise been a shameful and uncomfortable predicament and looked about for a place to empty the can. Not finding a suitable spot to my left and realizing Dave was guarding against my dumping it to my right, I raised the can precariously over my head and sloshed its contents against the ice behind me. Most of it melted in, but a little stream trickled under my bag. No matter, it would be frozen in seconds.

Dave calmly observed that my performance of holding the can was so skillful that I could damn well feed myself from now on.

I had heard Pirate's voice only two or three times throughout the day. Even though he lay along the opposite side of the cave, only four feet from me, I could barely hear his voice above the wind the few times he did speak. The altitude had cut off his exuberance and made him a slowed-down version of his old self. When I asked Dave whether Pirate was all right, he simply said that Pirate was worried about his feet, which had become worse than his hands. The swelling had levelled off, Dave told me, but most of his toes were insensitive to touch.

One particularly excruciating aspect of waiting was knowing that the longer we were held down the worse our frostbite would be. As our bodies began to dry up as a result of an inadequate liquid intake, they became more difficult to warm. Dave's toes were cold, but he didn't complain because he thought that was a good sign; better that they feel cold than numb. Only Dave and I had down booties, yet we had to frequently wiggle our toes to keep the circulation flowing through them. I considered lending my booties to Pirate, but the thought of my feet freezing while I slept discouraged me.

My main concern was my hands, which were swollen to nearly twice their normal size. To flex the tips of my fingers I had to painfully clench the muscles in my hand and forearm. I recalled the last time I had played my flute before leaving for McKinley. I had carefully watched my fingers run over the keys; I had wanted to appreciate them in case I lost them, and at the same time I had promised myself that I wouldn't lose them. I had begun to fear that was exactly what was happening every hour I lay in the cave. I caught myself wondering if I would still be able to play my flute with the first and second joints of my fingers missing.

Our stomachs hadn't really been full since we had left for the summit. An empty sort of craving had settled into my belly; I hoped it wouldn't develop into the cramps which I had heard afflict people suffering from malnutrition. The others down below would be running short of food soon. Maybe they would have to retreat down the mountain. I asked Dave whether he thought the others had given up on us. He didn't answer; maybe he was asleep. Surely they'd come looking for us when the wind died down.

That night, long after it was dark, I found myself repeating the words of a Dylan Thomas poem: "Light breaks where no sun shines." Before I'd come on McKinley I had known the verses by heart; now I couldn't remember the first one past "Where no sea runs the waters of the heart push in their tides." Further on there was something about the things of light filing through the flesh. I couldn't remember. Just the first line— "Light breaks where no sun shines"—ran over and over in my mind.

I lay a long time in the dark, unable to sleep. The wind, a persistent, audible ache in our heads, had been with us for so long that its incessant sounds were like a silence that had settled over our lives. That silent, paralytic quality in the wind recalled images of unalterable bleakness; I remembered seeing the wind run through the broken windows of an abandoned cabin, the wind in the dried grass of a beach in November after the birds had migrated, the wind over the delta of a frozen river.

I couldn't remember what it was like not to hear the wind, but the three of us knew that if we heard it in the morning, our situation would become critical. There appeared to be only enough gas to melt one more can of water.

Through more than 36 hours the wind had not even for a moment relinquished its hold on the mountain and on our lives. Surely, we reassured ourselves, the wind's force would be diminished by morning. . . .

March 3

The infernal noise filled our heads.

The wind's vicious, I told myself. It's diabolical. Silently cursing it became a pastime. I tried to think of all the words that described its evil nature—fiendish, wicked, malicious. I called it a vampire sucking the life out of us.

But the wind didn't hear me, and I knew my words were irrelevant anyway. The wind wasn't malevolent; it wasn't out to get us; it had no evil intentions, nor any intentions at all. It was simply a chunk of sky moving about. It was a weather pattern, one pressure area moving into another. Still, it was more satisfying, somehow more comforting, to personify the wind, make it something I could hate or respect, something I could shout at. I wished I were an old Eskimo shaman, seeing devils and demons in the storm and understanding the evil spirits that lived in the mountain. I thought that a good shaman would know a chant that would chase away the wind. But I didn't know any magic, and I knew all my cursing was only an attempt to escape the simple facts; we had to descend, we couldn't descend in the wind, and the wind showed no sign of letting up.

We needed water most desperately. There was very little gas left in the stove; I wanted Dave to melt ice with it. I tried to think of the most pleasant ways of reminding him that we needed to drink, but whatever I said he growled at. I knew he felt the strain of having to do all the chores for Pirate and me. I felt too thankful, too dependent, almost too much at the mercy of Dave to pester him about the water. He told me that "later" he would melt some ice and thaw the bacon or peas, but gradually the day slipped by without our eating or drinking. Yet, if my hands had been all right, I would have put off the cooking the way Dave did because the altitude had cut away our motivation; it was so much easier to say "later" because, though we didn't really believe it, we always thought the wind might suddenly stop, letting us run down to the cave at 17,200 feet.

It was toward the middle of the afternoon when I heard Dave beginning to coax the stove back to life. He fiddled with it for several minutes without any luck, then decided to let it sit while he opened one of the large cans of bacon, ham, or peas.

It was the moment I had waited for all day.

"Which one do we want first?" he asked.

"Mix 'em all together," Pirate suggested.

Dave scraped the ice off the can of bacon with his knife, clearing the top so he could open it. I could already taste the bacon.

"Damn!" Dave swore in disgust. "Holes in the can! We can't eat the bacon! It's rotten!"

He reached for a can of peas.

It could certainly not happen again. Those holes had been an accident. Nevertheless, Pirate and I listened intently as Dave cleared the ice from the can of peas.

When only about half the ice was off, he swore again. More holes! Than he tried the ham, our last can. It was the same!

We sank back into a numb depression. For two days we had anticipated the flavor of the bacon. We had let ourselves dream of the juice of the peas in our mouths. Suddenly the food we had counted on was gone. The gnawing cramps in our stomachs weren't going to be quieted.

Immediately we were angry for being so cruelly cheated, but only after several minutes did we realize how the spoiled food had transformed our trial with hunger into a confrontation with starvation. We had almost nothing left to eat—three bags of gorp, a dozen slices of cheese, some hard candies, a little coffee, a three-ounce can of chopped pork, and maybe a dozen cookies. The combined calorie count of our remaining food was probably adequate for one person for one day. Solemnly, Dave divided a little less than half of the remaining food into three equal portions.

Although Dave battled with the stove long after his fingers were insensitive from handling the cold metal, he failed to get it going. There was so little gas left that he couldn't build up enough pressure to vaporize it. At 30 below the gas was sluggish—he had to give up. Just like the punctured cans of food, our last drops of gas mocked us with their uselessness.

Our one hope was a gallon of gas Dave had cached on the far side of Denali Pass when he had climbed McKinley in the summer three years earlier. It might still be there; Dave had spotted the bottle of gas the first day we had tried for the summit. He thought we should take a look, but no one volunteered to go out. He said he had originally cached the gas only about 200 feet from where we lay. No one moved. Dave was the most fit to go out, and the most certain of the place it was cached, but the horror of entering the wind overcame the slightest inclination Dave might have had to go after it.

We tried to imagine what the others at 17,200 were doing. They had shelter, but only a limited supply of food. I remembered how a week or two before we had been concerned for the strength of John and George, about Shiro's cough and hemorrhoids, and about Gregg's unpredictable emotions in a crisis. Now they were entirely dependent on their own resources; and the three of us who had once been the strongest might soon come to depend on their judgment and strength to be rescued.

We hoped the others would not attempt anything rash for our sake—that the strain of their fear for us wouldn't break them. We thought of the gallon of gas. We imagined how delicious a cup of water would taste. We shifted our hips and shoulders to relieve the hard cold beneath us.

We talked very little. The grayness inside the cave faded into darkness. . . .

March 4

I woke elated. The wind had stopped. I heard a helicopter.

Just outside the cave I heard the steady whir. Gregg must have gotten a rescue started. It sounded as if the copter had already landed. People must be searching the pass for us. I was afraid they wouldn't find our cave; it was such a small hole in the ice. Maybe they'd give up and leave.

"Dave!" I rolled toward him. "Dave, do you hear the helicopter? We'd better get outside right away."

"Go to sleep . . . it's the wind."

"No! It can't be. It's too steady, too constant. It's a copter. . . . Dave. . . ."

He didn't answer.

"It's a copter," I repeated to myself. "It's the steady whir of a copter." I listened to be certain; but I wasn't certain. Maybe it was the wind; it couldn't be. I almost asked Dave to listen; but I knew he was right; yet I strained my ears for a voice, any sound that would let me believe there were rescuers outside.

There was only the wind.

After a long silence Dave admitted that he had been susceptible to my delusion; he had convinced himself for several minutes that the sound of the wind really was a rescue helicopter.

"But you know," Dave said, looking toward me, "it makes you feel kind of humble to know a helicopter couldn't possibly get to us."

Dave went on to explain how he felt good to know that no device of technology nor any effort on the part of our companions could conquer the storm, or even reach through it to help us. He said the three of us were alone in this sanctuary of the earth's wilderness, and that our only security lay in ourselves, in our individual abilities to endure, and in our combined capacities of will-power and judgment.

I said, "Dave, it may sound funny, but I feel closer to you than ever before."

Dave beamed and said "Yeah, I know what you mean. If we can't fight our way out of this storm, at least we can stick together, and try to live in harmony with it."

I thought to myself how the storm itself was helping to protect us from its own fury. Ever since the McKinley massif had been thrust upward out of a flat land, the wind had been packing the snow and ice of Denali Pass into contours of least resistance. We were sheltered inside ice that conformed to the pattern of the wind. We had suffered and nearly succumbed to the storm that first morning when we had fought it head-on in the open, but now all the force of the wind only pounded more stability into the roof of our cave as it swept across the slope above us.

The altitude riddled our attention span into fragments of thoughts. Discomfort was the only thing on which my mind seemed able to concentrate. My lips were deeply cracked in several places. Moving my tongue along the roof of my mouth I felt clumps of dried-up mucus; other experiences with dehydration had taught me that if I didn't get water soon, the rawest areas in my mouth would begin bleeding. The ligaments in my legs ached as they dried up. It was especially painful to stretch or change positions; unfortunately, the hardness of the ice made my hips and back sore whenever I remained still for more than a few minutes. I complained very little, not because I was naturally stoic, but because there was no one to complain to—each of us experienced the same discomforts; pain had become a natural condition of our life under the ice.

I was probably warmer than either Dave or Pirate because their sleeping bags were icing up faster than mine. Every time Dave had cooked, steam from the warm liquid had been absorbed into his bag, where it soon froze. As the down had matted together, its resilience had disappeared. It was particularly unsettling when Dave pointed out a number of lumps of ice mixed with the down. I didn't see how his bag could retain any warmth. Pirate's bag was a little better, but his down was fast becoming clogged with moisture from his breath because, against Dave's advice and mine, he persisted in burying his head in his bag, where his exhaled moisture had no escape. All of us sorely missed the foam pads. Without them, we were only able to place a spare wind parka or pair of wind pants under our buttocks and shoulders, leaving the rest of our sleeping bags on bare ice.

Pirate's hands were swollen, but he said he was worried most about his feet. He asked about my down booties. Though he didn't say it out-right, I could tell he wanted to wear them. I tried to ignore him, acting as if I hadn't heard. My feet were cold with the booties; without them I thought they would surely freeze while I slept, or even while I lay awake. I avoided thinking about it, but that was exactly what was hap-pening to Pirate's feet. He knew I didn't want to give them up, and didn't ask again. As he kicked his feet inside his bag to relieve their numbness, I knew he must be thinking of the warmth of my booties. Pretending to be asleep, I tried to forget about Pirate's feet.

I couldn't remember how many days we had been in the cave. The day we had gone to the summit, then that first day of the wind, the day we ate ham, then a day without water—it must have been the fourth day, but I was uncertain.

Sometime during the middle of the day Dave rationed us each a fig bar and two hard candies. Sucking on the candies brought a few min-utes of relief to the rawness in my mouth. I put the fig bar aside. I wanted to save it for later in the afternoon as a break in the monotony of hunger. After about an hour I couldn't wait any longer. I had looked forward to saliva coming back into my mouth as I chewed the fig bar, but the crumbs only stuck to the gums and roof of my mouth. With some effort I swallowed the sticky wad, feeling it tumble into my stomach, where it set off a series of cramps. The pain constructed a morbidly amusing pic-ture of four or five hands in my stomach grabbing for the fig bar, fight-ing each other for it, tearing and ripping at it. After a few minutes the cramps died down and the usual steady ache returned.

Silently I cursed the punctured cans of food. Some careless climbers must have punched holes in them with their ice axes as they tried to chip away the ice that covered them. We all wished we had never seen the cans. Without them we might have been able to accept our hunger, but knowing that ham and peas, rotten as they were, lay within arm's reach while we were gradually starving was almost unbearable. The cruelest twist to the irony was the uncertainty; the canned food might still be good. Perhaps the food had remained frozen ever since it had been brought to Denali Pass. It was doubtful that there were any bacteria living at 18,200 feet. At least a portion of the ham, peas, and bacon might not be rancid, but to find out would be risking food poisoning.

Early in the afternoon it became obvious that we were going to spend another night in the cave. Even if the wind let up toward evening, we wouldn't have the time, nor perhaps the strength, to descend. We knew our dehydration was critical. We hadn't drunk a cup of liquid for more than 36 hours. Because our circulation was down we were all chilly inside our bags with all our parkas and wind pants on. Occasionally, I could feel Dave's body tense and shake with shivers. We needed water, which meant we needed gas—which we didn't have.

The only possibility was the gas Dave had cached at Denali Pass three years before. If one of us went for the gallon of gas, he might not make it back through the wind to the cave. The gruesome reality of this possibility had kept us from retrieving the gas, but there was no longer any alternative. One of us had to go for the gas! Who? I couldn't go because of my hands, so I lay quietly in my bag, letting my silence ask someone else to go.

Dave resisted the thought of his going. He had dug the cave. He had cooked for us when there had been gas. He knew his efforts had kept Pirate and me alive. And we knew it.

It wasn't right that Dave go out into certain misery to possibly disappear in the wind. Yet, knowing Dave, I sensed he was struggling with his weariness and fear to find it in himself to go out. Since he was the only one of us who knew for certain where the gas should be, it was logical that he go. Neither Pirate nor I could ask him. Semiconscious from the altitude and the numbing hypnotism of the wind, we retained a sense of justice.

There was another reason we weren't anxious for Dave to go. He was our hands! We needed him to cook if we ever got some gas. We would need him to tie the rope around us and hold us on belay when we descended, whenever that might be.

Quietly—I don't remember hearing him say he would go—Pirate got out of his sleeping bag. When he started to pull on his boots, he found it difficult and painful to force his swollen feet into them. I offered him the use of my down booties. He took them and quickly had them tied on. Dave described the rocks among which the gas had been cached. Pirate pulled down his face mask.

The wind had become more erratic: there were gusts and then short—ten-to-30 second—lulls of comparative calm. Pirate lay on his stomach, facing the entrance, listening for the lull that sounded right to him. A resigned determination seemed to be all that was left of his former fierceness. Suddenly, he gave a short and not too loud "Arahhaa!" and began squirming out the entrance, uphill, through loose snow. Dave and I cheered, not loudly, but with all our remaining enthusiasm. For a moment we heard Pirate placing the pack across the entrance again. Then the lull ended abruptly, and all we heard was the wind.

For the longest time Dave and I listened without saying a word. Ten, 15 minutes passed. We knew Pirate should have returned, but we said nothing. He might call for help only ten feet from the cave and we'd never hear him. . . . I couldn't help imagining what we'd have to do if he failed to return. Maybe Dave would make a try for the gas. Maybe the two of us would attempt to dash down from the pass. If Pirate didn't return within a few minutes there would be no reason to go looking for him. Maybe Dave and I would simply lie in the cave, waiting until Gregg, Shiro, George, and John could reach us, or until we passed into delirium.

We heard a movement at the entrance. Two immediate whoops of sheer joy expressed our relief. A flurry of snow, then a plastic jug shot into the cave, followed by an exhausted Pirate.

"Bad!" He was gasping. "I couldn't stand up, even in the lulls. Something's wrong with my balance." I had never before heard Pirate say anything was rough or dangerous. "I crawled all the way, clawing into the ice with two ice axes. I can't feel my feet now."

We had gas! We could drink water!

With a merriment we'd forgotten ever existed Dave melted chunks of ice and piles of snow. The first can of water, especially, smelled and tasted sweet; we did not remember that the sweetness was the scent of urine. Dave heated can after can of water till they became hot. We drank, and drank, and always waited for yet another capful. For the first time in five days we went to sleep with full stomachs. That we were only full of water mattered not at all—or so we thought.

My feet had become colder. I had to constantly wiggle my toes to keep them from becoming numb. Still, I was glad I had not asked Pirate to return my booties after his trip for the gas. . . .

March 5

. . . The gusts and lulls of the wind sounded hopeful when we woke to another cold, gray morning under the ice. The ragged end of the storm seemed to be blowing itself out, and had we been strong we probably would have tried to dash down from the pass immediately. Unfortunately, we had become so weak that the wind would have to be completely gone before we could descend with any confidence. Yet, regardless of when the wind disappeared, this had to be our last day in the cave, because by the next morning there would be no food at all. For the three of us we had only a handful of gorp, four slices of cheese, and three little hard candies. When this food ran out the cold would take over our bodies unless we could make it down. We lay silent and brooding in our bags; cheerless as our situation was, I felt a curious sense of relief that it was so simple—without food, it was either descend or perish in this wretched cave.

Pirate refused to believe what the wind had done during the night.

On going to sleep, he had fixed a rope to the pack which closed the cave's entrance, then tied that rope around his arm to keep the pack from being blown away if a gust dislodged it. He woke to find both the rope and the pack gone. As the wind had begun packing the entrance full of snow, some loose, fine-grained crystals had sifted into Pirate's sleeping bag; the bag had so little warmth that the snow lay in it without melting. Pirate stared at the snow for ten or 15 seconds, then mumbled hoarsely that he'd leave the snow in his bag because it might help insulate him. His reasoning sounded absurd. I thought of telling him to get the snow out of his bag as fast as he could, but it was easier to lie silent than begin talking. Then I began wondering whether Pirate might be right about the snow helping to insulate him—his bag and Dave's were now little more than matted down and chunks of ice held together by the nylon shell.

Even after Pirate placed his boots and the gas bottle in the entrance to block the blowing snow from sealing us in, snow still blew through every time a gust of wind hit the slope above. Because the entrance wasn't tightly closed off from the storm, a steady draft circulated the minus 35-degree air through our cave. With the chill factor increased, I began shivering again. This wasn't particularly painful, but it was unnerving to watch my body shaking uncontrollably. What happens after you lose control of your body? I thought of asking Dave, but said nothing.

My thoughts wandered back to my childhood. I recalled my parents saying that when I was first learning to walk I enjoyed toddling around in the snow naked. I remembered the times when I was eight and nine and we'd run out into the spring windstorms that sweep across the plains of eastern Colorado; with bales of straw we built shelters from the driving wind and dust, and considered ourselves pioneers. In those days it had been great fun to run shouting from tree to tree in a thunderstorm or when the rain turned to hailstones the size of marbles and golf balls. How had those games in storms led to the desperate mess the three of us were trapped in? All I wanted now was to be free of the fear of freezing and being buried under the ice. I started imagining what we'd look like frozen solid. The feel of my mouth on Farine's cold lips came back. I saw his last expression frozen in his cheeks and eyelids. How much of a body could be frozen before the heart stopped? Was I acting cowardly to think this way? It wouldn't happen to us, not to me; yet, there was the cold in our hands and feet.

To get these thoughts out of my mind, I asked Dave if it seemed to him that the gusts were becoming less powerful and the periods of calm longer. He said, "Don't think about it." But I couldn't help being attentive to every fluctuation of the wind, even though I knew as well as Dave that it was only depressing to hear every lull end in a blast of wind.

Only food occupied our thoughts as much as the wind, especially the food in the punctured cans. Those cans haunted us. I felt the little holes staring at me whether the cans were in plain sight or hidden under a sleeping bag or out the entrance. After Dave had emptied the cans of their contents, he classified most of the food as definitely rotten, but there remained at least a pound of peas and a half pound of ham that he thought might be edible. He even thawed and heated some of the ham. It didn't smell or look bad; still, it had come from a partly spoiled can.

"Aw, I'm going to eat it," Pirate insisted.

But we wouldn't let him. There was no question in our minds that, weak as we were, food poisoning would do us in. As long as we could just resist the canned food we had a chance; if we gave in and ate the doubtful ham and peas we might eliminate that chance. Of course, the food might be good, and it could easily provide the extra strength we might need to get down.

As our stomachs tightened with cramps and the deafening repetition of gusts and lulls whittled away our patience, each of us changed our minds about eating the canned food. One moment Pirate would declare he was going to eat the ham, and the next he would be restraining Dave or me from trying it. So far we had been able to check ourselves, but every moment of hunger increased the temptation.

We dreamed about feasts, banquets, exotic dishes, all our favorite foods. For what seemed like hours Dave and I listed every type of food we could think of. Sometimes we would be silent for ten or 15 minutes, as if the conversation had ended; then as soon as I'd mention something like "crab," Dave would say "Wow, oh honcho boncho! I'd forgotten crab!" Another ten minutes might pass before one of us would remember a forgotten delicacy.

Once Dave said, "Stuffed green peppers!"

"Yeah . . . with lots of raisins in the stuffing!" I answered.

We tantalized each other with difficult choices between different foods. "Dave," I asked, "would you prefer a mushroom pizza or a pepperoni pizza?"

"Mushroom, and if you could have one fruit, what would it be?"

"Awaarraghaa. . . . I want some bloody meat!" Pirate interrupted. There was enough gas to make as much water as we could drink; however, Dave had only enough motivation to make a minimal amount. As our dehydration continued, our frostbite became more severe. The swelling in my fingers had started to go down; I didn't know whether this was a sign of improvement or an indication that my body simply didn't have enough liquid to keep the swelling up. Much as I worried over the blisters, I realized they were my body's way of trying to save the tissue that had been frozen.

Dave couldn't feel the large toe on his right foot, nor parts of several other toes. There was so little he could do for his feet—rub them, wiggle the toes. He said they were becoming steadily colder. The scabby, frostbitten skin on the end of his nose was sickening to look at, but not nearly as frightening as the freezing that was beginning in his feet. The frostbite on his nose was isolated and had come about because he happened to have a long nose which protruded from his face mask, while the frostbite taking hold in his feet was not isolated; it was a sign that the cold was steadily creeping into his body. It was happening to each of us.

At times I was surprised that I wanted Pirate to continue wearing my down booties, which I had previously guarded so selfishly. I knew I hadn't overcome my selfishness; Pirate was sort of included in it. Since his feet had suffered on his trip to get the gas, I had felt almost as protective toward his feet as toward my own. Later in the day Pirate passed one bootie back to me. Perhaps one bootie each would not be a practical way to halt the freezing in our feet, but, even if it was only a gesture, it was still the most touching thing I had ever seen Pirate do.

The one advantage of being dehydrated was that we rarely had to jeopardize ourselves by urinating into the can inside our sleeping bags. Likewise, our lack of food had saved us from the ordeal of a bowel movement in the wind. Nevertheless, our hour of reckoning came. We had postponed the moment until it appeared we wouldn't be safe another minute. To go outside would be risking the possibility of contracting a humiliating case of frostbite while our pants were down. By comparison, it was almost pleasant to contemplate attempting the feat inside our sleeping bags. Dave's ingenuity developed a technique which produced little packages, nicely wrapped in toilet paper. With some coaching from him I managed to get my bundles safely wrapped and out the cave's entrance. However, Pirate, who hadn't been very attentive, got himself into trouble. Soon after he had completely disappeared into his sleeping bag we heard him begin to mumble and swear. When the shape of his sleeping bag began shifting frantically, we offered him some advice.

"Oh, you had paper?" he moaned. "I didn't know you guys had used paper."

During the first days of the wind, sleep had been an effective way of waiting. Now it had become a continual twisting of hips and shoulders away from the hardness of the ice, a twisting away from the cold that seeped into our bags from the ice beneath. None of us had even a momentary respite from hunger cramps and the cramps and aches in our dried-up ligaments and muscles. Nevertheless, wakefulness continued to be a worse kind of half-consciousness; pain was felt more acutely by a more alert mind, and we realized that we weren't dreaming, that we were not going to wake up to find everything friendly and warm.

At times I was unable to tell for certain whether I was awake or asleep. Dreams of Farine lying on the ice, of John calling from the bottom of that crevasse, of Shiro coughing, of our hands and feet turning black, filled my sleep and drifted over into the different levels of wakefulness that stretched through the day. Hours no longer existed. I once asked Dave how long we had been trapped under the ice; he said he didn't know.

In the afternoon, during one period of what I thought was clear-sightedness, it seemed as though the wind was finally dying. The lulls had become much longer, maybe as long as five or six minutes, and the gusts were less frequent and no longer hit with the force which had shaken our cave for so many days. I dozed fitfully, then woke in the dark to a strange sound. I was startled. To ears that had become unaccustomed to quietness, the silence sounded nearly as loud as the wind's roar had that first morning.

"Dave, the wind's gone! We can descend!"

"Yeah man, I'm cooking us up a farewell dinner to this awful hole," Dave said. In a moment his headlamp flicked on and several minutes later I heard the cheery purr of the stove. It was all over; we thought we had made it through. Our farewell dinner was a farewell to the very last of our food, to the cave, and, we hoped, to the wind. Dave passed the hot water and divided up the four slices of cheese.

March 6

. . . In the gray light and quietness we anxiously prepared to leave the cave, but it took us several hours to get ready. Dave melted ice. Pirate was a long time cramming his swollen feet into his boots. My feet and Dave's weren't swollen, but during the night we had both lost feeling in several toes. With my hands still mostly useless, I relied on Dave to stuff my feet into my boots, then lace them up.

Keyed-up by our departure, we felt more alert than we had at any time since the first day of the wind. When I decided to give the mental tests before we went down, Dave helped me with the stop-watch and the sheet of subtraction problems since my fingers were unable to hold them. Dave said he was thinking as clearly as he ever had; the test results did not agree. It took each of us twice as much time to answer a series of subtraction problems as we had needed to answer a similar series down on the Kahiltna. Although this was only a rough indication of one way in which our logical thought processes were impaired, I made a mental note to be damn careful if we had to make an important decision.

But we weren't really worried. There was no wind. After sticking out the storm we felt there was nothing we couldn't do. In a few hours we'd reach 17,300 feet; we might descend all the way to the 14,400-foot igloos before night. It was going to be great to walk in on the others; they had probably given up on us by now. A new excitement quickened our movements. We were going down, going home! Dave was the first outside. With one word he cut short all our excitement.

"Whiteout!"

"Whiteout." The word hung in the air. We had never considered the possibility of a whiteout after the wind. Dave could see only 20 to 30 feet. A mile of ice stretched between us and the 17,200-foot camp if we took a direct course; but on the slope below us there were four or five square miles of ice, in the basin below there were another four or five square miles of ice, and the basin fell away through 40 or 50 square miles of heavily crevassed glacier. Blinded by the whiteout, we might wander about the ice forever, or rather, until we collapsed, or walked off an edge, or fell into a crevasse.

We hoped the whiteout was merely a small passing cloud that would sift away in an hour or two. We dreaded to think of what would become of us if the whiteout proved to be the beginning of a week-long snowstorm.

I followed Pirate out of the cave only to see his hunched form stumble into Dave, who was also unable to straighten his back. For a moment I just watched the two lean against each other like drunks trying to maintain their balance. A mist of ice crystals crept silently over the rocks behind them.

With short, painful jerks of his head, Pirate twisted his face up to look Dave in the eye: "Dave," he said in a hoarse whisper, "I think I'm too weak to go down."

For the first time since the night we had pulled Farine out of the crevasse, Dave's face went blank with shock. In an instant his confidence had been broken. It wasn't only Pirate's words that had shaken him. In the half-light of our cave we had been unable to see each other's features clearly, but now nothing was hidden. Pirate's appearance was the most appalling. It was as if he had emerged from the cave 20 years older; his voice was that of an old man; his face was furrowed with lines we had never seen before; his eyes were faded and glazed and sunk back into their sockets.

I felt shaky getting to my hands and knees and was unable to stand on my feet without Dave's help. I tumbled over with the first step I tried, hitting the ice with my shoulder to avoid falling onto my swollen hands. None of us had a sense of balance. Our legs were dried up and, along with our backs, were stiff from lying immobile for days. We practiced walking, but it took ten or 15 minutes of stretching and limbering up before we regained enough coordination to walk in a relatively straight line.

To be able to walk again was an achievement, but hardly a consolation, because even if the whiteout cleared, we didn't have nearly enough balance to climb down the hundreds of yards of steep ice that separated us from 17,200 feet. Yet waiting in the cave would be suicide, since one more day without food would certainly leave us without the strength to descend.

Dave grew nervous. Pirate leaned against a rock and mumbled to himself. Desperation made us begin to voice wild plans for escaping from the pass. We discussed the possibility of just Dave and I trying to make it out. Pirate said he'd wait by himself in the cave until we could get a rescue party to him; but of course assistance would not reach him for at least two days, and that would be too late. Once, feeling I was the strongest, I said I wanted to try it alone. I reasoned that if I made it down I could send in help, and if I didn't make it Dave and Pirate would still have a chance if the weather cleared.

How easy it might have been if I could have fully deceived myself. I knew my reasons for a solo descent were flimsily constructed excuses to conceal my desire to save Art Davidson above all else. I became afraid that my fear of our situation was stripping away my sentiments of loyalty to the others. I didn't want Dave or Pirate to see my ruthless self-centeredness. But then, wasn't this need to save myself a sense of self-preservation? And wasn't this healthy, even necessary?

As I began to feel panicky, my eyes glanced swiftly over the ice and rocks and at the whiteness all around us. Dave looked at me. Pirate appeared lost in his thoughts. I didn't know what to say. Despite the urgency of my desire to try it alone, that other sense of being unalterably bound to Dave and Pirate persisted. Maybe this inclination to stick it out with the others was only a reaction to loneliness, but perhaps it was a basic reaction I couldn't violate.

My fingers began to throb and my head felt light. I didn't seem to have control of my thoughts. I wanted to take off by myself, but I couldn't abandon Dave and Pirate. I had to save myself at any cost, but I wouldn't be alive now if it hadn't been for Dave and Pirate. What good was there in perishing together? If I had a better chance of making it alone, shouldn't I forget about Dave and Pirate and take off without them?

I felt I had to scream or run across the ice. To relieve my tension I looked at the clouds. I studied the different shades of grayness that walled us in. And it worked. My panic disappeared as quickly as it had rushed up.

Dave said we ought to hold off deciding what to do because the whiteout might clear. I nodded. Pirate looked at the hole in the ice that was our cave's entrance.

Clouds clung to the pass, filtering the sun's light into a bleak variety of flat grays and whites. An eerie quietness had settled over the mountain; soundless and still, it seemed impossible that this was the same pass the wind had stormed through. The sky that had been terrifyingly alive hung around us lifelessly. The entire range, which had seemed to be some sort of living being during the days the wind had howled, now was only a frozen waste of ice and rock.

Hiding under the ice from all the fury, I'd felt closed in, but this day, standing outside in the stillness of the whiteout, I began to feel brief moments of claustrophobia, as if I were being smothered along with the mountain and all the peaks around us. Standing on our patch of ice it seemed as if the whiteout had cut us off from the world. The sky was gone, and we had only our little island of light in this immense grayness.

Pirate said we had to do something. We continued to stare into the cloud, hoping it would break open to let us descend. *Hoping*—we had come to understand it so well that it had lost much of its meaning; but none of its appeal. I decided that to hope was to ignore the reality of our situation in favor of a wishful belief that some stroke of luck would befall us. No one could come for us through this whiteout. I berated myself for ever hoping, and warned myself never to hope again. Faith was what I lacked. I needed faith that this whiteout, like any stretch of foul weather, would eventually end; and faith that we'd have the presence of mind and stamina to take advantage of that moment when it came. I told Dave we'd be lost if we stopped believing in ourselves; he looked puzzled and said, "Huh?"

Several minutes later I realized I was once again staring at the clouds, hoping they'd part.

As we grew weary of waiting for the whiteout to clear we searched among the rocks for food—a cache someone else might have left behind or some of our own supplies that had been blown away—but found nothing. We stood at the edge of the pass, looking down toward the 17,200-foot camp. Through the grayness I tried to picture Gregg, Shiro, John, and George camped in the cave, waiting patiently for a chance to look for us. Then I remembered they would have run out of food by now. But surely they hadn't left us.

For many minutes no one spoke. All our mountaineering experience told us that we should not descend into the whiteout because we would almost certainly lose our way, or else, weak and without a sense of balance, we would fall. At the same time, we were certain of what would be in store for us if we waited in the cave.

Hours had slipped by since we had first crawled out of the cave.

Although the lateness of the hour was beginning to force us to make up our minds, every alternative still appeared futile. It seemed absurd to choose. I thought that if we ever decided there was no chance at all of our getting down, I'd use my last energies to wander up toward McKinley's north summit.

I told myself that was another desperate thought that ought to be discouraged. Our situation demanded thoughtfulness which we weren't certain we were capable of. The most frustrating part of having our minds affected by the altitude was our inability to know to what extent we were affected. Probably the duller we became, the less we realized we were dull at all.

At length it became apparent that our greatest chance lay in trying to find our way down the ice wall, instead of waiting for the whiteout to clear. Besides, we were disgusted with the cave; Pirate said crawling back into it would be the same as crawling into our grave. By descending we would at least be active, be trying. Dave said we'd better get our crampons on. Pirate said O.K., and I didn't say anything.

Dave, with Pirate lagging behind, headed back up the 50 yards or so to the cave, where we had left our crampons. I waited near the edge of the pass because Dave had thoughtfully offered to bring down my crampons and gear after he was set himself. As Pirate passed the scattered ruins of a large cache, I called after him to ask if he had checked it for food. He said that he and Dave had looked all through it without finding anything edible. Nonetheless, Pirate plowed again through the rubble of a shredded tarp, pieces of wooden crates which must have been airdropped, torn clothes, silverware, all sorts of things we couldn't eat. I figured the cache was most likely one that Washburn had carefully prepared after one of his scientific expeditions, but 20 years of storms and curious climbers had left it a trash heap half buried in the ice. After a minute, Pirate stopped searching and looked at me without speaking. I asked if he had found anything.

"No." Very slowly he continued on up to get his crampons.

I stood in a daze, not wanting to do anything until someone came to take care of me. Staring at the cache, I remembered advice Shiro had once given me; since it was urging me to move, I tried to suppress the thought. Yet it nagged me: "When there is only one way to survive in the mountains, you must check every possibility to the very end in order to find the one that works." The cache was a possibility. Just possibly some food remained hidden toward the bottom of the rubbish; but the cache was 40 feet away, 40 feet uphill. I stood still, without the energy or desire to move. Shiro's words kept repeating themselves in my mind. I heard them in his soft accent: ". . . check every possibility to the very end." I resisted checking the cache; a waste of energy, I rationalized. Then, not realizing I had started, I was walking toward the cache. To get a grip on my ice axe I forced my fingers around the shaft, no longer caring whether my blisters broke—I was going to dig.

I whacked at the ice where it held the canvas tarp; my hands, revolting at the pain, dropped the axe. The tarp hadn't budged. I picked up the axe, and by the time I had swung a couple more times I was in a frenzy. I slashed and beat at the canvas frozen into the ice. I pried and yanked. Hitting with my axe as hard as I could, I must have struck a rock, because the axe's metal adze broke.

I became furious. I couldn't stop. I smashed at the pieces of wood, lashing out with my axe until I collapsed onto my knees. I was out of breath and dizzy, but as soon as my head began to clear I started swinging at the debris again. Still on my knees, I uncovered bits of rotten rope, pots, old socks, ladles, odd boots; and of all the absurd, useless luxuries there was even a colander.

I attacked the cache, driven by an obsession to reach the bottom of it. My hands throbbed with pain and my feet had become numb, but all that mattered was that I check every last inch of the trash. A rage drove me to see what was underneath. When I discovered another layer, I was careful not to destroy anything. I opened a box, but it was full of clothes.

I kicked some of the surface junk aside with my boots, then dug in again with my axe. Ice and splintered wood and strips of canvas were frozen around each other. I grabbed and yanked and kicked, and swung the axe, and eventually I reached another unopened box. I pried it open: more clothes on top, but underneath lay several cloth bags, small, white bags. Excited and exhausted, I felt my heart beating wildly as I fumbled to see what was in one of the bags. The drawstring came loose, and as I looked into the bag I'm certain I would have cried, if my body had had enough water to spare for tears.

Dried potatoes!

Farther inside the crate sat a box of raisins packaged in a wrapper that had gone out of style at least 15 years ago! I found two more bags of potatoes and even uncovered a can of ham without holes in it!

We ate!

Dave enlarged the cave. Crouched on his knees the circulation to his legs was partly cut off. He mentioned that his feet were icy-cold below the arches, and mumbled about warming them on someone's stomach, but he didn't want to bother Pirate or me. I heard him ramble on to himself: "Oh, well, a couple toenails lost, nothing new . . . It won't happen to you, Dave baby . . . don't sweat it. . . ."

Far into the night Dave brewed hot drinks and made quantities of raisin, ham, and potato stew. Life seemed easy again. Our cave was more comfortable and we had the security of knowing there would be something to eat the next day. We settled in, determined to hold out another week if necessary but hoping, as we had hoped for the last six nights, that we could descend in the morning.

March 7

I dreamed that a kindly man cut off my feet every time they grew too large. There would be several minutes of relief each time he sliced them off and set them on a shelf, but always my feet, glowing a bright chartreuse, would swell again to the size of basketballs and ache as if about to burst until they were cut off. I was lying in a small, dark cellar, and before long the shelves that lined the walls were filled with huge, luminous, green feet.

Dave woke me to say my tossing was keeping him awake. A sharp, pulsating ache made both my feet feel as if they were about to explode. They had become partly frozen while I had dug for the food. I wasn't sure whether they had thawed or frozen some more during the night. The only way to relieve the pain was to shift their position; sleeping, I had dreamed of each shift as a thoughtful slice of my friend's knife.

The wind was gone and the whiteout had disappeared. Soon we were all awake, eating, drinking, and wondering where we would meet Gregg, Shiro, and the others. Pirate tried to get us to laugh by saying they had probably scratched us off and flown on home. They must have descended to the 14,400-foot igloos for food, but I figured that they would be coming up to look for us and that we'd run into them on the wall below our cave or perhaps down at 17,200 feet. Dave, not quite so optimistic, said we wouldn't see them until we reached the igloos.

Two hours after waking we attempted to pull on our boots. Once I screamed out loud as Dave shoved and jammed my feet into my boots. Since Pirate's hands were as bad as mine, Dave had to help force his boots on too. When he got around to putting his own boots on, Dave had more trouble than he had with either Pirate or me. The ends of both his feet were swollen.

After crawling out of the cave, we bumped into each other and sprawled onto the ice as we tried to control the uncoordinated blocks of pain that were our feet. Every time one of our boots touched the ice a burning sensation shot up the calf. Pirate spotted a four-engine plane circling the summit. We were not just about to rush down onto the open ice toward 17,200 feet, where the plane could easily spot us. Before setting foot on the steep ice below the pass we had to learn to walk and climb on our injured feet. We stepped in place and practiced traversing a gentle slope. Unfortunately, walking downhill was the most painful and difficult because all our weight jarred onto our frozen and half-frozen toes. Dave strapped on my crampons, then helped Pirate tighten his. Because his were the only hands that hadn't been frozen Dave also took the important anchor position at the end of the rope when we finally decided we were ready to start down.

The ice wall fell away from the pass at an angle of 30 to 40 degrees. At sea level we could have almost played tag on ice no steeper than this; however, at 18,000 feet we had climbed this ice gingerly on the ascent, when our legs had been relatively strong and our balance keen. Now, as we wobbled on spindly, dried-up remnants of legs, each step was near the limit of our capability.

"Don't charge off, Pirate!" I felt I had to warn Pirate, who was leading, to go slowly even though he only crept out onto the ice wall. We tested each position of our feet before trusting our weight onto them.

Because the wind had stolen our packs we had our sleeping bags draped around our shoulders; they hung to our feet, sometimes snagging our crampons, but it was the only way we could carry the bags.

"Slower, Pirate!"

The only thing certain about each step was the pain it would send through our feet. Step after step Pirate led us across and down the ice. The rope tied us together with only a psychological protection; if one of us slipped, we would all peel off the wall. A belay was impossible. If we did come off there would be nothing we could do to arrest our fall until we crashed into the basin 600 feet below.

Pirate stopped.

"Oh, God!" I whispered to myself. One of his crampons had loosened. We were caught on the steepest section of ice. Dave and I chopped out small ledges to relieve some of the strain on our ankles. Pirate's fingers had been too stiff to tie his crampon laces when we had started, but now they had to bind his crampon to his boot.

Dave called anxiously at Pirate to hurry up. My ankles felt on the verge of buckling. Pirate grappled with the stiff straps, cursing at the cold cutting into his fingers—he had to handle the metal crampon with bare fingers. He knew everything depended on him. Should he lose his balance while tugging at the frozen bindings, all our efforts to hold out during the storm would be for nothing.

Pirate straightened; he grabbed his ice axe. I sighed with relief and turned to see Dave grinning behind me.

"All right, you guys. . . . We're goin' down!"

Tense with caution, we placed one foot in front of the other. Each step was carefully considered. The large military plane which Pirate had noticed earlier swung out over the Kahiltna. Even if the plane located us, there was no way it could help us now. We didn't see Gregg, John, Shiro, and George climbing up toward us. Their absence began to worry me because I knew they'd be here to help us down the ice if they could possibly manage it.

"Slow down, Pirate!"

With the steepest ice behind us, Pirate quickened his pace. Actually, he was taking a step only every two or three seconds, but that seemed dangerously fast to me.

"You're gettin' us down, Pirate—you crazy honcho!"

Pirate paused to turn and holler, "Aaahaaaa. . . ."

The rough but level ice of the basin began passing beneath us. "We did it, we did it," I repeated to myself.

However, as the ice rose ever so slightly toward the rocks, our feet became so heavy that we were soon stopping to rest every seven or eight steps. The rocks appeared unfamiliar. When Dave motioned for Pirate to turn right, I said I thought we had to head for the rocks to the left. After discussing the difference of opinion for a moment, we decided that none of us were certain which particular outcrop of rocks the cave was next to. Tired as we were, it was discouraging to think we might go 50 or 100 feet out of our way if we climbed toward the wrong rocks. We compromised by striking out in a line running directly between the two main rock outcroppings. Ten and then 20 yards of ice were covered; Pirate called out that he could see a bamboo pole sticking out of the ice. It looked to be about ten feet high. Since we had not brought a bamboo pole to this point, we figured a helicopter must have landed rescuers who had left the pole behind. But where were they now? Maybe the others had had an accident. Anyway, the cave had to be near the pole.

Weary and growing apprehensive, we slowly approached the pole. One moment it was hundreds of feet away, then we suddenly realized it was only ten feet away and wasn't a bamboo pole at all. It was simply a willow wand. Our eyes had fooled us. Somehow the altitude or our dehydration or perhaps even our lack of food had affected our sense of depth perception. It was particularly startling because each of us had been deceived in the same way.

We passed by the willow wand and approached the cave. Just before we peered into it, I was seized with a sudden fear that we might see bodies. They could have been trapped here and could have never made it down for more food. We looked in; to my relief the cave was deserted. In one corner a small pile of food was stacked against a stove. They must have descended thinking we'd never come down; yet on the slight chance that we would they had left us the most favored delicacies— sausage, coconut balls Gregg's wife had made, and some of the fruitcake my grandmother had baked for us.

While we ate, the circling plane spotted us. Then Sheldon's silver Cessna 180 appeared and flew low over the basin. We waved. He swung around, came in lower yet, and dropped a bag. I retrieved it. Bits of a smashed orange were scattered on the ice. I picked up a carefully wrapped kit but couldn't figure out what it should be used for. Although it was tempting to leave it where it had fallen, I decided the others might be able to determine what it was. I felt somewhat foolish when Pirate immediately recognized it as a radio; the altitude was affecting me more than I wanted to admit. Either our minds were too fuzzy to operate the radio or else it had been damaged when dropped, because we couldn't get it to send or receive.

Filled with food and a little water, we continued the descent. With extreme caution we inched our way down among the rocks along the ridge. We were climbing several times more slowly than we had ever ascended this section of the route. Reaching the fixed ropes, we lowered our bags in front of us to free our arms for handling the ropes.

Our feet suffered a cutting pain every time our boots hit the ice. It became almost unbearable for Pirate and me to grip the rope with our frostbitten hands. Once I slipped, and as I grabbed the rope to halt my fall I could feel the skin and blisters tearing across my fingers.

Near the end of the ropes we entered a cloud. Despite the whiteout, there could be no thought of waiting because we had to avoid bivouacking for another night. Since Dave had climbed this part of the route more often than Pirate or I, he took the lead. We climbed down deeper into the cloud. The tops of the high ridges on either side disappeared. Somewhere ahead in the grayness were two igloos and our friends; beyond the igloos lay an ice fall of enormous crevasses. Should we pass by the igloos, we would walk blindly over the edge of a crevasse. The grayness grew so thick that from my position in the middle of the rope I could see neither Dave nor Pirate.

Dave stopped, then started again. My knees and ankles seemed on the verge of collapsing. Slack rope on the snow in front of me indicated Dave had stopped again. We were lost.

Gray cloud and gray ice appeared the same; the glacier and the sky had become one wall of grayness. Since we couldn't see the slope where we set our feet, I began stumbling onto my hands with a crunching of stiff, swollen flesh.

I shouted into the grayness that I thought the igloos were to our right. The rope jerked me to a halt from behind; Pirate must have fallen onto the ice. I heard him yell that we should head more to the left. Dave said nothing. I lay flat on the ice myself, waiting for Pirate to pick himself up and retighten a loose crampon. After several minutes Dave called, "Let's go!"; with considerable effort I got to my feet, and we started staggering on through the whiteout. As we passed through the endless grayness, I began to think we had already gone beyond the igloos. I tried to pull my befuddled mind together to be ready to throw myself onto the ice in arrest position should Dave plunge into a crevasse. I still could not see him and the rope disappeared in the grayness about ten feet in front of me. We might have passed within ten feet of the camp without spotting it. As the snow became deeper, I began wondering whether the igloos would be buried. Dave plodded on.

Blind, and uncertain that my legs could manage another step, I let the rope running to Dave pull me on.

"Waahoooo. . . ." A call in front of me—unable to see Dave, I wasn't sure it had been his voice.

"Igloos!" It was Dave's voice.

With luck or an astonishing instinct he had led us straight to the igloos.

Dave waited for Pirate and me to appear out of the whiteout so the three of us could share that first moment of greeting the others. Nearly delirious with relief and joy we shoveled the entrance of the main igloo free of some drifted snow, then pulled back the tarp which closed the igloo from the weather. We peered inside.

Darkness! The igloo was empty. We found the other igloo also deserted and dark. There wasn't even a note. Were we alone on the mountain? Where were they? None of us felt like voicing our disappointment that the others were gone, that they must have given up on us.

We attacked the food left in the largest igloo. Mashed potatoes, rice, jello, gorp, freeze-dried meat—never had food been so satisfying, but never before had our appetites been really insatiable. Long after we were full we continued to stuff food into our mouths—we had a compulsion to devour everything that was edible. It seemed irreverent to leave any food uneaten.

Despite the excitement of our feast, we ate quietly because we were weary and apprehensive about the fate of the other four.

from The Mountain of My Fear
by David Roberts

David Roberts (b. 1943) is one of the world's best climbing writers, largely on the strength of two early books: Deborah *(1968) and* The Mountain of My Fear *(1970). It is no surprise to learn that he was both a climbing and writing mentor to Jon Krakauer. As a very young man, Roberts made several notable climbs of Alaskan routes, including the first ascent of Mt. Huntington's intimidating west face in 1965. Roberts here describes that success and its tragic aftermath.*

J uly 29 dawned clear. Our fifth perfect day in a row, it was almost more than we could believe. Don and Ed got moving by 7:30 am. Quickly over the Nose, from there on, they faced unclimbed rock and ice. Ed started to lead the first new pitch. Suddenly he remembered he'd forgotten his ice ax in the rush to get started. It was down by the tent.

"What a dumb thing to do," he said to Don. "You think we should go back for it?"

"No. It would take too much time. We can make do with an icelite."

So Don and Ed took turns leading with Don's ax, while the second man used one of our aluminum daggers for balance and purchase. Although it was awkward, it seemed to work.

To make things more unsettling, they had only five or six fixed ropes and about a dozen pitons. Matt and I had not yet been able to bring up supplies to them; they could expect us to reach the tent sometime today with more of everything, but the beautiful weather couldn't be wasted. They would go as high as they reasonably could.

Ed led the next pitch, a traverse on steep, crunchy snow, quickly and well, needing only a piton at the top to belay from. Don managed the same economy on the next, our 37th pitch, though the snow was becoming ice in which he had to chop steps. At the top of the 55-degree pitch he found a protruding block of granite, but there didn't seem to be any good cracks in it. At last he hammered a short, stubby piton in about three-quarters of an inch, tied a loop around its blade to minimize the torque if a pull should come on it, and belayed Ed up. The pitch above required another steep traverse, again on the shallow snow-ice that lay uncomfortably close to the rock beneath. Ed led it carefully. Don could see him silhouetted against the sky all the way. The sun was beginning to hit the face, and they welcomed it after their first pitches in cold shadow. To be sure, sooner or later the sun might loosen the snow, but it would be very hard to climb difficult rock without its warmth. And it looked as if they would have to climb a steep cliff very soon.

They left fixed ropes on the first three pitches, then decided to save their few remaining ones, placing them only on the worst pitches, where they would be most helpful on the descent. Don led another pitch, their easiest yet. With excitement he realized at the top of it that he was standing beside the large smooth pillar we had noticed in the Washburn pictures, and which he knew marked the beginning of the last rock barrier. Ed led into a steep couloir, now hard blue ice in which he laboriously and precariously had to chop steps. But he reached rock on the opposite side where he could get in a good anchor. So far they had used only five pitons in five pitches—the absolute minimum, certainly fewer than they would have used had they had plenty to spare. But they had climbed fast. The snow was still solid, but the rock was warming up. It looked as if they might be able to climb the 70-degree cliff above them barehanded. They certainly couldn't climb all of it with mittens on.

Don began the cliff. At least it had a few fine, sharpedged holds. Trying to save the pitons, he went 40 feet before he put one in. It rang solidly as he pounded it—thank God for the fine rock on this route! Thirty feet above that he was faced by a blank section, unclimbable, free. He hammered in a poor piton, one that wouldn't go all the way in, but vibrated noisily as he hit it. But at last it would hold his weight, and with a stirrup he surmounted the blank stretch. Difficult as it was, the climbing exhilarated him, especially knowing, as both Ed and he did, that above the cliff lay only the long, steep summit ice field. Don climbed into a wide chimney, moved up 15 feet, and found the top blocked by a little ceiling. There was a way out to the left if there was even one handhold at the top of his reach. Except for a thin crack, though, there was nothing. Choosing his smallest piton, he was able to hammer it in about half an inch. He tested it cautiously, putting a carabiner through the piton's eye to hold onto. It felt insecure, but didn't budge; it would probably hold. He was 40 feet above the bad piton, 70 feet above his good one. Moving delicately, putting as little weight on the piton as possible, he swung himself up and around the corner. Ed, watching tensely, saw Don step onto the snow above the highest rock. The cliff was climbed. Don quickly brought Ed up. Ed led a short pitch of crusty snow above, which seemed to lie just below the edge of something. Topping the rim, he looked ahead in amazement. The smooth expanse of the summit ice field lay above him, swooping upward at an unbroken 50-degree angle to the summit. After a month of climbing among jagged towers, inside chimneys, up enclosed couloirs, the summit ice field looked nightmarishly bare. It was like hacking one's way out of a jungle suddenly to stand on the edge of an empty desert.

It meant that they might have a chance for the summit that very day. Ed finished the pitch and brought Don up. Together they planned their attack. It was early afternoon, and going for the summit would undoubtedly require a bivouac. Four hundred feet above them stood the only bit of rock in the whole expanse, an outcrop about ten feet high. They decided to aim for it.

Four quick pitches on the unnervingly open slope brought them to it. The last 50 feet before the rock were steeper, and the sun had started to undermine the ice. They reached the rock with a feeling of relief, and agreed that the snow conditions would get worse for the next few hours. Choosing the one small ledge the rock offered, they chopped a little platform on it and pitched the tiny two-man bivouac tent Don had made. It was crowded inside, but consequently warm. Holding a stove on their laps, they could melt ice chips to make water. It was about five in the afternoon. They decided to wait for night, then go all out for the summit. It was still a long way, perhaps five more hours if things went well. But it was within reach. There was still not a cloud in the sky, no wind to disturb even a grain of snow. The afternoon sun gleamed on the mountains around them as they sat, drunk with the excitement of height, looking over the wilderness below them. For the first time they could see all of the Tokositna Glacier, even the dirty tongue sprawled on the tundra in the hazy distance, whose last ice Belmore Browne had crossed 60 years before. . . .

Matt and I had started at 11:15 am from the Alley Camp. On a hunch, I had suggested that we take our down jackets and an extra lunch, as well as the ropes and pitons we were relaying up to Don and Ed. We made very good time, reaching their tent beneath the Nose in only three and a half hours. It was still early; it seemed pointless to go down at once. We decided to climb above the Nose; at least we could put in extra rope and pitons to safeguard the route behind the leaders for their descent. We were encouraged by the fact that we couldn't hear their shouts; they must be far above.

As we were preparing to climb the Nose, Matt noticed Ed's ax beside the tent. That was very strange; why hadn't he taken it? Unable to think of a more ominous reason, we assumed he had simply forgotten it as he climbed the difficult ceiling and, once above, had decided it wasn't worth going back for. Matt put the ax in his pack so that we could give it to Ed if we caught them, or at least leave it hanging from a piton where they couldn't help finding it on their way down.

At the top of the Nose we saw the newly placed fixed rope stretching around the corner. Without much trouble we followed their steps. Matt led the first pitch, I the second. It was about 3:30 pm; the snow was just beginning to deteriorate in the sun. The steps they had chopped in the ice, therefore, occasionally seemed uncomfortably small; we enlarged a few of them. At the top of the 37th pitch I saw that the anchor piton was a poor one and looked around for a place to put a new one. About five minutes later I gave up and tied into the eye of the piton. Since I wasn't sure how long the piton's blade was, I had no way of judging how far into the crack it had been hammered. But there was a fixed rope leading above to the next piton, so it seemed reasonably safe.

Matt started to lead, holding the fixed rope wrapped around his left arm. Only four feet above me he stopped on a steep ice-step to tighten his right crampon, which seemed to be coming off. As he pulled on the strap his foot slipped and he fell on top of me. Not alarmed, I put up a hand to ward off his crampon, holding him on belay with the other. As his weight hit me, I felt the snow platform I had stomped for my feet collapse. But I was tied in with only a foot or two of slack, and I knew that the anchor would catch me immediately, and I would have no trouble catching Matt a foot or two below me. Yet we were sliding suddenly, unchecked. I realized the piton must have pulled out, but wondered in a blur why the fixed rope wasn't holding me; had it come loose, too? We were falling together, gaining speed rapidly. Matt was on top of me. We began to bounce, and each time we hit I had the feeling, without any pain, that I was being hurt terribly. Everything was out of control. I was still probably holding the rope in a belay, but I could do nothing to stop us. The mountain was flashing by beneath us, and with detachment I thought, This is what it's like. . . .

Suddenly we stopped. Matt was sitting on top of me. For an instant we didn't dare breathe. Then we carefully tried to stand on the steep ice.

"Don't move yet!" I said. "We could start going again!"

Now the fear, which we hadn't had time to feel as we fell, swept over us.

"Are you all right?" Matt asked urgently.

I couldn't believe those bounces hadn't broken any bones. I could move all right and I didn't seem to be bleeding. "I think so. Are you?"

"I guess. I lost my ice ax, though."

Then I realized my glasses were missing. As I looked around I saw them balanced on the tip of my boot. I grabbed them and put them on.

"We've got to get a piton in immediately," I said.

I managed to hammer in several poor ones. We could relax a little now, but trying to relax only made us more frightened. Matt had lost the crampon he was adjusting and both mittens. I had lost the dark clip-ons to my glasses. My right crampon had been knocked off, but it hung from my ankle by the strap. We were bruised but otherwise unhurt. The fall seemed to have been selectively violent.

What had stopped us? Matt still had his hand wrapped around the fixed rope, yet we had been falling without any apparent retardation. I looked up. The fixed rope, no longer attached to the anchor I had been belaying from, still stretched in one long chain to the anchor on the next pitch beyond. We saw Matt's ax, too, planted in the ice where his fall had started. Then we saw that the climbing rope had snagged above us on a little nubbin of rock. That was apparently what had stopped us.

It was safer, at least at first, to go up than to go down. I led, soon getting a very good piton in. I traversed back into our steps. As I passed the nubbin that had caught the rope, I looked at it. It was rounded, no bigger than the knuckle of one of my fingers.

Finally I got to a safe anchor above the bad one. As Matt came up, I tried to figure out what had happened. Just after we stopped falling, I had noticed the piton dangling at my feet, still tied to me, but unconnected to the fixed rope. I realized that I had attached myself to the piton's eye, while the fixed ropes had been tied around its blade. When the piton came out, we were no longer connected to the fixed ropes, except by the grasp of Matt's left hand.

We were extremely shaken. We discussed whether to go back or go on. I wanted to go on. The accident, though it had scared us badly, shouldn't affect our general resolve, I said. I had the feeling, too, that if we went back now we might develop an overwhelming, irrational fear and never want to go above the Nose. Matt reluctantly agreed. Fortunately, I had an extra pair of mittens for him. I could get along without the dark glasses, since it was growing late; but the loss of Matt's crampon was more serious. If I led the rest of the pitches, though, enlarging the right-foot steps for him, we thought it would work.

We continued, still shaky and nervous. Now we deliberately overpitoned the route, making it as safe as was humanly possible. As we climbed, we regained confidence. Soon we no longer had Ed's and Don's fixed ropes to follow, but their steps were clear. Wondering where they had climbed the cliff, I caught sight of a fixed rope dangling. The sight was more than exciting; it was reassuring as well.

I led the cliff, marveling at the difficulties Ed and Don had overcome with only three pitons. I put in about five more. As the sun passed over Foraker, low to the west, I emerged on the summit ice field. There was still no sign of Don and Ed, but as I belayed Matt up, I heard Ed shout to us from somewhere above.

"Where are you?" I yelled back.

"In the rock outcrop!"

We couldn't see them, but hearing their voices again was thrilling. Matt and I hurried up the steep ice to join them. The conditions were at their worst now, even though it was 8:00 pm. Twice I had to hammer rock pitons into the ice for anchors, never a dependable technique.

At last we were reunited. It was wonderful to see them. Ed said at once, "You didn't happen to bring my ice ax up, did—you did? What a couple of buddies!" Then, trying not to overstate it, we described our near-accident. Ed, especially, seemed disturbed; but the safety of numbers and the realization that now we could go to the summit together, as a rope of four, made up for all our misgivings. We ate a few candy bars as the sun set behind McKinley and the mountains faded into the dusky pallor of early night. Around 10:00 pm we started.

Since we had only two ropes, we had to tie in at 90 foot intervals instead of the usual 140. Don went first, I second, Matt third, while Ed brought up the rear. In order to save time, I belayed Don above me with one rope and one hand and Matt below me with the other simultaneously. It was growing dark rapidly. Soon I could see Don only as a faint silhouette in the sky, seeming to walk toward Cassiopeia. We were getting tired; the darkness made our effort seem more private, more detached from the mountain beneath us. After five pitches, at half-past midnight, we reached the summit ridge. We could scarcely tell we were there, except by the gradual leveling of the steep slope. We knew the far side was festooned with cornices overhanging the Ruth Glacier, so we didn't go all the way up to the ridge's level crest.

Now all that remained was the quarter-mile across to the summit, a narrow, airy walkway with a 5,000-foot drop on the left and a 6,000-foot drop on the right. This was the first and only part of our climb that coincided with the French route. Although it was such a short distance to the top, we knew we couldn't afford to underestimate it, for it had taken the French four and a half hours to reach the summit from here a year and a month before. For 600 feet we moved continuously, a ghostly walk in the sky. The night seemed to muffle all sound, and I had the illusion for an instant that we were the only people alive in the world. Soon we faced two flutings, short walls of vertical snow carved and crusted by the incessant wind, which spared the ridge only a few days each year. Perhaps we had been lucky enough to hit one of them. Here it was imperative that the four of us spread as far apart as possible. Don started up toward the first fluting as I belayed from a not very solid ice ax. Traversing high, he stuck his foot through the cornice and quickly pulled it back. Through the hole he could see the dull blueness of the Ruth Glacier below. He returned to my belay spot near exhaustion from the tension and exertion of a whole day of leading. We traded places and I started for the fluting, approaching it lower. The light was returning; an orange wall of flame lit the tundra north of McKinley. I could see the contours of the nearby snow now, glimmering palely. As I neared the bottom of the first wall, I thought I saw something sticking out of the snow. I climbed over to it. Stretched tight in the air, a single, frail foot of thin rope emerged from the ice. I pulled on it, but it was stuck solid. The sight was strangely moving. It testified, in a way, both to the transience and to the persistence of man. That bit of French fixed rope was the only human thing not our own that we had found during the whole expedition. It even seemed to offer a little security. I clipped into it although I knew it was probably weather-rotten.

It seemed best to attack the fluting high, probably even on top of the cornice. If it broke off, at least there would be the weight of the other three on the opposite side of the ridge to hold me. The snow was terrible, made more out of air than anything else. I used one of our longest aluminum daggers in my left hand, my ax in the right, trying to plant something in the snow I could hold onto. At last, by hollowing a kind of trough out of the fluting, I could half climb, half chimney up. Just beyond its top the second fluting began. Don came up to belay me for the new obstacle. It was a little harder, but with a last spurt of energy I got over it. Though things seemed to be happening quickly to me, I took a long time on each fluting, and Matt and Ed grew cold waiting at the other end of the rope. Eventually all four of us were up, however. Then there were only three pitches left, easy ones, and suddenly I stood on top, belaying the others up. The summit itself was a cornice, so we had to remain a few feet below it, but our heads stood higher.

It was 3:30 am. We'd been going for 16 hours without rest. Now we were too tired even to exult. The sun had just risen in the northeast; 130 miles away we could see Deborah, only a shadow in the sky. As Don looked at it I said, "This makes up for a lot." He nodded.

There was no one to tell about it. There was, perhaps, nothing to tell. All the world we could see lay motionless in the muted splendor of sunrise. Nothing stirred, only we lived; even the wind had forgotten us. Had we been able to hear a bird calling from some pine tree, or sheep bleating in some valley, the summit stillness would have been familiar; now it was different, perfect. It was as if the world had held its breath for us. Yet we were so tired . . . the summit meant first of all a place to rest. We sat down just beneath the top, ate a little of our lunch, and had a few sips of water. Ed had brought a couple of firecrackers all the way up; now he wanted to set one off, but we were afraid it would knock the cornices loose. There was so little to do, nothing we really had the energy for, no gesture appropriate to what we felt we had accomplished: only a numb happiness, almost a languor. We photographed each other and the views, trying even as we took the pictures to impress the sight on our memories more indelibly than the cameras could on the film. If only this moment could last, I thought, if no longer than we do. But I knew even then that we would forget, that someday all I should remember would be the memories themselves, rehearsed like an archaic dance; that I should stare at the pictures and try to get back inside them, reaching out for something that had slipped out of my hands and spilled in the darkness of the past. And that someday I might be so old that all that might pierce my senility would be the vague heart-pang of something lost and inexplicably sacred, maybe not even the name Huntington meaning anything to me, nor the names of three friends, but only the precious sweetness leaving its faint taste mingled with the bitter one of dying. And that there were only four of us (four is not many), and that surely within 80 years and maybe within five (for climbing is dangerous) we would all be dead, the last of our deaths closing a legacy not even the mountain itself could forever attest to.

We sat near the summit, already beginning to feel the cold. I got up and walked a little bit beyond, still roped, down the top of the east ridge, which someday men would also climb. From there I could see the underside of the summit cornice and tell that we had judged right not to step exactly on top. We had touched it with our ice axes, reaching out, but it might not have borne our weight.

Ed, who was normally a heavy smoker, had sworn off for the whole expedition. Now, out of his inexhaustible pockets, he pulled three cigarettes. He had no trouble lighting them; after smoking two, though, he felt so light-headed he had to save the third. One of the things he must have looked forward to, I realized, was that ritual smoke on the summit, partly because of the surprise he knew it would cause. But that was only one of Ed's reasons for being there, a minor one. I thought then, much as I had when Matt and I sat on the glacier just after flying in, that I wanted to know how the others felt and couldn't. Trying to talk about it now would have seemed profane; if there was anything we shared, it was the sudden sense of quiet and rest. For each of us, the high place we had finally reached culminated ambitions and secret desires we could scarcely have articulated had we wanted to. And the chances are our various dreams were different. If we had been able to know each others', perhaps we could not have worked so well together. Perhaps we would have recognized, even in our partnership, the vague threats of ambition, like boats through a fog: the unrealizable desires that drove us beyond anything we could achieve, that drove us in the face of danger; our unanswerable complaints against the universe—that we die, that we have so little power, that we are locked apart, that we do not know. So perhaps the best things that happened on the summit were what we could see happening, not anything beneath. Perhaps it was important for Don to watch me walk across the top of the east ridge; for Matt to see Ed stand with a cigarette in his mouth, staring at the sun; for me to notice how Matt sat, eating only half his candy bar; for Ed to hear Don insist on changing to black-and-white film. No one else could see these things; no one else could even ask whether or not they were important. Perhaps they were all that happened.

It was getting a little warmer. We knew we had to get down before the sun weakened the snow, especially on the summit ice field. Each of us as we left took a last glance back at the summit, which looked no different than when we had come, but for the faint footprints we had left near it.

We put fixed ropes in on all the difficult pitches, refusing to let up or get careless now that we were so tired. For the same reason we didn't take dexedrine tablets, though we carried them. When we reached the bivouac tent, we split into pairs to continue down. Ed and I went first, while Don and Matt packed up the little camp before following us. The sun, high in a still perfect sky, had taken the magic out of the mountain's shapes. Only the soft early light and the tension of our expectancy could have left it as beautiful as it had been. At last, after 25 straight hours of technical climbing, we rappelled off the Nose and piled, all four together, into the tent.

Now we could relax at last, but the tent was far too crowded. We felt giddy, and laughed and shouted as the edge of our alertness wore off. We had brought up our pint of victory brandy—blackberry-flavored— and now indulged in a few sips, toasting everything from Washburn to Kalispell. Each of us managed to doze off at some time or other, with someone else's foot or elbow in his face. In the afternoon it grew unbearably hot and stuffy inside, and the Nose began to drip (appropriately enough), pouring water through the roof of the tent. We cooked all our favorite delicacies, robbing the two food boxes rapaciously. By 6:00 pm it had started to cool again, and we saw that, finally, the weather might be turning bad, after six consecutive perfect days, a spell almost unheard of in Alaska. It was as if the storms had politely waited for us to finish our climb. We slept a little more, but still couldn't get comfortable. Around 9:00 pm Ed suggested that he and I go down in the night to the Alley Camp. We were still tired, but it wouldn't be a difficult descent. Once he and I got to the Camp, moreover, all four of us could rest in luxurious comfort, a sleeping bag each, room to stretch out full length, and plenty of food to wait out any storm. We dressed and were ready to go by 9:40 pm.

＊ ＊ ＊

The snow was in poorer condition than we liked; it hadn't refrozen yet, and might not that night since a warm wind was coming in. I knew the pitches below better than Ed, having been over them five times to his one, so I tried to shout instructions to him when the route was obscure. It got to be too dark to see a full rope-length. I went down the 29th pitch, our ice-filled chimney, feeling rather than seeing the holds. But the fixed ropes helped immensely, and since I came last on the two hard pitches (29th and 27th), Ed didn't have to worry so much about not knowing the moves. Despite the conditions, we were moving efficiently.

At the top of the 26th pitch, the vertical inside corner Don had led so well in crampons, we stopped to rappel. We stood, side by side, attached to the bottom of the fixed rope we had just used on the pitch above. In the dark, we could discern only the outlines of each other's faces. Under our feet, we felt our crampons bite the ice. Just below the little ledge we stood on, the rock shrank vertically away, and empty space lurked over the chasm below. It was too dark to see very far down. Above us, the steepest part of the face, which we had just descended, loomed vaguely in the night. Up there, on another ledge, Don and Matt were probably sleeping. Beside us, in the mild darkness, icicles dripped trickles of water that splashed on the rocks. The fixed rope was wet; here and there ice, from the splashing, had begun to freeze on it.

We didn't have an extra rope, so we untied and attached ourselves to the fixed line, setting up a rappel with the climbing rope. Ed attached a carabiner to the anchor, through which he clipped the climbing rope, so that we could pull it down from the bottom. He wrapped the rope around his body and got ready to rappel. We were tired, but were getting down with reasonable speed. It was ten minutes before midnight.

"Just this tough one," I said. "Then it's practically walking to camp."

"Yeah," Ed answered.

He leaned back. Standing about five feet from him, I heard a sharp scraping sound. Suddenly Ed was flying backward through the air. I could see him fall, wordless, 50 feet free, then strike the steep ice below.

"Grab something, Ed!" But even as I shouted, he was sliding and bouncing down the steep ice, tangled in the rappel rope. He passed out of sight, but I heard his body bouncing below. From the route photos I knew where he had fallen; there wasn't a chance of his stopping for 4,000 feet.

Perhaps five seconds had passed. No warning, no sign of death—but Ed was gone. I could not understand. I became aware of the acute silence. All I could hear was the sound of water dripping near me. "Ed! Ed! Ed!" I shouted, without any hope of an answer. I looked at the anchor—what could have happened? The piton was still intact, but the carabiner and rope were gone with Ed. It made no sense.

I tried to shout for help to Matt and Don. But they were nearly 1,000 feet above, hidden by cliffs that deflected and snow that absorbed my voice. I realized they couldn't hear me. Even the echo of my shouts in the dark seemed tiny. I couldn't just stand there; either I must go up or I must go down. It was about an equal distance either way, but the pitches above were more difficult. I had no rope. There was no point going up, because there was nothing we could do for Ed.

His body lay now, as far as anyone could ever know, on the lower Tokositna, inaccessible. An attempt even by the three of us to descend the 4,000 feet to look for him would be suicidally dangerous, especially since we would have only one rope for all of us. If I went up, I should eventually have to go down again. All it could do was add to the danger. I realized these things at the time. Yet the instinct, in my isolation, to try to join Matt and Don was so compelling that for a while I didn't even consider the other possibility. But it became obvious I had to go down.

At least the fixed ropes were still in. I used two carabiners to attach myself to them, then began to climb down the steep pitch we had started to rappel. I moved jerkily, making violent efforts, telling myself to go more slowly. But I had to use the adrenaline that was racing through me now; it was the only thing that could keep the crippling fear and grief temporarily from me.

I managed to get down the hard pitch. The snow on the Upper Park was in poor condition. I broke steps out beneath me, but held my balance with the fixed rope. I realized that I was going far too fast for safety, but slowing down was almost impossible. As I traversed to the Alley, I was sure the weak snow would break under my feet, but it held. At last I arrived at the tent. The seven pitches had taken 18 minutes, dangerously fast. But I was there; now there was nothing to do but wait alone.

I crawled into the tent. It was full of water. Matt and I had left the back door open! In the dark I sponged it out, too tired to cry, in something like a state of shock. I took two sleeping pills and fell asleep.

In the morning I gradually woke out of a gray stupor. It seemed to be snowing lightly. I felt no sudden pang about the accident; even in sleep I must have remained aware of it. I forced myself to cook and eat a breakfast, for the sake of establishing a routine, of occupying myself. I kept thinking, *What could have happened?* The carabiner and rope were gone; nothing else had been disturbed. Perhaps the carabiner had flipped open and come loose; perhaps it had broken; perhaps Ed had clipped in in such a way that he wasn't really clipped in at all. Nothing seemed likely. It didn't matter, really. All that mattered was that our perfect expedition, in one momentary mechanical whim, had turned into a trial of fear and sorrow for me, as it would for Matt and Don when they learned, and into sudden blankness for Ed. His death had come even before he could rest well enough to enjoy our triumph.

The time passed with terrible slowness. I knew Matt and Don would be taking their time now that it was snowing. I grew anxious for their arrival, afraid of being alone. I tried to relax, but I caught myself holding my breath, listening. Occasionally a ball of snow would roll up against the tent wall. I was sure each time that it was one of them kicking snow down from above. I would stick my head out the tent door, looking into the empty whiteness for a sign of them. My mind magnified even the sound of snowflakes hitting the tent into their distant footsteps.

I made myself eat, write in my diary, keep the tent dry, keep a supply of ice near the door. But I began to worry about Matt and Don, too. I knew there was no reason to expect them yet, but what if they had had an accident, too?

There were some firecrackers in the tent. We had tentatively arranged on the way up to shoot them off in an emergency. I might have done that now, but there was no emergency. It would be more dangerous to communicate with them than not to, because in their alarm they might abandon caution to get down fast.

I began to wonder what I would do if they didn't come. What if I heard them calling for help? I would have to go up, yet what could I do alone? I calculated that they had at most five days' food at the Nose Camp. I had enough for 20 days at the Alley Camp. I would wait five or six days, and if there was no sign of them, I would try to finish the descent alone. At the cave I could stamp a message for Sheldon; if he flew over, he would see it. If he didn't, I would eventually start to hike out, 70 miles down an unknown glacier, across rivers, through the tundra. . . .

But these were desperate thoughts, the logical extremes of possible action I might have to take; I forced myself to consider them so that no potential course of events could lurk unrealized among my fears.

Already I had begun to miss Ed in a way separate from the shock and loneliness. I longed for his cheeriness, that fund of warmth that Matt, Don, and I lacked. I had wanted so much to relax in the tent, talking and joking with him, reliving the long summit day. I hadn't climbed with him since July 11. Now it was the last day of the month, and he was gone.

I went outside the tent only to urinate. Each time, I tied a loop around my waist and clipped into a piton outside, not only because I was afraid but because I couldn't be sure that the sleeping pills and the shock (if it was actually shock) were not impairing my judgment or balance. I felt always tense, aware that I was waiting, minute by minute. I could think of very little but the accident; I couldn't get the sight of Ed falling, sudden and soundless, out of my head.

The snow continued to fall lightly, but the tent got warmer as the hidden sun warmed the air. In the afternoon I began to hear a high, faint whining sound. It was like nothing human, but I couldn't place it. Could it be some kind of distress signal from Matt or Don? Impossible. . . . Could it be the wind blowing through a carabiner somewhere above? But there was almost no wind. Was it even real? I listened, holding my breath, straining with the effort to define the sound. I couldn't even tell if it was above the camp or below. I sang a note of the same pitch to convince myself the sound was real. It seemed to stop momentarily, but I couldn't be sure I hadn't merely begun to ignore it. Finally I noticed that when I went outside the tent, I couldn't hear it. Therefore the sound had to come from inside. At last I found it—vaporized gas, heated by the warmth of the day, was escaping from the stove's safety valve! I felt silly but measurably relieved.

I tried to relive every moment Ed and I had had together the last day, as if doing so could somehow salvage something from the tragedy. My recollections had stuck on a remark he had made in the Nose Camp as we rested after the summit. I had told him that it had been the best day I'd ever had climbing. Ed had said, "Mine too, but I don't know if I'd do the whole thing again."

I thought he was still upset about Matt's and my near-accident, and suggested so. Ed thought a moment, then said, "No. It's not only that."

We hadn't pursued it, but his attitude had seemed strange to me. For me, there was no question but that it would have been worth doing all over again. Nor for Don. And I thought Matt would have said so, too. But Ed had climbed less than we had; perhaps he wasn't so sure that climbing was the most important thing in his life, as we would have said it was in ours.

Now his remark haunted me. The accident, ultimately inexplicable beyond its mechanical cause, which itself we would never be sure of, seemed that much more unfair in view of what Ed had said. It would have been better, fairer, perhaps, had it happened to me. Yet not even in the depth of anguish could I wish that I had died instead. And that irreducible selfishness seemed to prove to me that beyond our feeling of "commitment" there lay the barriers of our disparate self-love. We were willing to place our lives in each other's hands, but I wouldn't have died for Ed. What a joke we played on ourselves—the whole affair of mountaineering seemed a farce then. But the numbness returned; I told myself to wait, to judge it all in better perspective, months, years from now.

By that night there had still been no sign of Matt or Don. I took another sleeping pill and finally dozed off. Sometime in the night, on the edge of sleeping and waking, I had a vision of Ed stumbling, bloody, broken, up to the tent, yelling out in the night, "Why didn't you come to look for me?" I woke with a jolt, then waited in the dark for the dream to dissolve. I hadn't considered, after the first moments, trying to look for Ed's body. For me alone, without a rope, to try to descend the 4,000 feet would certainly have been suicide. Yet because there was nothing to do, and because I hadn't seen Ed's dead body, a whisper of guilt had lodged in my subconscious, a whisper that grew to Ed's shout in my nightmare.

I took a sip of water and fell asleep again. In the morning I discovered my watch had stopped. An unimportant event, it hit me with stunning force. It was as if one more proof of reality were gone, one more contact with the others, Matt and Don first of all, everyone else alive in the world eventually. I set the watch arbitrarily and shook it to get it started.

That day, August 1, dragged by as the last one had. I was no more relaxed than I had been before. The weather was good for a few minutes in the morning, then clouded up again; but at least it had stopped snowing. I felt surer now that Matt and Don would get to me, but I began to dread their arrival, for it would open the wounds of shock in them, and I would have to be the strong one, at first.

I thought of how rarely an expedition is both successful and tragic, especially a small expedition. Something like 95 percent of the dangers in a climb such as ours lay in the ascent. But we had worked for 31 days, many of them dangerous, on the route without a serious injury before finally getting to the summit. Going down should have taken only two or three days, and it is usually routine to descend pitches on which fixed ropes have been left. I was reminded of the first ascent of the Matterhorn, when only hours after its conquest the climbing rope broke, sending four of Edward Whymper's seven-man party to their deaths. Then I realized that the Matterhorn had been climbed 100 years, almost to the day, before our ascent. I thought, also, of the ascent of Cerro Torre in Patagonia in 1959, still regarded by many as the hardest climb ever done. On its descent Toni Egger, one of the best mountaineers in the world, had fallen off a cold rappel to his death, leaving only Cesare Maestri to tell of their victory. But thinking of those climbs explained ours no better. I knew that Whymper, after the Matterhorn, had been persecuted by the public, some of whom even suggested he had cut the rope. I knew that, even in an age that understands mountaineering a little better than the Victorians did, vague suspicions still shrouded the Cerro Torre expedition. But even if we could explain Ed's death to mountaineers, how could we ever explain it to those who cared more about him than about any mountain?

Around 4:00 pm I heard the sound of a plane, probably Sheldon's, flying near the mountain. I couldn't see anything through the mist, but perhaps his very presence meant that it was clear up above, possibly that he could see our steps leading to the summit.

Around 10:00 pm I thought I heard a shout. I looked out of the tent, but saw nothing, and was starting to attribute the sound to a random noise of the mountain, ice breaking loose somewhere or a rock falling, when suddenly Matt came in sight at the top of the Alley. He let out a cheery yell when he saw me. I couldn't answer, but simply stared at him. Pretty soon Don came in sight and yelled, "How are things down there?" I pretended I couldn't hear him. Matt said later that they had seen our tracks from high on the mountain and therefore known that Ed and I hadn't completed the descent to the cave. This had disturbed them a little, and their mood had acquired gloominess during the treacherous last descent, on steps covered by new snow, using ice-coated fixed ropes, once belaying in a waterfall that had frozen their parkas stiff. But as they approached, Matt had seen my head poking out of the tent and for an instant had thrown off his worries. Yet my silence made him uneasy again; then, before he got to the tent, he saw that there was only one pack beside it. Then I said, "Matt, I'm alone."

He belayed Don all the way down before either of us said anything to him. When Matt told him, Don stood there frozen momentarily, looking only at the snow. Then, in a way I cannot forget, he seemed to draw a breath and swallow the impact of the shock. He said, "All right. Let's get inside the tent." His voice, calm as ever, was heavy with a sudden fatigue. But once they knew, once I saw that they were taking it without panic, being strong, I felt an overwhelming gratitude toward them: out of my fear, an impulse like love.

from Everest: The West Ridge
by Tom Hornbein

Mountaineers still consider Tom Hornbein's (b. 1930) and Willi Unsoeld's 1963 traverse of Everest one of climbing's greatest achievements. The two ascended the mountain's unclimbed West Ridge, then continued over the top and down the South Col route, staging an emergency bivouac at 28,000 feet. Hornbein, recounting a climb that defined an era in American mountainering, doesn't seem especially impressed; his concern is to convey his experience.

A t four the oxygen ran out, a most effective alarm clock. Two well-incubated butane stoves were fished from inside our sleeping bags and soon bouillon was brewing in the kitchen. Climbing into boots was a breathless challenge to balance in our close quarters. Then overboots, and crampons.

"Crampons, in the tent?"

"Sure," I replied, "It's a hell of a lot colder out there."

"But our air mattresses!"

"Just be careful. We may not be back here again, anyway. I hope."

We were clothed in multilayer warmth. The fishnet underwear next to our skin provided tiny air pockets to hold our body heat. It also kept the outer layers at a distance which, considering our weeks without a bath, was respectful. Next came Duofold underwear, a wool shirt, down underwear tops and bottoms, wool climbing pants, and a lightweight wind parka. In spite of the cold our down parkas would be too bulky for difficult climbing, so we used them to insulate two quarts of hot lemonade, hoping they might remain unfrozen long enough to drink during the climb. Inside the felt inner liners of our reindeer-hair boots were innersoles and two pairs of heavy wool socks. Down shells covered a pair of wool mittens. Over our oxygen helmets we wore wool balaclavas and our parka hoods. The down parka-lemonade muff was stuffed into our packs as padding between the two oxygen bottles. With camera, radio, flashlight, and sundry mementos (including the pages from Emerson's diary), our loads came close to 40 pounds. For all the prior evening's planning it was more than two hours before we emerged.

I snugged a bowline about my waist, feeling satisfaction at the ease with which the knot fell together beneath heavily mittened hands. This was part of the ritual, experienced innumerable times before. With it came a feeling of security, not from the protection provided by the rope joining Willi and me, but from my being able to relegate those gray brooding forbidding walls, so high in such an unknown world, to common reality—to all those times I had ever tied into a rope before: with warm hands while I stood at the base of sun-baked granite walls in the Tetons, with cold hands on a winter night while I prepared to tackle my first steep ice on Longs Peak. This knot tied me to the past, to experience known, with that which man might do. To weave the knot so smoothly with clumsily mittened hands was to assert my confidence, to assert some competence in the face of the waiting rock, to accept the challenge.

Hooking our masks in place we bade a slightly regretful goodbye to our tent, sleeping bags, and the extra supply of food we hadn't been able to eat. Willi was at the edge of the ledge looking up the narrow gully when I joined him.

"My oxygen's hissing, Tom, even with the regulator turned off."

For the next 20 minutes we screwed and unscrewed regulators, checked valves for ice, to no avail. The hiss continued. We guessed it must be in the valve, and thought of going back to the tent for the spare bottle, but the impatient feeling that time was more important kept us from retracing those 40 feet.

"It doesn't sound too bad," I said. "Let's just keep an eye on the pressure. Besides if you run out we can hook up the sleeping T and extra tubing and both climb on one bottle." Willi envisioned the two of us climbing Everest in lockstep, wed by six feet of rubber hose.

We turned to the climb. It was ten minutes to seven. Willi led off. Three years before in a tent high on Masherbrum he had expounded on the importance of knee-to-toe distance for step-kicking up steep snow. Now his anatomical advantage determined the order of things as he put his theory to the test. Right away we found it was going to be difficult. The Couloir, as it cut through the Yellow Band, narrowed to ten or 15 feet and steepened to 50 degrees. The snow was hard, too hard to kick steps in, but not hard enough to hold crampons; they slid disconcertingly down through this wind-sheltered, granular stuff. There was nothing for it but to cut steps, zigzagging back and forth across the gully, occasionally finding a bit of rock along the side up which we could scramble. We were forced to climb one at a time with psychological belays from axes thrust a few inches into the snow. Our regulators were set to deliver two liters of oxygen per minute, half the optimal flow for this altitude. We turned them off when we were belaying to conserve the precious gas, though we knew that the belayer should always be kept at peak alertness in case of a fall.

We crept along. My God, I thought, we'll never get there at this rate. But that's as far as the thought ever got. Willi's leads were meticulous, painstakingly slow and steady. He plugged tirelessly on, deluging me with showers of ice as his ax carved each step. When he ran out the hundred feet of rope he jammed his ax into the snow to belay me. I turned my oxygen on to "2" and moved up as far as I could, hoping to save a few moments of critical time. By the time I joined him I was completely winded, gasping for air, and sorely puzzled about why. Only late in the afternoon, when my first oxygen bottle was still going strong, did I realize what a low flow of gas my regulator was actually delivering.

Up the tongue of snow we climbed, squeezing through a passage where the walls of the Yellow Band closed in, narrowing the Couloir to shoulder width.

In four hours we had climbed only 400 feet. It was 11 am. A rotten bit of vertical wall forced us to the right onto the open face. To regain the Couloir it would be necessary to climb this 60-foot cliff, composed of two pitches split by a broken snow-covered step.

"You like to lead this one?" Willi asked.

With my oxygen off I failed to think before I replied, "Sure, I'll try it."

The rock sloped malevolently outward like shingles on a roof—rotten shingles. The covering of snow was no better than the rock. It would pretend to hold for a moment, then suddenly shatter and peel, cascading down on Willi. He sank a piton into the base of the step to anchor his belay.

I started up around the corner to the left, crampon points grating on rusty limestone. Then it became a snowplowing procedure as I searched for some sort of purchase beneath. The pick of my ax found a crack. Using the shaft for gentle leverage, I moved carefully onto the broken strata of the step. I went left again, loose debris rolling under my crampons, to the base of the final vertical rise, about eight feet high. For all its steepness, this was a singularly poor plastering job, nothing but wobbly rubble. I searched about for a crack, unclipped a big angle piton from my sling, and whomped it in with the hammer. It sank smoothly, as if penetrating soft butter. A gentle lift easily extracted it.

"Hmmm. Not so good," I mumbled through my mask. On the fourth try the piton gripped a bit more solidly. Deciding not to loosen it by testing, I turned to the final wall. Its steepness threw my weight out from the rock, and my pack became a downright hindrance. There was an unlimited selection of handholds, mostly portable. I shed my mittens. For a few seconds the rock felt comfortably reassuring, but cold. Then not cold anymore. My eyes tried to direct sensationless fingers. Flakes peeled out beneath my crampons. I leaned out from the rock to move upward, panting like a steam engine. Damn it, it'll go; I know it will, T, I thought. My grip was gone. I hadn't thought to turn my oxygen up.

"No soap," I called down. "Can't make it now. Too pooped."

"Come on down. There may be a way to the right."

I descended, half rappeling from the piton, which held. I had spent the better part of an hour up there. A hundred feet out we looked back. Clearly we had been on the right route, for above the last little step the gully opened out. A hundred feet higher the Yellow Band met the gray of the summit limestone. It had to get easier.

"You'd better take it, Willi. I've wasted enough time already."

"Hell, if you couldn't make it, I'm not going to be able to do it any better."

"Yes you will. It's really not that hard. I was just worn out from putting that piton in. Turn your regulator clear open, though."

Willi headed up around the corner, moving well. In ten minutes his rope was snapped through the high piton. Discarding a few unsavory holds, he gripped the rotten edge with his unmittened hands. He leaned out for the final move. His pack pulled. Crampons scraped, loosing a shower of rock from beneath his feet. He was over. He leaned against the rock, fighting for his breath.

"Man, that's work. But it looks better above."

Belayed, I followed, retrieved the first piton, moved up, and went to work on the second. It wouldn't come. "Guess it's better than I thought," I shouted. "I'm going to leave it." I turned my oxygen to four liters, leaned out from the wall, and scrambled up. The extra oxygen helped, but it was surprising how breathless such a brief effort left me.

"Good lead," I panted. "That wasn't easy."

"Thanks. Let's roll."

Another rope length and we stopped. After six hours of hiss Willi's first bottle was empty. There was still a long way to go, but at least he could travel ten pounds lighter without the extra cylinder. Our altimeter read 27,900. We called Base on the walkie-talkie.

Willi: West Ridge to Base. West Ridge to Base. Over.

Base (Jim Whittaker, excitedly): This is Base here, Willi. How are you? How are things going? What's the word up there? Over.

Willi: Man, this is a real bearcat! We are nearing the top of the Yellow Band and it's mighty tough. It's too damned tough to try to go back. It would be too dangerous.

Base (Jim): I'm sure you're considering all about your exits. Why don't you leave yourself an opening? If it's not going to pan out, you can always start your way down. I think there is always a way to come back.

Willi: Roger, Jim. We're counting on a further consultation in about two or three hundred feet. It should ease up by then! Goddammit, if we can't start moving together, we'll have to move back down. But it should be easier once the Yellow Band is passed. Over.

Base (Jim): Don't work yourself up into a bottleneck, Willi. How about rappeling? Is that possible, or don't you have any *reepschnur* or anything? Over.

Willi: There are no rappel points, Jim, absolutely no rappel points. There's nothing to secure a rope to. So it's up and over for us today. . . .

While the import of his words settled upon those listening 10,000 feet below, Willi went right on:

Willi (continuing): . . . and we'll probably be getting in pretty late, maybe as late as seven or eight o'clock tonight.

As Willi talked, I looked at the mountain above. The slopes looked reasonable, as far as I could see, which wasn't very far. We sat at the base of a big, wide-open amphitheater. It looked like summits all over the place. I looked down. Descent was totally unappetizing. The rotten rock, the softening snow, the absence of even tolerable piton cracks only added to our desire to go on. Too much labor, too many sleepless nights, and too many dreams had been invested to bring us this far. We couldn't come back for another try next weekend. To go down now, even if we could have, would be descending to a future marked by one huge question: what might have been? It would not be a matter of living with our fellow man, but simply living with ourselves, with the knowledge that we had had more to give.

I listened, only mildly absorbed in Willi's conversation with Base, and looked past him at the convexity of rock cutting off our view of the gully we had ascended. Above—a snowfield, gray walls, then blue-black sky. We were committed. An invisible barrier sliced through the mountain beneath our feet, cutting us from the world below. Though we could see through, all we saw was infinitely remote. The ethereal link provided by our radio only intensified our separation. My wife and children seemed suddenly close. Yet home, life itself, lay only over the top of Everest and down the other side. Suppose we fail? The thought brought no remorse, no fear. Once entertained, it hardly seemed even interesting. What now mattered most was right here: Willi and I, tied together on a rope, and the mountain, its summit not inaccessibly far above. The reason we had come was within our grasp. We belonged to the mountain and it to us. There was anxiety, to be sure, but it was all but lost in a feeling of calm, of pleasure at the joy of climbing. That we couldn't go down only made easier that which we really wanted to do. That we might not get there was scarcely conceivable.

Willi was still talking.

Willi: Any news of Barrel and Lute? Over.

Jim: I haven't heard a word from them. Over.

Willi: How about Dingman?

Jim: No word from Dingman. We've heard nothing at all.

Willi: Well listen, if you do get hold of Dingman, tell him to put a light in the window because we're headed for the summit, Jim. We can't possibly get back to our camp now. Over.

I stuffed the radio back in Willi's pack. It was 1 pm. From here we could both climb at the same time, moving across the last of the yellow slabs. Another 100 feet and the Yellow Band was below us. A steep tongue of snow flared wide, penetrating the gray strata that capped the mountain. The snow was hard, almost ice-hard in places. We had only to bend our ankles, firmly plant all 12 crampon points, and walk uphill. At last, we were moving, though it would have appeared painfully slow to a distant bystander.

As we climbed out of the Couloir the pieces of the puzzle fell into place. That snow rib ahead on the left skyline should lead us to the Summit Snowfield, a patch of perpetual white clinging to the North Face at the base of Everest's final pyramid. By three we were on the Snowfield. We had been climbing for eight hours and knew we needed to take time to refuel. At a shaly outcrop of rock we stopped for lunch. There was a decision to be made. We could either cut straight up the northeast ridge and follow it west to the summit, or we could traverse the face and regain the West Ridge. From where we sat, the Ridge looked easier. Besides, it was the route we'd intended in the first place.

We split a quart of lemonade that was slushy with ice. In spite of its down parka wrapping, the other bottle was already frozen solid, as were the kippered snacks. They were almost tasteless but we downed them more with dutiful thoughts of calories than with pleasure.

To save time we moved together, diagonaling upward across down-sloping slabs of rotten shale. There were no possible stances from which to belay each other. Then snow again, and Willi kicked steps, fastidiously picking a route between the outcropping of rocks. Though still carting my full load of oxygen bottles, I was beginning to feel quite strong. With this excess energy came impatience, and an unconscious anxiety over the high stakes for which we were playing and the lateness of the day. Why the hell is Willi going so damned slow? I thought. And a little later: He should cut over to the Ridge now; it'll be a lot easier.

I shouted into the wind, "Hold up, Willi!" He pretended not to hear me as he started up the rock. It seemed terribly important to tell him to go to the right. I tugged on the rope. "Damn it, wait up, Willi!" Stopped by a taut rope and an unyielding Hornbein, he turned, and with some irritation anchored his ax while I hastened to join him. He was perched, through no choice of his own, in rather cramped, precarious quarters. I sheepishly apologized.

We were on rock now. One rope length, crampons scraping, brought us to the crest of the West Ridge for the first time since we'd left camp 4W yesterday morning. The South Face fell 8,000 feet to the tiny tents of Advanced Base. Lhotse, straight across the face, was below us now. And near at hand a 150 feet higher, the South Summit of Everest shone in the afternoon sun. We were within 400 feet of the top! The wind whipped across the ridge from the north at nearly 60 miles an hour. Far below, peak shadows reached long across the cloud-filled valleys. Above, the Ridge rose, a twisting, rocky spine.

We shed crampons and overboots to tackle this next rocky bit with the comforting grip of cleated rubber soles. Here I unloaded my first oxygen bottle though it was not quite empty. It had lasted ten hours, which obviously meant I'd be getting a lower flow than indicated by the regulator. Resisting Willi's suggestion to drop the cylinder off the South Face, I left it for some unknown posterity. When I resaddled ten pounds lighter, I felt I could float to the top.

The rock was firm, at least in comparison with our fare thus far. Climbing one at a time, we experienced the joy of delicate moves on tiny holds. The going was a wonderful pleasure, almost like a day in the Rockies. With the sheer drop to the Cwm beneath us, we measured off another four rope lengths. Solid rock gave way to crud, then snow. A thin, firm, knife-edge of white pointed gently toward the sky. Buffeted by the wind, we laced our crampons on, racing each other with rapidly numbing fingers. It took nearly 20 minutes. Then we were off again, squandering oxygen at three liters per minute since time seemed the shorter commodity at the moment. We moved together, Willi in front. It seemed almost as if we were cheating, using oxygen; we could nearly run this final bit.

Ahead the North and South ridges converged to a point. Surely the summit wasn't that near? It must be off behind. Willi stopped. What's he waiting for, I wondered as I moved to join him. With a feeling of disbelief I looked up. Forty feet ahead tattered and whipped by the wind was the flag Jim had left three weeks before. It was 6:15. The sun's rays sheered horizontally across the summit. We hugged each other as tears welled up, ran down across our oxygen masks, and turned to ice.

Just rock, a dome of snow, the deep blue sky, and a hunk of orange-painted metal from which a shredded American flag cracked in the wind. Nothing more. Except two tiny figures walking together those last few feet to the top of the earth.

For 20 minutes we stayed there. The last brilliance of the day cast the shadow of our summit on the cloud . . . plain a hundred miles . . . to the east. Valleys were filled with the indistinct purple haze of evening, concealing the dwellings of man we knew were there. The chill roar of wind made speaking difficult, heightened our feeling of remoteness. The flag left there seemed a feeble gesture of man that had no purpose but to accentuate the isolation. The two of us who had dreamed months before of sharing this moment were linked by a thin line of rope, joined in the intensity of companionship to those inaccessibly far below, Al and Barry and Dick—and Jake.

From a pitch of intense emotional and physical drive it was only partly possible to become suddenly, completely the philosopher of a balmy afternoon. The head of steam was too great, and the demands on it still remained. We have a long way to go to get down, I thought. But the prospect of descent of an unknown side of the mountain in the dark caused me less anxiety than many other occasions had. I had a blind, fatalistic faith that, having succeeded in coming this far, we could not fail to get down. The moment became an end in itself.

There were many things savored in this brief time. Even with our oxygen turned off we had no problem performing those summit obeisances, photographing the fading day (it's a wonderful place to be for sunset photographs), smiling behind our masks for the inevitable "I was there" picture. Willi wrapped the kata given him by Ang Dorje about the flag pole and planted Andy Bakewell's crucifix alongside it in the snow; Lhotse and Makalu, below us, were a contrast of sun-blazed snow etched against the darkness of evening shadow. We felt the lonely beauty of the evening, the immense roaring silence of the wind, the tenuousness of our tie to all below. There was a hint of fear, not for our lives, but of a vast unknown which pressed upon us. A fleeting disappointment—that after all those dreams and questions this was only a mountaintop—gave way to the suspicion that maybe there was something more, something beyond the three-dimensional form of the moment. If only it could be perceived.

But it was late. The memories had to be stored, the meaning taken down. The question of why we had come was not now to be answered, yet something up here must yield an answer, something only dimly felt, comprehended by senses reaching farther yet than the point on which we stood; reaching for understanding, which hovered but a few steps higher. The answers lay not on the summit of Everest, nor in the sky above it, but in the world to which we belonged and must now return.

Footprints in the snow told that Lute and Barrel had been here. We'd have a path to follow as long as light remained.

"Want to go first?" Willi asked. He began to coil the rope.

Looking down the corniced edge, I thought of the added protection of a rope from above. "Doesn't matter, Willi. Either way."

"O.K. Why don't I go first then?" he said, handing me the coil. Paying out the rope as he disappeared below me I wondered, Is Unsoeld tired? It was hard to believe. Still he'd worked hard; he had a right to be weary. Starting sluggishly, I'd felt stronger as we climbed. So now we would reverse roles. Going up had been pretty much Willi's show; going down would be mine. I dropped the last coil and started after him.

Fifty feet from the top we stopped at a patch of exposed rock. Only the summit of Everest, shining pink, remained above the shadow sea. Willi radioed to Maynard Miller at Advance Base that we were headed for the South Col. It was 6:35 pm.

We almost ran along the crest, trusting Lute and Barrel's track to keep us a safe distance from the cornice edge. Have to reach the South Summit before dark, I thought, or we'll never find our way. The sun dropped below the jagged horizon. We didn't need goggles any more. There was a loud hiss as I banged against the ice wall. Damn! Something's broken. I reached back and turned off the valve. Without oxygen, I tried to keep pace with the rope disappearing over the edge ahead. Vision dimmed, the ground began to move. I stopped till things cleared, waved my arms and shouted into the wind for Willi to hold up. The taut rope finally stopped him. I tightened the regulator, then turned the oxygen on. No hiss! To my relief it had only been jarred loose. On oxygen again, I could move rapidly. Up 20 feet, and we were on the South Summit. It was 7:15.

Thank God for the footprints. Without them, we'd have had a tough time deciding which way to go. We hurried on, facing outward, driving our heels into the steep snow. By 7:30 it was dark. We took out the flashlight and resumed the descent. The batteries, dregs of the Expedition, had not been helped by our session with Emerson's diary the night before; they quickly faded. There was pitiful humor as Willi probed, holding the light a few inches off the snow to catch some sign of tracks. You could order your eyes to see, but nothing in the blackness complied.

We moved slowly now. Willi was only a voice and an occasional faint flicker of light to point the way. No fear, no worry, no strangeness, just complete absorption. The drive which had carried us to a nebulous goal was replaced by simple desire for survival. There was no time to dwell on the uniqueness of our situation. We climbed carefully, from years of habit. At a rock outcrop we paused. Which way? Willi groped to the right along a corniced edge. In my imagination, I filled in the void.

"No tracks over here." Willi called

"Maybe we should dig in for the night."

"I don't know. Dave and Girmi should be at 6."

We shouted into the night, and the wind engulfed our call. A lull. Again we shouted. "Helloooo," the wind answered. Or was it the wind?

"Hellooo," we called once more.

"Hellooo," came back faintly. That wasn't the wind!

"To the left, Willi."

"O.K., go ahead."

In the blackness I couldn't see my feet. Each foot groped cautiously, feeling its way down, trusting to the pattern set by its predecessor. Slowly left, right, left, crampons biting into the snow, right, left. . . .

"*Willeeee!*" I yelled as I somersaulted into space. The rope came taut, and with a soft thud I landed.

"Seems to be a cornice there," I called from beneath the wall. "I'll belay you from here."

Willi sleepwalked down the edge. The dim outline of his foot wavered until it met my guiding hand. His arrival lacked the flair of my descent. It was well that the one of lighter weight had gone first.

Gusts buffeted from all directions, threatening to dislodge us from the slope. Above a cliff we paused, untied, cut the rope in half, and tied in again. It didn't help; even five feet behind I couldn't see Willi. Sometimes the snow was good, sometimes it was soft, sometimes it lay shallow over rocks so we could only drive our axes in an inch or two. With these psychological belays, we wandered slowly down, closer to the answering shouts. The wind was dying, and so was the flashlight, now no more than an orange glow illuminating nothing. The stars, brilliant above, cast no light on the snow. Willi's oxygen ran out. He slowed, suddenly feeling much wearier.

The voices were close now. Were they coming from those two black shapes in the snow? Or were those rocks?

"Shine your lights down here," a voice called.

"Where? Shine yours up here," I answered.

"Don't have one," came the reply.

Then we were with them—not Dave and Girmi, but Lute and Barrel. They were near exhaustion, shivering lumps curled on the snow. Barrel in particular was far gone. Anxious hungering for air through the previous night, and the near catastrophe when their tent caught fire in the morning, had left him tired before they even started. Determination got him to the top, but now he no longer cared. He only wanted to be left alone. Lute was also tired. Because of Barrel's condition he'd had to bear the brunt of the climbing labor. His eyes were painfully burned, perhaps by the fire, perhaps by the sun and wind. From sheer fatigue they had stopped thinking. Their oxygen was gone, except for a bit Lute had saved for Barrel; but they were too weak to make the change.

At 9:30 we were still 1,000 feet above Camp 6. Willi sat down in the snow, and I walked over to get Lute's oxygen for Barrel. As I unscrewed Lute's regulator from the bottle, he explained why they were still there. Because of the stove fire that had sent them diving from the tent, they were an hour late in starting. It was 3:30 pm when they reached the summit. Seeing no sign of movement down the west side, they figured no one would be any later than they were. At 4:15 they started down. Fatigue slowed their descent. Just after dark they stopped to rest and were preparing to move when they heard shouts. Dave and Girmi, they thought. No—the sounds seemed to be coming from above. Willi and Tom! So they waited, shivering.

I removed Barrel's regulator from his empty bottle and screwed it into Lute's. We were together now, sharing the support so vigorously debated a week before. Lute would know the way back to their camp, even in the dark. All we had to do was help them down. Fumbling with unfeeling fingers, I tried to attach Barrel's oxygen hose to the regulator. Damn! Can't make the connection. My fingers scraped uncoordinatedly against the cold metal. Try again. There it goes. Then, quickly, numb fingers clumsy, back into mittens. Feeling slowly returned, and pain. Then, the pain went and the fingers were warm again.

Willi remembered the Dexedrine I had dropped into my shirt pocket the evening before. I fished out two pills—one for Barrel and one for Lute. Barrel was better with oxygen, but why I had balked at his communal use of Lute's regulator, I cannot say. Lack of oxygen? Fatigue? it was 15 hours since we'd started the climb. Or was it that my thoughts were too busy with another problem? We had to keep moving or freeze.

I led off. Lute followed in my footsteps to point out the route. Lost in the darkness 60 feet back on our ropes, Willi and Barrel followed. The track was more sensed than seen, but it was easier now, not so steep. My eyes watered from searching for the black holes punched in the snow by Lute's and Barrel's axes during their ascent. We walked to the left of the crest, three feet down, ramming our axes into the narrow edge. Thirty feet, and the rope came taut as Barrel collapsed in the snow, bringing the entire caravan to a halt. Lute sat down behind me. Got to keep moving. We'll never get there.

We had almost no contact with the back of the line. When the rope came taut, we stopped, when it loosened we moved on. Somewhere my oxygen ran out, but we were going too slow for me to notice the difference. Ought to dump the empty bottle, I thought, but it was too much trouble to take off my pack.

Heat lightning flashed along the plains to the east, too distant to light our way. Rocks that showed in the snow below seemed to get no closer as the hours passed. Follow the ax holes. Where'd they go? Not sure. There's another.

"Now where, Lute?"

"Can't see, Tom." Lute said. "Can't see a damn thing. We've got to turn down a gully between some rocks."

"Which gully. There's two or three."

"Don't know, Tom."

"Think, Lute. Try to remember. We've got to get to 6."

"I don't know. I just can't see."

Again and again I questioned, badgering, trying to extract some hint. But half blind and weary, Lute had no answer. We plodded on. The rocks came closer.

Once the rope jerked tight, nearly pulling me off balance. Damn! What's going on? I turned and looked at Lute's dim form lying on the snow a few feet further down the Kangshung Face. His fall had been effectively if uncomfortably arrested when his neck snagged the rope between Willi and me.

We turned off the crest, toward the rocks. Tongues of snow pierced the cliffs below. But which one? It was too dangerous to plunge on. After midnight we reached the rocks. It had taken nearly three hours to descend 400 feet, maybe 15 minutes' worth by daylight.

Tired. No hope of finding camp in the darkness. No choice but to wait for day. Packs off. Willi and I slipped into our down parkas. In the dark, numb fingers couldn't start the zippers. We settled to the ground, curled as small as possible atop our pack frames. Lute and Barrel were somewhere behind, apart, each alone. Willi and I tried hugging each other to salvage warmth, but my uncontrollable shivering made it impossible.

The oxygen was gone, but the mask helped a little for warmth. Feet, cooling, began to hurt. I withdrew my hands from the warmth of my crotch and loosened crampon binding and boot laces, but my feet stayed cold. Willi offered to rub them. We removed boots and socks and planted both my feet against his stomach. No sensation returned.

Tired by the awkward position, and frustrated by the result, we gave up. I slid my feet back into socks and boots, but couldn't tie them. I offered to warm Willi's feet. Thinking that his freedom from pain was due to high tolerance of cold, he declined. We were too weary to realize the reason for his comfort.

The night was overpoweringly empty. Stars shed cold unshimmering light. The heat lightning dancing along the plains spoke of a world of warmth and flatness. The black silhouette of Lhotse lurked half sensed, half seen, still below. Only the ridge on which we were rose higher, disappearing into the night, a last lonely outpost of the world.

Mostly there was nothing. We hung suspended in a timeless void. The wind died, and there was silence. Even without wind it was cold. I could reach back and touch Lute or Barrel lying head to toe above me. They seemed miles away.

Unsignaled, unembellished, the hours passed. Intense cold penetrated, carrying with it the realization that each of us was completely alone. Nothing Willi could do for me or I for him. No team now, just each of us, imprisoned with his own discomfort, his own thoughts, his own will to survive.

Yet for me, survival was hardly a conscious thought. Nothing to plan, nothing to push for, nothing to do but shiver and wait for the sun to rise. I floated in a dreamlike eternity, devoid of plans, fears, regrets. The heat lightning, Lhotse, my companions, discomfort, all were there—yet not there. Death had no meaning, nor, for that matter, did life. Survival was no concern, no issue. Only a dulled impatience for the sun to rise tied my formless thoughts to the future.

About 4:00 the sky began to lighten along the eastern rim, baring the bulk of Kangchenjunga. The sun was slow in following, interminably slow. Not till after 5:00 did it finally come, its light streaming through the South Col, blazing yellow across the Nuptse Wall, then onto the white wave crest of peaks far below. We watched as if our own life was being born again. Then as the cold yellow light touched us, we rose. There were still miles to go.

＊ ＊ ＊

The rest is like a photograph with little depth of field, the focused moments crystal sharp against a blurred background of fatigue. We descended the gully I had been unable to find in the dark. Round the corner, Dave and Girmi were coming toward us. They thought they heard shouts in the night and had started up, but their own calls were followed only by silence. Now as they came in search of the bodies of Lute and Barry they saw people coming down—not just two, but four. Dave puzzled a moment before he understood.

The tents at Camp 6—and we were home from the mountain. Nima Dorje brought tea. We shed boots. I started blankly at the marble-white soles of Willi's feet. They were cold and hard as ice. We filled in Emerson's diary for the last time, then started down.

With wind tearing snow from its rocky plain, the South Col was as desolate and uninviting as it had always been described. We sought shelter in the tents at Camp 5 for lunch, then emerged into the gale. Across the Geneva Spur, out of the wind, onto the open sweep of the Lhotse Face we plodded in somber procession. Dave led gently, patiently; the four behind rocked along, feet apart to keep from falling. Only for Willi and me was this side of the mountain new. Like tourists we looked around, forgetting fatigue for a moment.

At Camp 4 we stopped to melt water, then continued with the setting sun, walking through dusk into darkness as Dave guided us among crevasses, down the Cwm. It was a mystery to me how he found the way. I walked along at the back, following the flashlight. Sometimes Willi stopped and I would nearly bump into him. We waited while Dave searched, then moved on. No one complained.

At 10:30 pm we arrived at Advance Base. Dick, Barry, and Al were down from the Ridge, waiting. Frozen feet and Barrel's hands were thawed in warm water. Finally to bed, after almost two days. Short a sleeping bag, Willi and I shared one as best we could.

May 24 we were late starting, tired. Lute, Willi, and Barrel walked on thawed feet. It was too dangerous to carry them down through the Icefall. Willi, ahead of me on the rope, heeled down like an awkward clown. The codeine wasn't enough to prevent cries of pain when he stubbed his toes against the snow. I cried as I walked behind, unharmed.

At Camp 1 Maynard nursed us like a mother hen, serving us water laboriously melted from ice samples drilled from the glacier for analysis.

Then down through the Icefall, past Jake's grave—and a feeling of finality. It's all done. The dream's finished.

No rest. The next day, a grim gray one, we departed Base. From low-hanging clouds wet snow fell. Willi, Barrel, and Lute were loaded aboard porters to be carried down over the rocky moraine. It was easier walking.

At Gorak Shep we paused. On a huge boulder a Sherpa craftsman had patiently carved:

IN MEMORY OF JOHN E. BREITENBACH,
AMERICAN MOUNT EVEREST EXPEDITION, 1963.

Clouds concealed the mountain that was Jake's grave.

As we descended, the falling snow gave way to a fine drizzle. There was nothing to see; just one foot, then another. But slowly a change came, something that no matter how many times experienced, is always new, like life. It was life. From ice and snow and rock, we descended to a world of living things, of green—grass and trees and bushes. There was no taking it for granted. Spring had come, and even the gray drizzle imparted a wet sheen to all that grew. At Pheriche flowers bloomed in the meadows.

Lying in bed, Willi and I listened to a sound that wasn't identifiable, so foreign was it to the place—the chopping whir as a helicopter circled, searching for a place to light. In a flurry of activity Willi and Barrel were loaded aboard. The helicopter rose from the hilltop above the village and dipped into the distance. The chop-chop-chop of the blades faded, until finally the craft itself was lost in the massive backdrop. The departure was too unreal, too much a part of another world, to be really comprehended. Less than five days after they had stood on the summit of Everest, Barrel and Willi were back in Kathmandu. For them the Expedition was ended. Now all that remained was weeks in bed, sitting, rocking in pain, waiting for toes to mummify to the time for amputation.

Up over barren passes made forbidding by mist and a chill wind, we traveled. Hard work. Then down through forests of rain-drenched rhododendrons, blossoming pastels of pink and lavender. Toes hurt.

Two weeks to Kathmandu. Feet slipped on the muddy path. Everything was wet.

We were finished. Everest was climbed; nothing to push for now. Existence knew only the instant, counting steps, falling asleep each time we stopped to rest beside the trail. Lester, Emerson, and I talked about motivation; for me it was all gone. It was a time of relaxation, a time when senses were turned to perceive, but nothing was left to give.

Pleasure lay half-hidden beneath discomfort, fatigue, loneliness. Willi was gone. The gap where he had been was filled with question: Why hadn't I known that his feet were numb? Surely I could have done something, if only . . . I was too weary to know the question couldn't be resolved. Half of me seemed to have gone with him; the other half was isolated from my companion by an experience I couldn't share and by the feeling that something was ending that had come to mean too much. Talk of home, of the first evening in the Yak and Yeti Bar, of the reception that waited, was it really so important? Did it warrant the rush?

We'd climbed Everest. What good was it to Jake? To Willi, to Barrel? To Norman, with Everest all done now? And to the rest of us? What waits? What price less tangible than toes? There must be something more to it than toiling over the top of another, albeit expensive, mountain. Perhaps there was something of the nobility-that-is-man in it somewhere, but it was hard to be sure.

Yes, it satisfied in a way. Not just climbing the mountain, but the entire effort—the creating something, the few of us molding it from the beginning. With a lot of luck we'd succeeded. But what had we proved?

Existence on a mountain is simple. Seldom in life does it come any simpler: survival, plus the striving toward the summit. The goal is solidly, three-dimensionally there—you can see it, touch it, stand upon it—the way to reach it well defined, the energy of all directed toward its achievement. It is this simplicity that strips the veneer off civilization and makes that which is meaningful easier to come by—the pleasure of deep companionship, moments of uninhibited humor, the tasting of hardship, sorrow, beauty, joy. But it is this very simplicity that may prevent finding answers to the questions I had asked as we approached the mountain.

Then I had been unsure that I could survive and function in a world so foreign to my normal existence. Now I felt at home here, no longer overly afraid. Each step toward Kathmandu carried me back toward the known, yet toward many things terribly unknown, toward goals unclear, to be reached by paths undefined.

Beneath fatigue lurked the suspicion that the answers I sought were not to be found on a mountain. What possible difference could climbing Everest make? Certainly the mountain hadn't been changed. Even now wind and falling snow would have obliterated most signs of our having been there. Was I any greater for having stood on the highest place on earth? Within the wasted figure that stumbled weary and fearful back toward home there was no question about the answer to that one.

It had been a wonderful dream, but now all that lingered was the memory. The dream was ended.

Everest must join the realities of my existence, commonplace and otherwise. The goal, unattainable, had been attained. Or had it? The questions, many of them, remained. And the answers? It is strange how when a dream is fulfilled there is little left but doubt.

from K2: The Savage Mountain
by Robert Bates and Charles Houston

The members of the 1953 Third American Karakoram Expedition would be uncomfortable with the label, but they were heroes of a sort. When climber Art Gilkey developed thrombophlebitis, his exhausted teammates set out to lower him over 9,000 feet of difficult ground, through a storm. It was an impossible task, but they were willing to die attempting it. Team members Charlie Houston (b. 1913) and Robert Bates (b. 1912) wrote an account of the expedition; this passage is by Bates.

We all knew now that some of us might never get down the mountain alive. Each had long recognized the near impossibility of evacuating an injured man from the upper ledges of K2. We had told one another that "if somebody broke a leg, you never could get him down the mountain," but now that we were faced with Gilkey's helplessness, we realized that we *had* to get him down. We didn't know how, but we knew that we had to do it.

Schoening in particular, and also Bob Craig and Dee Molenaar, had done a lot of mountain rescue work, and the rest of us placed great confidence in their faith that somehow we could get our casualty to Base Camp. Gilkey's high morale and his confidence in us was a great boost to our spirits and we faced the job ahead with strong determination. When on the morning of August 10 Charlie Houston thrust his shoulders through the tunnel entrance of the tent where Schoening, Streather, and I, shoulder rubbing shoulder, had tossed during the long night hours, we spoke almost in unison: "How is he?"

"We've got to take him down," said the doctor. "His other leg has a clot now and he can't last long *here*."

The wind was hammering the tent fabric so hard that we had to yell at one another. Drifts of fine powder snow were sifting in through a strained seam in the tent vestibule, though we had done our best to keep the shelter airtight, and we could feel the whole tent vibrate as gusts stretched the fabric to the utmost.

"What? Move in this storm?" said someone.

"We've got to," said Houston. "He'll soon be dead if we don't get him down."

Nothing needed saying after that, for we knew what this decision meant. All of us had fought mountain storms before, but we had never seen anything like the duration and violence of this furious wind and snow that was still battering us. We all knew the story of the storm on Nanga Parbat in 1934, when nine members of a German expedition had died of exhaustion while battling the wind and snow. Willy Merkl, Uli Wieland, and Willi Welzenbach had been famous mountaineers, but a storm had exhausted them and killed them one by one. Here on K2 we had not only the storm to fight but the steepest part of the mountain, and we were trying to bring down these precipitous slopes a crippled companion as well!

We all realized that our adventure had now become grim, for the odds against getting Art down were obvious, and our own position was getting more critical all the time. While Houston and Schoening were easing Art out of his tent into the storm, the rest of us began packing light loads to take down. We would need one tent in case of emergency, and we took the Gerry tent, our lightest one. We also might need a stove and pot, and some meat bars, chocolate, or quick-energy food that needed no cooking. Often the effects of altitude so weaken one's determination that doing nothing becomes a positive pleasure, but this was no time for lethargy, and as we moved purposefully out of the tents into the stinging blasts of snow, we knew that we had to move fast, while fingers and toes still had feeling. Little was spoken. Each of us realized that he was beginning the most dangerous day's work of his lifetime.

Gilkey seemed in no pain as we wrapped him in the smashed tent, put his feet in a rucksack, and tied nylon ropes to him in such a way that they cradled him. Four ropes, tied to this cradle, could be held by one man ahead, one man behind, and one on either side. We had already put on all our warm clothing—sweaters, wool jackets, down jackets, and nylon parkas—and stripped our packs to the minimum. As we worked, the disabled man watched the preparations silently. He was an experienced mountaineer and realized what all of us were up against. But he knew also that we would never leave him, and that we would bring him down safely if it were humanly possible. Art's cap was pulled down over his face, which looked drawn and bluish-gray, but he gave a wan smile whenever someone asked, "How is it going?"

"Just fine," he would say. "Just fine." And his mouth would smile. He never showed a moment's fear or the slightest lack of confidence, but he realized of course that he had been stricken by something that was likely to be fatal, that his condition was getting worse, and that he was 9,000 feet above Base Camp in a terrible monsoon storm. The nearest tent, at Camp VI, was 2,000 feet below. He knew that we could not carry him down the tricky route we had come up, and that we must go only where we could lower him. Even in perfect weather with all men in top physical condition, the task might prove impossible—yet Art Gilkey could smile, and his smile gave us strength.

While we were adjusting the tow ropes, Schoening and Molenaar strapped on their crampons and disappeared into the storm. They were to find the best route past the dangerous avalanche slope that had blocked us a few days before, and to go over to the Camp VII cache to get a climbing rope that was strung on the ice slope just above. It would be useful in the descent. After their departure Houston called Base Camp on the walkie-talkie and told Ata-Ullah our plans. "It's pretty desperate, Ata," he said grimly, "but we can't wait. We're starting down now. We'll call you at three o'clock."

Each man took his place on a rope tied to Gilkey and for a couple of hundred yards we lunged hard at the tow ropes to pull Art through the knee-deep drifts of powder snow; then gravity took over and we had to hold back just as strongly to keep our helpless 185-pound load from plunging into the abyss. The steep slope we were on disappeared below us into nothingness. Was there a cliff there, a jumping-off place? We strained our eyes peering into the storm, but we could not wait for clearing weather. Instead we had to depend on Schoening and Molenaar, who had gone ahead to scout out the way. As we descended, Craig and Bell pulled the front ropes, one on each side, and Houston directed operations from a point immediately behind Gilkey, while Streather and I anchored the rope higher up. Gradually we worked our way to a rock ridge, climbed down alongside it, and then began to lower Gilkey down a steep snow slope leading to a snow chute and an ice gully below. This route was not the one we would have taken had Gilkey been able to walk, but now we had no choice: we could go only where we could lower our companion, and we had faith that the two men ahead would find a route down. Once we were well started, return to Camp VIII would be impossible for any of us.

The wind and cold seeped insidiously through our layers of warm clothing so that by the end of the third hour none of us had feeling in his toes any longer, and grotesque icicles hung from our eyebrows, beards, and mustaches. Goggles froze over and we continually raised them on our foreheads in order to see how to handle the rope. Moving the sick man was frightfully slow. We had to belay one another as well as Gilkey, and our numb fingers would not move quickly. Somehow, when we got to the steepest pitch, however, someone managed to tie two 120-foot nylon ropes together and we started to lower Gilkey down, down in the only direction the slope would permit. Houston and I, braced on the storm-swept ridge, backs to the wind, could feel the terrible gusts trying to hurl us off the rocks. We could not see where we were lowering Art, but we could hear faint shouts from Schoening and Molenaar, who were out of sight below. As we slowly payed out the coils of rope, thankful that they were of nylon and would not freeze in kinks, Bob Craig unroped from us and climbed down alongside the injured man to direct the descent. Soon he was completely obscured, too, but Streather climbed down to where he could see Craig's arm signals, yet still see us, and so we belayers had communication with Craig and Gilkey and knew whether to lower or to hold the rope. Alternately we anchored and payed out line until we were nearly frozen, and our arms were strained when Tony Streather, whom we could barely see, turned and shouted, "Hold tight! They're being carried down in an avalanche!"

We held. Our anchorage was good and the rope stretched taut. For a moment snow flurries blotted out everything, and then we could hear a muffled shout from Streather. "They're still there!" The rope had broken loose a wind-slab avalanche of powder snow that had roared down over both men, blotting them from sight. Craig clung to the rope to Gilkey, and held onto it for his life. The pull of the hissing particles must have been terrible, but the avalanche was of unconsolidated snow. The falling powder slithered out of sight and down off the side of the mountain, where it must have kept falling long after we could hear it. When it was gone, Craig still clung to the rope, gray and very chilled. Both men were safe. The grim descent continued.

Schoening and Molenaar, who were not far from Camp VII, soon were able to reach Gilkey, but it seemed like hours to the four of us on the icy rocks of the wind-swept ridge before they shouted up that they had him strongly belayed "on the edge of a cliff," and we could climb down. Stiffly we shifted from our frozen positions, and climbed clumsily down the steep, crumbly rocks to the snow chute above the ice gully. Houston and I were on one rope, Bell and Streather on the other. All were so cold, so near exhaustion, that moving down over dangerous, snow-covered ice stretched us to the limit. Through the murk of blowing snow we saw Schoening standing in front of a large, rounded rock that had become frozen onto a narrow ledge. His ice ax was thrust deep into the snow above the rock, and the rope with which he held Art Gilkey was looped tightly around the shaft of the ax. The sick man was at the edge of a 20-foot cliff, beneath which we could glimpse the ice gully dropping off steeply into the storm toward the Godwin-Austen Glacier nearly two miles below.

Schoening looked like a man from another world. So much frost had formed on our beards that faces were unrecognizable, and we knew that we were fast reaching the breaking point. We could not continue much longer without shelter from the driving storm and food to renew our energy. Some 150 yards below us to the east was the tiny shelf, nicked into the ice slope, where Schoening and Gilkey had spent the night of July 30 during their reconnaissance above Camp VI. We had called it Camp VII, or Camp VII cache. None of us had expected anyone to spend another night there, but Bob Craig, whose struggle against the avalanche had so completely exhausted him temporarily that he could hardly tie a crampon strap, had been belayed over to this site to rest and clear some of the avalanche snow that had seeped under his parka. We yelled to him to try to enlarge the ledge. Meanwhile, with Schoening anchoring the rope, we lowered Gilkey slowly over the short rock cliff until he was resting against the 45-degree ice slope. Streather, who was roped to Bell, climbed down to Gilkey. Schoening held Gilkey's rope firmly while Houston belayed me across a delicate pitch of steep, hard ice, and then Houston climbed down to a point opposite the man suspended against the slope.

The problem now was not to get Gilkey down, but to swing him across the steep ice slope to the ice shelf at Camp VII. Our plan was to get a firm anchorage and then pendulum him across, but unfortunately the ice near him was too hard for axes to be driven in and the slope was relentlessly steep.

Even during the best weather conditions the maneuver would have been dangerous, and our position at that moment I shall never forget. Schoening was belaying Gilkey, who hung 60 feet below him, suspended against the sharply angled ice. On the same level as Gilkey, and 40 feet across from him, five of us, facing into the stinging, drifting snow, were searching for a place where we could stand and anchor the rope to Gilkey as we pulled him across the ice in the direction of Craig on the ice shelf. With our spiked crampons biting the hard ice, Streather, Houston, Molenaar, and I stood close together. Bell and Streather were roped together, Houston and I were on a rope together—and Molenaar had just "tied in" to a loose rope to Gilkey. He had done this when Craig had unroped and gone over to the ice shelf to rest, and it was Molenaar's precaution that saved us all. For George Bell, who was some 60 feet above us, began to descend a delicate stretch of hard ice in order to help with Gilkey's ropes. At that moment, what we had all been dreading occurred. Something threw Bell off balance and he fell.

I never saw Bell fall, but to my horror I saw Streather being dragged off the slope and making desperate efforts to jam the pick of his ax into the ice and stop. Streather had been standing above the rope from Houston to me. In almost the same instant I saw Houston swept off, and though I turned and lunged at the hard ice with the point of my ax, a terrible jerk ripped me from my hold and threw me backward headfirst down the slope. *This is it!* I thought as I landed heavily on my pack. There was nothing I could do now. We had done our best, but our best wasn't good enough. This was the end. Since nobody was on the rope with Houston and me, there was no one else to hold us, and I knew that nothing could stop us now. On the slope below, no rock jutted on which the rope between us could catch. Only thousands of feet of empty space separated us from the glacier below. It was like falling off a slanting Empire State Building six times as high as the real one.

Thrown violently backward, with the hood of my down jacket jammed over my eyes, I had a feeling of unreality, of detachment. The future was beyond my control. All I knew was that I landed on my pack with great force, bouncing faster and faster, bumping over rocks in great thumps. The next bound I expected to take me over a cliff in a terrible drop that would finish it all, when, by a miracle, I stopped sliding.

I was on my back with my hood over my eyes and my head a yard below my feet. My arms, stretched over my head, were so completely tangled with the taut rope that I could not loosen them. I was helpless, and when I tried to move, I realized that I was balanced on the crest of some rocks and that a change of position might throw me off the edge.

The rope had apparently snagged on a projection—though how and where I couldn't imagine—but it might not be securely caught. Whether it was firmly held, whether anyone else was alive, I did not know, but I didn't need to wait. Almost immediately I heard a groan coming from nearly on top of me. "Get me loose," I called, and immediately I felt the pressure of a leg braced against my shoulder and the rope was pulled off my arms.

Grabbing a rock, I swung my head around. Dee Molenaar and I were clinging to a rocky outcrop at the side of a steep ice slope, studded with rocks, about 150 to 200 feet below the place where we had been working on the ropes to Gilkey. Blood from Dee's nose trickled across his mustache and beard, and he looked badly shaken. My rope was tight to someone or something above, and I heard a distant yell, "Get your weight off the rope!" Fifty feet higher, through a mist of blowing snow, I could see Tony Streather staggering to his feet, a tangle of ropes still tight about his waist. Below me I heard a cry, "My hands are freezing!" and, looking down, to my amazement I saw George Bell, who seconds before had been 60 feet above me. Now about 60 feet *below*, he was climbing up over the edge of nothingness. He wore neither pack nor glasses and was staggering up over the steep rocks, obviously dazed, with his hands held out grotesquely in front of him. His mittens had been ripped off in the fall, and already the color of his hands had turned an ugly fish-belly white. If his hands were badly frozen, of course, we might never be able to get him down off the mountain.

Turning to Molenaar, I thrust my pack into his arms. Most of the lashing had ripped loose and the walkie-talkie radio, which had been on top, was gone; my sleeping bag was half off, held by a single twist of line. Without sleeping bags we were unlikely to survive the night, no matter how we tried! Since Molenaar wore no pack, I imagined that his sleeping bag also had been torn off in the fall. Whether or not the tent someone had been carrying had survived the fall, I didn't know. "For God's sake, hold this," I yelled above the wind, placing my load in Molenaar's arms. (For all I knew, mine was the only sleeping bag to survive the fall, and we must not lose it now.) The loose pack was awkward to hold securely while we were standing on such steep rock, but Molenaar grasped it and I unroped and started to climb shakily down to meet Bell. As I climbed down, I wondered about the ropes that had saved us. They were snagged to something up above, but the driving snow kept us from seeing what was holding them. Luckily I had a spare pair of dry, loosely woven Indian mitts in the pouch pocket of my parka, and when I reached Bell, whose face was gray and haggard, I helped him to put them on. Already his fingers were so stiff with cold that he couldn't move them, but balancing on projections of rock on the steep slope, we struggled to save his hands and finally forced the big white mittens past his stiff thumbs and down over his wrists.

Bell's fall had ended with him suspended over the edge of a ledge, below which the slope dropped away precipitously for thousands of feet. The weight of his pack pulled him head down, and he had lost it while trying to get right side up and back over the ledge. While Bell crouched down, working desperately to warm his hands under his parka, I left him, for Molenaar and I had seen a crumpled figure lying below a 30-foot cliff on a narrow shelf that seemed to be projecting over utter blankness below. It was Houston. Somehow a rope to him was snagged high above us, too. Climbing unsteadily but cautiously, for I was not roped and felt shaken by the fall, I worked my way down the steep rocks and across to the ledge. Houston was unconscious, but his eyes opened as I touched his shoulder. When he staggered to his feet, I felt relief it is impossible to describe.

"Where are we?" he asked. "What are we doing here?"

He was obviously hurt. His eyes did not focus and he appeared to be suffering from a concussion. Again and again I tried to persuade him to climb up the cliff, while Molenaar anchored the rope still attached to him from above. He didn't understand. "Where are we?" he kept saying, for my replies did not convey any meaning to him in his confused state.

The wind and blowing snow were searing our faces. We were all near exhaustion and in danger of crippling frostbite. If we were to survive, we had to get shelter at once, or we would be so numbed by exposure that we could not protect ourselves. What had happened in that Nanga Parbat storm which had taken so many men was a grim reminder. All of us working together did not now have strength enough to pull or carry Houston up the steep rock and snow to the ice ledge, 150 feet above, which we had called Camp VII.

"Charlie," I said with the greatest intensity, looking directly into his eyes, "if you ever want to see Dorcas and Penny again [his wife and daughter], climb up there *right now!*"

Somehow this demand penetrated to his brain, for, with a frightened look and without a word, he turned and, belayed by Molenaar, fairly swarmed up the snowy rocks of the cliff. Instinct and years of climbing helped him now in his confused condition, for he climbed brilliantly up to Molenaar. I followed more slowly because, being fully conscious, I had great respect for this steep rock wall, and with great care I pulled myself up over the snow-covered slabs. When I reached Molenaar, he was looking puzzled and very unhappy as he tried to answer Houston's repeated question, "What are we doing here?"

When I reached Molenaar, I still did not know what had caused the near disaster or how all five of us who fell had been saved. Up above, through the murk of blinding snow, I caught glimpses of Art Gilkey, anchored where he had been before the fall, but now Bob Craig was near him. Tony Streather, in a direct line above me, seemed to be untangling himself from a confused snarl of nylon climbing ropes, one of which led down to me.

Much later I learned the sequence of events that had put us in this position and marveled even more at our escape. When Bell fell, he pulled off Streather, who was hurled into the rope between Houston and me and became tangled with it. We were in turn knocked off by the impact, and all three of us—Streather, Houston, and I—began tumbling in a blind, uncontrolled whirl toward the glacier far below. Nothing we could do could stop us now. But our time had not come. For Molenaar was standing below us on the slope, farther away from the sick man, and he had just tied one of the loose ropes from Art Gilkey about his waist. That circumstance saved us, for our wild fall sent us all into and across the rope from Gilkey to Molenaar, and somehow Streather fouled onto this rope too. But our impact had thrown Molenaar headfirst down the slope, and we all bounded on unchecked until stopped by the tightening of the rope from Gilkey to Molenaar—a rope in which Streather was now completely tangled. Gilkey was not pulled loose, for he was anchored by Schoening, who stood on a rock ledge 60 feet above him, and the whole strain of the five falling men, plus Gilkey, was transmitted to Schoening, the youngest member of the party. Fortunately for us all, Schoening is an expert belayer, and his skill and quick thinking saved our lives. Later he told us how he did it.

By the time I returned to Molenaar and Houston, it was clear that through some miracle every climber was still able to move under his own power, but our exposure to the wind-driven snow was chilling us dangerously; we had to move fast to take shelter before we became too numb to set up a tent or became so crippled by frostbite that we would never be able to continue the descent. Since Molenaar's leg hurt and he didn't feel like moving much, I took Charlie Houston's rope and began climbing slowly up toward the ice ledge at Camp VII. I couldn't hurry to save my life. Houston was obviously confused, but by instinct he climbed well and did what was asked. I hadn't climbed far when Tony Streather threw me a rope-end, and then Bob Craig returned from anchoring Art Gilkey and he and Streather took over the task of escorting Houston to the ledge. Craig had not seen the fall, but had looked up suddenly and been horrified to see the slope bare except for Schoening and Gilkey and a solitary ice ax with its pick end jabbed into the ice. At that moment a cloud of snow had blown across the ice, blotting out everything. When it cleared, Schoening, whose tight grip on the rope was freezing his hands, called to Craig to help him to anchor

Gilkey. The sick man had not fallen, and he lay suspended against the ice as he had been at the time of the accident. He was probably the warmest of us all, but we could not continue to move him until the injured were cared for and we had more manpower to help get him across the slope.

When Craig reached him, Art handed over his ice ax, which he had retained for use in the descent. To make a secure anchorage was not easy, and Craig, still exhausted from his struggle against the avalanche, was not secured by anyone while he did it, but he skillfully found firm snow and drove in Art's ice ax right up to the head. He told the sick man that we would return for him as soon as we had a tent up. Gilkey understood. Not until then, when Craig had an ice ax firmly embedded, could Pete Schoening release his grip—which had held six men!—and begin to warm his freezing hands. Craig had not been involved in the accident, but all the rest of us owed our lives to Schoening's skill, courage, and technique.

Fortunately the tent had not been in one of the lost packs, but as I started to unroll it, the wind threatened to sweep it off the mountain. Craig and I were trying to wrestle the corners of the tent into position when Streather, who had now anchored Gilkey with a second ice ax, joined us to help pin the flapping edges under loose rocks till we could get anchorage for the guy ropes. The slope was so steep that the outer third of the tent was off the ledge and overhanging, so that it was impossible to keep the wind from sucking under the tent and trying to tear it away.

We were fortunate that this was our smallest two-man tent, for it held the ledge better than a wider one. Actually, in Exeter before the expedition, we had thought it too small for two men and had almost failed to bring it. Pitching the tent was frustrating, for each time we would secure one corner, another corner would shudder loose. Finally we tied the front guy rope to a rock piton and lashed the inside corners as well as we could to projecting rocks. When Bob Craig later pounded in a Bernays ice piton, we felt somewhat safer, though the nylon shroud line attached to it didn't look too strong and the outer section of the tent bulged out over the slope. If someone inside forgot how precariously the tent was poised and leaned against the outer wall, we knew that the fabric would probably tear or the whole tent pull loose from the little ledge, and with everyone in it roll down the mountain into space.

The moment the tent was up, we moved Bell and Houston inside, where they would be under shelter and their weight would be useful in anchoring the tent. Molenaar at this point joined them to help take care of Houston, for Dee by now had lashed my loose pack together and carried it to the ledge. His left thigh hurt and he had a cracked rib.

While these men were trying to warm themselves in the tent, the rest of us began to hack out another platform in the ice for Schoening's bivouac tent, which had previously been cached on the ledge as a safeguard for Streather and me on the day when we climbed from Camp VI to Camp VIII. This tent was meant for one person or in an emergency two, but if we could get it up, we meant to use it for three men to huddle inside.

At this moment Peter Schoening climbed down to us and declared laconically, "My hands are freezing." He too crawled into the tent to try to save his hands. All of us were still too busy to find out how Schoening had held us, for it seemed as if we would never get a platform flat enough or wide enough to pitch the bivouac tent. All our strength and energy went into chipping out an ice platform, for we had to get shelter from the bitter blast for everyone; but when we did get an uneven floor carved out, the wind whipped the fabric violently. It was like working in the slipstream behind an airplane as it taxied across the snow, spraying stinging particles behind. Finally Pete crawled out to help us insert the poles and we fastened the tent insecurely to rocks and pitons near the shelf of ice. It too overhung in an alarming manner.

The moment the bivouac tent was up, three of us prepared to go back for Art Gilkey. He was only 150 feet away, but a low rib of rock hid from sight the ice gully where we had left him suspended from the two widely separated ice axes, each firmly thrust into the snow. Gilkey had called to us a couple of times while we were desperately hacking at the slope to make a platform for the bivouac tents, but the severity of the storm and the position of the gully made it impossible to distinguish words. Gilkey sounded as if he were shouting encouragement, but the wind blurred his words, as it must have muffled our answering shouts to him. He knew that we were making a shelter and would come for him as soon as we could.

About ten minutes after Gilkey's last shout, Streather, Craig, and I roped up and began to cross the slope to reach the injured man and move him somehow to the ice ledge where we now had two small tents. We knew that moving him even this short distance would take every bit of strength we had left, and we roped together carefully and braced ourselves for the effort.

Schoening would have come with us, but as he emerged from the tent, he began a fit of coughing so long and painful that it doubled him up and made us urge him to crawl back into the tent. Pete had gulped in deep draughts of frigid air while climbing up to collect the fixed rope above Camp VII earlier in the day, and apparently the cold had somehow temporarily affected his lungs. He coughed until he seemed exhausted. At the moment we were particularly dismayed by Schoening's near collapse, because he had always been strong and we were counting heavily on him to help in moving Gilkey and in getting the party down the mountain. We didn't know at the moment what his trouble was or how serious it might be, and in great distress we started out into the wind to traverse the slope to Art Gilkey. Streather and I had had our snow glasses off most of the day, because snow had frozen over the lenses, turning them almost to blinders. Apparently we had developed a touch of snow blindness, because we now seemed to be seeing everything through a very light mist. This mist was hard to distinguish from blowing snow, and we seemed to be moving in a dream. Fortunately, the wind had dropped as we reached the rock rib and looked into the gully where Art had been left suspended. What we saw there I shall never forget. The whole slope was bare of life. Art Gilkey was gone!

Our sick comrade, who had called to us a few minutes before, had disappeared. Even the two ice axes used to anchor him safely had been torn loose. The white, windswept ice against which he had been resting showed no sign that anyone had ever been there. It was as if the hand of God had swept him away.

The shock stunned us. Blowing snow stung our faces as we silently stared and stared, but the slope remained empty. Something about it had changed, however, for there seemed to be a groove on the lower part of the slope that had not been there before. A snow or ice avalanche must have swept the sick man away scant minutes before we came to get him. As Craig and I belayed Streather out onto the center of the gully, he looked down past his cramponed feet to where the slope disappeared into the storm below. We called and shouted, but all of us knew that there would be no answer. Nobody could slide off that slope out of sight and remain alive. Dazed and incredulous, we turned and plodded back to the tents.

Gilkey's death, though anticipated for other reasons, was a violent shock. He had been very close to us, and we could not forget his many kindnesses to each of us in the past weeks. We had admired him and loved him. But too many immediate problems faced us to permit brooding over our loss now. Several men were injured. Whether they were in condition to climb down the mountain without help, we didn't know; nor did we know whether we could get them down if they could not walk. We would never leave anybody, but our struggle to lower Art Gilkey had shown us that to get a helpless man down the upper slopes of K2 under storm conditions required more strength and manpower than we now had. The route down from Camp VII to Camp VI would be longer and infinitely more difficult for rescue work than anything we had yet descended.

At Schoening's request, I moved into the Gerry tent alongside Houston. Four of us were now crowded into this little shelter with our backs to the ice slope and our feet resting lightly on the one-third of the tent which bellied out and overhung the slope. Luckily we had an air mattress, and once this was inflated and worked under the men inside, it gave some insulation from the cold. I opened my sleeping bag and placed the outer bag under our feet on the droopy side of the tent, while the inner half I wrapped around Houston, who was in a state of shock.

By this time the sky was darkening, but to our great relief the wind had dropped. We wore all our clothes and though they were damp we were not too cold, yet the night was a ghastly experience. George Bell, his hands and feet frozen, had jammed his great bulk into one end of the little Gerry tent. He cannot see well without glasses, and the pair he was wearing and the spare pair in his pack had disappeared in the fall. That night he must have realized the effort that would be required of him next day, for the steepest part of the route lay immediately below our ledge, and it would be impossible for us to carry him if he could not climb down. At the opposite end of the tent lay Dee Molenaar, a deep cut stiffening his left thigh and a bruised or cracked rib making his breathing painful. What he was thinking during the long hours of darkness I don't know, but he insisted on covering up Houston in his down jacket, even though he himself was lying exposed just inside the doorway of the tent.

Between Molenaar and Bell were Houston and I. Charlie Houston usually is bursting with energy, and if he had had his normal strength that night he would have been far too powerful for us. At first he was in a state of shock, but he soon stopped shivering and began to ask question after question, "Where are we?" "Where is Pete?" "How is Art?" Some things he seemed to understand, but he would ask the same questions again and again. A dozen times at least during the night he would ask, "How's Pete?" I would say, "He's all right," but Charlie wouldn't believe me. Then I would call across to the tiny bivouac tent, which was swelled to bursting by the three men inside, "Hey, Pete, tell Charlie you're all right."

Pete Schoening would call out, "I'm fine, Charlie. Don't worry about me."

"Oh, that's fine; that's fine," Charlie would say, and for a moment he would be quiet. Then again he would say solicitously, "How's

Tony?" and the rigmarole would begin all over again. We were touched by his anxiety about us but we were more concerned about him.

During the fall Houston had evidently struck his forehead against a rock, causing a concussion and a hemorrhage which blurred the vision in his right eye. Another blow had given him a painful chest injury, which so affected his breathing that any deep breath was painful. In his confused state he thought that the pain in his chest when he breathed was caused by lack of oxygen in the tent, and so he tried to remedy the situation by clawing a hole in the fabric. Then, to keep from breathing deeply, he would take short breaths, faster and faster, until he would slump over unconscious and breathe normally until he became conscious again. When he became unconscious, we would shift position and try to get more comfortable, for the moment he was conscious he would become active again and we would have to restrain him.

Somehow—I still don't know how—the three men crammed into the bivouac tent, which was just as precariously pitched, were able to make tea and pass it in to us occasionally. There wasn't a great deal, but those swallows of tea were a godsend. They helped us to keep awake. Molenaar even opened the tent door to humor Charlie, but he still wanted to cut a hole in the tent. "I know about these things," he would say. "I have studied them. We'll all be dead in three minutes if you won't let me cut a hole in the tent." And again his breathing would speed up tremendously and he would collapse.

The night seemed unbearably long, but at least we could converse with those in the other tent and the tea cheered us. During the long darkness we asked each man about his injuries and each man told a compressed story of what had happened to him in the fall. Schoening wasn't saying much, but we kept calling over to him, "How did you do it, Pete?"

"What kind of a belay did you have?"

"If you can stop five men at 25,000 feet, how many could you stop at 15,000?"

Pete's story was brief. "Well, I was lucky," he said. "My ice ax was dri-

ven into the snow and braced against the upper side of that big boulder frozen in the ice. The rope passed around the ax to where I stood
in front of the boulder, and went around my body, so that the force was
widely distributed. Of course I was belaying Art anyway, and when I
saw George slip and then Tony and the others pulled off, I swung
weight onto the head of the ax and held on as the rope slid a bit. The
force must have come in a series of shocks. The strain on me was not
too great, but at the ice ax that seven-sixteenth-inch nylon rope
stretched until it looked like a quarter-inch line, and I was scared stiff
the boulder would be pulled loose. If that happened, the ax, which was
braced against it, would go, too, and we would be lost. For minutes, it
seemed, the rope was taut as a bowstring. Snow squalls blotted out
everything below, and I couldn't tell what was happening. My hands
were freezing, but of course I could not let go. Then the air cleared a bit
and I yelled to Bob Craig, who was over at Camp VII, to come and
anchor Art. By the time he reached him, most of the weight was off the
rope, and from below I could hear someone calling, 'Charlie's hurt.'
Once Art was secured, I came down to thaw out."

This simple story failed to stress the remarkable fact that one man
had held five men who slid 150 to 300 feet down a 45-degree slope
and that he had done it at nearly 25,000 feet, where the mere job of
survival absorbs most of the strength of a man. Such magnificent belay
work has rarely been recorded in mountaineering anywhere. Nor have
I read of any other climbing miracle when three separate ropes fouled
together to save the lives of five men. Bad luck had forced us to move
in storm and had placed us where the fall had swept us off, but good
luck, the resilience of nylon rope, and a remarkable tangle had saved
our lives.

When the long hours finally wore away and the first rays of daylight
came, a dour gray sky showed that more storm was coming fast. Silent,
haggard, exhausted, we waited until Bob Craig had first made some tea
and then cooked a little cereal. We had only one pot. During the night
someone had placed the other pot outside the door of the crowded
tent and it had immediately slid off the mountain. At the first light

Houston crawled to the door and thrust out his shoulders. He seemed astonished that he didn't find more oxygen or easier breathing outside the tent. The morning air was raw and we were sore and weary. Everyone's eyes looked dead. But there was no question about the next move. We had to go down.

from Annapurna
by Maurice Herzog

The 1950 French Himalayan Expedition was the first to scale one of the world's fourteen 8,000-meter peaks. Their climb of Annapurna (26,493 feet) was in many ways a more impressive achievement than the British ascent of Everest three years later. The French had to find their mountain before they could climb it. Approach routes were unknown. Team leader Maurice Herzog (b. 1919) and Chamonix guide Louis Lachenal were understandably weakened by summit day. But their troubles were just beginning.

O n the third of June, 1950, the first light of dawn found us still clinging to the tent poles at Camp V. Gradually the wind abated, and with daylight, died away altogether. I made desperate attempts to push back the soft, icy stuff which stifled me, but every movement became an act of heroism. My mental powers were numbed: thinking was an effort and we did not exchange a single word.

What a repellent place it was! To everyone who reached it, Camp V became one of the worst memories of their lives. We had only one thought—to get away. We should have waited for the first rays of the sun, but at half-past five we felt we couldn't stick it any longer.

"Let's go, Biscante," I muttered. "Can't stay here a minute longer."

"Yes, let's go," repeated Lachenal.

Which of us would have the energy to make tea? Although our minds worked slowly we were quite able to envisage all the movements that would be necessary—and neither of us could face up to it.

It couldn't be helped—we would just have to go without. It was quite hard enough work to get ourselves and our boots out of our sleeping-bags—and the boots were frozen stiff so that we got them on only with the greatest difficulty. Every movement made us terribly breathless. We felt as if we were being stifled. Our gaiters were stiff as a board, but I succeeded in lacing mine up; Lachenal couldn't manage his.

"No need for the rope, eh, Biscante?"

"No need," replied Lachenal laconically.

That was two pounds saved. I pushed a tube of condensed milk, some nougat and a pair of socks into my sack; one never knew, the socks might come in useful—they might even do as Balaclavas. For the time being I stuffed them with first-aid equipment. The camera was loaded with a black and white film; I had a color film in reserve. I pulled the movie-camera out from the bottom of my sleeping-bag, wound it up and tried letting it run without film. There was a little click, then it stopped and jammed.

"Bad luck after bringing it so far," said Lachenal.

In spite of our photographer Ichac's precautions taken to lubricate it with special grease, the intense cold, even inside the sleeping-bag, had frozen it. I left it at the camp rather sadly: I had looked forward to taking it to the top. I had used it up to 24,600 feet.

We went outside and put on our crampons, which we kept on all day. We wore as many clothes as possible; our sacks were very light. At six o'clock we started off. It was brilliantly fine, but also very cold. Our super-lightweight crampons bit deep into the steep slopes of ice and hard snow up which lay the first stage of our climb.

Later the slope became slightly less steep and more uniform. Sometimes the hard crust bore our weight, but at others we broke through and sank into soft powder snow which made progress exhausting. We took turns in making the track and often stopped without any word having passed between us. Each of us lived in a closed and private world of his own. I was suspicious of my mental processes; my mind was working very slowly and I was perfectly aware of the low state of my intelligence. It was easiest just to stick to one thought at a time—safest, too. The cold was penetrating; for all our special eider-down clothing we felt as if we'd nothing on. Whenever we halted, we stamped our feet hard. Lachenal went as far as to take off one boot which was a bit tight; he was in terror of frostbite.

"I don't want to be like Lambert," he said. Raymond Lambert, a Geneva guide, had to have all his toes amputated after an eventful climb during which he got his feet frostbitten. While Lachenal rubbed himself hard, I looked at the summits all around us; already we over-topped them all except the distant Dhaulagiri. The complicated struc-ture of these mountains, with which our many laborious explorations had made us familiar, was now spread out plainly at our feet.

The going was incredibly exhausting, and every step was a struggle of mind over matter. We came out into the sunlight, and by way of marking the occasion made yet another halt. Lachenal continued to complain of his feet. "I can't feel anything. I think I'm beginning to get frostbite." And once again he undid his boot.

I began to be seriously worried. I realized very well the risk we were running; I knew from experience how insidously and quickly frostbite can set in if one is not extremeley careful. Nor was Lachenal under any illusions. "We're in danger of having frozen feet. Do you think it's worth it?"

This was most disturbing. It was my responsibility as leader to think of the others. There was no doubt about frostbite being a very real dan-ger. Did Annapurna justify such risks? That was the question I asked myself; it continued to worry me.

Lachenal had laced his boots up again, and once more we contin-ued to force our way through the exhausting snow. The whole of the Sickle glacier was now in view, bathed in light. We still had a long way to go to cross it, and then there was that rock band—would we find a gap in it?

My feet, like Lachenal's, were very cold and I continued to wriggle my toes, even when we were moving. I could not feel them, but that was nothing new in the mountains, and if I kept on moving them it would keep the circulation going.

Lachenal appeared to me as a sort of specter—he was alone in his world, I in mine. But—and this was odd enough—any effort was slightly *less* exhausting than lower down. Perhaps it was hope lending us wings. Even through dark glasses the snow was blinding—the sun beating straight down on the ice. We looked down upon precipitous ridges which dropped away into space, and upon tiny glaciers far, far below. Familiar peaks soared arrow-like into the sky. Suddenly Lachenal grabbed me:

"If I go back, what will you do?"

A whole sequence of pictures flashed through my head: the days of marching in sweltering heat, the hard pitches we had overcome, the tremendous efforts we had all made to lay seige to the mountain, the daily heroism of all my friends in establishing the camps. Now we were nearing our goal. In an hour or two, perhaps, victory would be ours. Must we give up? Impossible! My whole being revolted against the idea. I had made up my mind, irrevocably. Today we were consecrating an ideal, and no sacrifice was too great. I heard my voice clearly:

"I should go on by myself."

I would go alone. If he wished to go down it was not for me to stop him. He must make his own choice freely.

"Then I'll follow you."

The die was cast. I was no longer anxious. Nothing could stop us now from getting to the top. The psychological atmosphere changed with these few words, and we went forward now as brothers.

I felt as though I were plunging into something new and quite abnormal. I had the strangest and most vivid impressions, such as I had never before known in the mountains. There was something unnatural in the way I saw Lachenal and everything around us. I smiled to myself at the paltriness of our efforts, for I could stand apart and watch myself making these efforts. But all sense of exertion was gone, as though there were no longer any gravity. This diaphanous landscape, this quintessence of purity—these were not the mountains I knew: they were the mountains of my dreams.

The snow, sprinkled over every rock and gleaming in the sun, was of a radiant beauty that touched me to the heart. I had never seen such complete transparency, and I was living in a world of crystal. Sounds were indistinct, the atmosphere like cotton wool.

An astonishing happiness welled up in me, but I could not define it. Everything was so new, so utterly unprecedented. It was not in the least like anything I had known in the Alps, where one feels buoyed up by the presence of others—by people of whom one is vaguely aware, or even by the dwellings one can see in the far distance.

This was quite different. An enormous gulf was between me and the world. This was a different universe—withered, desert, lifeless; a fantastic universe where the presence of man was not foreseen, perhaps not desired. We were braving an interdict, overstepping a boundary, and yet we had no fear as we continued upward. I thought of the famous ladder of St. Theresa of Avila. Something clutched at my heart.

Did Lachenal share these feelings? The summit ridge drew nearer, and we reached the foot of the ultimate rock band. The slope was very steep and the snow interspersed with rocks.

"Couloir!"

A finger pointed. The whispered word from one to another indicated the key to the rocks—the last line of defense.

"What luck!"

The couloir up the rocks though steep was feasible.

The sky was a deep sapphire blue. With a great effort we edged over to the right, avoiding the rocks; we preferred to keep to the snow on account of our crampons and it was not long before we set foot in the couloir. It was fairly steep, and we had a minute's hesitation. Should we have enough strength left to overcome this final obstacle?

Fortunately the snow was hard, and by kicking steps we were able to manage, thanks to our crampons. A false move would have been fatal. There was no need to make handholds—our axes, driven in as far as possible, served us for an anchor.

Lachenal went splendidly. What a wonderful contrast to the early days! It was a hard struggle here, but we kept going. Lifting our eyes occasionally from the slope, we saw the couloir opening out onto . . . well, we didn't quite know, probably a ridge. But where was the top—left or right? Stopping at every step, leaning on our axes we tried to recover our breath and to calm down our racing hearts, which were thumping as though they would burst. We knew we were there now—that nothing could stop us. No need to exchange looks—each of us would have read the same determination in the other's eyes. A slight détour to the left, a few more steps—the summit ridge came gradually nearer—a few rocks to avoid. We dragged ourselves up. Could we possibly be there?

Yes!

A fierce and savage wind tore at us.

We were on top of Annapurna! 8,075 meters, 26,493 feet.

Our hearts overflowed with an unspeakable happiness.

"If only the others could know. . . ."

If only everyone could know!

The summit was a corniced crest of ice, and the precipices on the far side which plunged vertically down beneath us, were terrifying, unfathomable. There could be few other mountains in the world like this. Clouds floated halfway down, concealing the gentle, fertile valley of Pokhara, 23,000 feet below. Above us there was nothing!

Our mission was accomplished. But at the same time we had accomplished something infinitely greater. How wonderful life would now become! What an inconceivable experience it is to attain one's ideal and, at the very same moment, to fulfill oneself. I was stirred to the depths of my being. Never had I felt happiness like this—so intense and yet so pure. That brown rock, the highest of them all, that ridge of ice—were these the goals of a lifetime? Or were they, rather, the limits of man's pride?

"Well, what about going down?"

Lachenal shook me. What were his feelings? Did he simply think he had finished another climb, as in the Alps? Did he think one could just go down again like that, with nothing more to it?

"One minute, I must take some photographs."

"Hurry up!"

I fumbled feverishly in my sack, pulled out the camera, took out the little French flag which was right at the bottom, and the pennants. Useless gestures, no doubt, but something more than symbols—eloquent tokens of affection and goodwill. I tied the strips of material—stained by sweat and by the food in the sacks—to the shaft of my ice-axe, the only flagstaff at hand. Then I focused my camera on Lachenal.

"Now, will you take me?"

"Hand it over—hurry up!" said Lachenal.

He took several pictures and then handed me back the camera. I loaded a color-film and we repeated the process to be certain of bringing back records to be cherished in the future.

"Are you mad?" asked Lachenal. "We haven't a minute to lose: we must go down at once."

And in fact a glance round showed me that the weather was no longer gloriously fine as it had been in the morning. Lachenal was becoming impatient.

"We must go down!"

He was right. His was the reaction of the mountaineer who knows his own domain. But I just could not accustom myself to the idea that we had won our victory. It seemed inconceivable that we should have trodden those summit snows.

It was impossible to build a cairn; there were no stones; everything was frozen. Lachenal stamped his feet; he felt them freezing. I felt mine freezing too, but paid little attention. The highest mountain to be climbed by man lay under our feet! The names of our predecessors on these heights raced through my mind: Mummery, Mallory and Irvine, Bauer, Welzenbach, Tilman, Shipton. How many of them were dead—how many had found on these mountains what, to them, was the finest end of all?

My joy was touched with humility. It was not just one party that had climbed Annapurna today, but a whole expedition. I thought of all the others in the camps perched on the slopes at our feet, and I knew it was because of their efforts and their sacrifices that we had succeeded. There are times when the most complicated actions are suddenly summed up, distilled, and strike you with illuminating clarity: so it was with this irresistible upward surge which had landed us two here.

Pictures passed through my mind—the Chamonix valley, where I had spent the most marvelous moments of my childhood; Mont Blanc, which so tremendously impressed me! I was a child when I first saw "the Mont Blanc people" coming home, and to me there was a queer look about them; a strange light shone in their eyes.

"Come on, straight down," called Lachenal.

He had already done up his sack and started going down. I took out my pocket aneroid: 8,500 meters. I smiled. I swallowed a little condensed milk and left the tube behind—the only trace of our passage. I did up my sack, put on my gloves and my glasses, seized my ice-axe; one look around and I, too, hurried down the slope. Before disappearing into the couloir I gave one last look at the summit which would henceforth be all our joy and all our consolation.

Lachenal was already far below; he had reached the foot of the couloir. I hurried down in his tracks. I went as fast as I could, but it was dangerous going. At every step one had to take care that the snow did not break away beneath one's weight. Lachenal, going faster that I thought he was capable of, was now on the long traverse. It was my turn to cross the area of mixed rock and snow. At last I reached the foot of the rock band. I had hurried and I was out of breath. I undid my sack. What had I been going to do? I couldn't say.

"My gloves!"

Before I had time to bend over, I saw them slide and roll. They went further and further straight down the slope. I remained where I was, quite stunned. I watched them rolling down slowly, with no appearance of stopping. The movement of those gloves was engraved in my sight as something irredeemable, against which I was powerless. The consequences might be most serious. What was I to do?

"Quickly, down to Camp V."

Rébuffat and Terray would be there. My concern dissolved like magic. I now had a fixed objective again: to reach the camp. Never for a minute did it occur to me to use as gloves the socks which I always carry in reserve for just such a mishap as this.

On I went, trying to catch up with Lachenal. It had been two o'clock when we reached the summit; we had started out at six in the morning, but I had to admit that I had lost all sense of time. I felt as if I were running, whereas in actual fact I was walking normally, perhaps rather slowly, and I had to keep stopping to get my breath. The sky was now covered with clouds, everything had become gray and dirty-looking. An icy wind sprang up, boding no good. We must push on! But where was Lachenal? I spotted him a couple of hundred yards away, looking as if he was never going to stop. And I had thought he was in indifferent form!

The clouds grew thicker and came right down over us; the wind blew stronger, but I did not suffer from the cold. Perhaps the descent had restored my circulation. Should I be able to find the tents in the mist? I watched the rib ending in the beak-like point which overlooked the camp. It was gradually swallowed up by the clouds, but I was able to make out the spearhead rib lower down. If the mist should thicken I would make straight for that rib and follow it down, and in this way I should be bound to come upon the tent.

Lachenal disappeared from time to time, and then the mist was so thick that I lost sight of him altogether. I kept going at the same speed, as fast as my breathing would allow.

The slope was now steeper; a few patches of bare ice followed the smooth stretches of snow. A good sign—I was nearing the camp. How difficult to find one's way in thick mist! I kept the course which I had set by the steepest angle of the slope. The ground was broken; with my crampons I went straight down walls of bare ice. There were some patches ahead—a few more steps. It was the camp all right, but there were two tents!

So Rébuffat and Terray had come up. What a mercy! I should be able to tell them that we had been successful, that we were returning from the top. How thrilled they would be!

I got there, dropping down from above. The platform had been extended, and the two tents were facing each other. I tripped over one of the guy-ropes of the first tent; there was movement inside, they had heard me. Rébuffat and Terray put their heads out.

"We've made it. We're back from Annapurna!

* * *

Rébuffat and Terray received the news with great excitement.

"But what about Biscante?" asked Terray anxiously.

"He won't be long. He was just in front of me! What a day—started out at six this morning—didn't stop . . . got up at last."

Words failed me. I had so much to say. The sight of familiar faces dispelled the strange feeling that I had experienced since morning, and I became, once more, just a mountaineer.

Terray, who was speechless with delight, wrung my hands. Then the smile vanished from his face: "Maurice—your hands!" There was an uneasy silence. I had forgotten that I had lost my gloves: my fingers were violet and white and hard as wood. The other two stared at them in dismay—they realized the full seriousness of the injury. But, still blissfully floating on a sea of joy remote from reality, I leaned over towards Terray and said confidentially, "You're in such splendid form, and you've done so marvelously, it's absolutely tragic you didn't come up there with us!"

"What I did was for the Expedition, my dear Maurice, and anyway you've got up, and that's a victory for the whole lot of us."

I nearly burst with happiness. How could I tell him all that his answer meant to me? The rapture I had felt on the summit, which might have seemed a purely personal, egotistical emotion, had been transformed by his words into a complete and perfect joy with no shadow upon it. His answer proved that this victory was not just one man's achievement, a matter for personal pride; no—and Terray was the first to understand this—it was a victory for us all, a victory for mankind itself.

"Hi! Help! Help!"

"Biscante!" exclaimed the others.

Still half intoxicated and remote from reality I had heard nothing. Terray felt a chill at his heart, and his thoughts flew to his partner on so many unforgettable climbs; together they had so often skirted death, and won so many splendid victories. Putting his head out, and seeing Lachenal clinging to the slope 100 yards lower down, he dressed in frantic haste.

Out he went. But the slope was bare now; Lachenal had disappeared. Terray was horribly frightened, and he could only utter unintelligible cries. It was a ghastly moment for him. A violent wind sent the mist tearing by. Under the stress of emotion Terray had not realized how it falsified distances.

"Biscante! Biscante!"

He had spotted him, through a rift in the mist, lying on the slope much lower down than he had thought. Terray set his teeth, and glissaded down like a madman. How would he be able to brake without crampons, on the wind-hardened snow? But Terray was a first-class skier, and with a jump turn he stopped beside Lachenal, who was suffering from concussion after his tremendous fall. In a state of collapse, with no ice-axe, balaclava, or gloves, and only one crampon, he gazed vacantly around him.

"My feet are frost-bitten. Take me down . . . take me down, so that Oudot can see to me."

"It can't be done," said Terray sorrowfully. "Can't you see we're in the middle of a storm. . . . It'll be dark soon."

But Lachenal was obsessed by the fear of amputation. With a gesture of despair he tore the axe out of Terray's hands and tried to force his way down; but soon saw the futility of his action and resolved to climb up to the camp. While Terray cut steps without stopping, Lachenal, ravaged and exhausted as he was, dragged himself along on all fours.

Meanwhile I had gone into Rébuffat's tent. He was appalled at the sight of my hands and, as rather incoherently I told him what we had done, he took a piece of rope and began flicking my fingers. Then he took off my boots with great difficulty for my feet were swollen, and beat my feet and rubbed me. We soon heard Terray giving Lachenal the same treatment in the other tent.

For our comrades it was a tragic moment: Annapurna was conquered, and the first eight-thousander had been climbed. Every one of us had been ready to sacrifice everything for this. Yet, as they looked at our feet and hands, what can Terray and Rébuffat have felt?

Outside the storm howled and the snow was still falling. The mist grew thick and darkness came. As on the previous night we had to cling to the poles to prevent the tents being carried away by the wind. The only two air-mattresses were given to Lachenal and myself while Terray and Rébuffat both sat on ropes, rucksacks, and provisions to keep themselves off the snow. They rubbed, slapped and beat us with a rope. Sometimes the blows fell on the living flesh, and howls arose from both tents. Rébuffat persevered; it was essential to continue painful as it was. Gradually life returned to my feet as well as to my hands, and circulation started again. Lachenal, too, found that feeling was returning.

Now Terray summoned up the energy to prepare some hot drinks. He called to Rébuffat that he would pass him a mug, so two hands stretched out towards each other between the two tents and were instantly covered with snow. The liquid was boiling though scarcely more than 60 degrees centigrade (140 degrees Fahrenheit). I swallowed it greedily and felt infinitely better.

The night was aboslutely hell. Frightful onslaughts of wind battered us incessantly, while the never-ceasing snow piled up on the tents.

Now and again I heard voices from next door—it was Terray massaging Lachenal with admirable perseverance, only stopping to ply him with hot drinks. In our tent Rébuffat was quite worn out, but satisfied that warmth was returning to my limbs.

Lying half unconscious I was scarcely aware of the passage of time. There were moments when I was able to see our situation in its true dramatic light, but the rest of the time I was plunged in an inexplicable stupor with no thought for the consequences of our victory.

As the night wore on the snow lay heavier on the tent, and once again I had the frightful feeling of being slowly and silently asphyxiated. I tried, with all the strength of which I was capable, to push off with both forearms the mass that was crushing me. These fearful exertions left me gasping for breath and I fell back into the same exhausted state. It was much worse than the previous night.

"Rébuffat! Gaston! Gaston!"

I recognized Terray's voice.

"Time to be off!"

I heard the sounds without grasping their meaning. Was it light already? I was not in the least surprised that the other two had given up all thought of going to the top, and I did not at all grasp the measure of their sacrifice.

Outside the storm redoubled in violence. The tent shook and the fabric flapped alarmingly. It had usually been fine in the mornings: did this mean the monsoon was upon us? We knew it was not far off—could this be its first onslaught?

"Gaston! Are you ready?" Terray called again.

"One minute," answered Rébuffat. He didn't have an easy job: he had to put my boots on and do everything to get me ready. I let myself be handled like a baby. In the other tent Terray finished dressing Lachenal whose feet were still swollen and would not fit into his boots. So Terray gave him his own, which were bigger. To get Lachenal's onto his own feet he had to make slits in them. As a precaution he put a sleeping-bag and some food into his sack and shouted to us to do the same. Were his words lost in the storm? Or were we too intent on leaving this hellish place to listen to his instructions?

Lachenal and Terray were already outside.

"We're going down!" they shouted.

Then Rébuffat tied me on the rope and we went out. There were only two ice-axes for the four of us, so Rébuffat and Terray took them as a matter of course. For a moment as we left the two tents of Camp V, I felt childishly ashamed at leaving all this good equipment behind.

Already the first rope seemed a long way down below us. We were blinded by the squalls of snow and we could not hear each other a yard away. We had both put on our *cagoules,* for it was very cold. The snow was apt to slide and the rope often came in useful.

Ahead of us the other two were losing no time. Lachenal went first and, safeguarded by Terray, he forced the pace in his anxiety to get down. There were no tracks to show us the way, but it was engraved on all our minds—straight down the slope for 400 yards then transverse to the left for 150 to 200 yards to get to Camp IV. The snow was thinning and the wind less violent. Was it going to clear? We hardly dared to hope so. A wall of seracs brought us up short.

"It's to the left," I said, "I remember perfectly."

Somebody else thought it was to the right. We started going down again. The wind dropped completely, but the snow fell in big flakes. The mist was thick, and, not to lose each other, we walked in line: I was third and I could barely see Lachenal who was first. It was impossible to recognize any of the pitches. We were all experienced enough mountaineers to know that even on familiar ground it is easy to make mistakes in such weather. Distances are deceptive, one cannot tell whether one is going up or down. We kept colliding with hummocks which we had taken for hollows. The mist, the falling snow-flakes, the carpet of snow, all merged into the same whitish tone and confused our vision. The towering outlines of the seracs took on fantastic shapes and seemed to move slowly around us.

Our situation was not desperate, we were certainly not lost. We would have to go lower down; the traverse must begin further on—I remembered the serac which served as a milestone. The snow stuck to our *cagoules,* and turned us into white phantoms noiselessly flitting against a background equally white. We began to sink in dreadfully, and there is nothing worse for bodies already on the edge of exhaustion.

Were we too high or too low? No one could tell. Perhaps we had better try slanting over to the left! The snow was in a dangerous condition, but we did not seem to realize it. We were forced to admit that we were not on the right route, so we retraced our steps and climbed up above the serac which overhung us. No doubt, we decided, we should be on the right level now. With Rébuffat leading, we went back over the way which had cost us such an effort. I followed him jerkily, saying nothing, and determined to go onto the end. If Rébuffat had fallen I could never have held him.

We went doggedly on from one serac to another. Each time we thought we had recognized the right route, and each time there was fresh disappointment. If only the mist would lift, if only the snow would stop for a second! Only Terray and Rébuffat were capable of breaking the trail and they relieved each other at regular intervals, without a word and without a second's hesitation.

I admired this determination of Rébuffat's for which he is so justly famed. He did not intend to die! With the strength of desperation and at the price of super-human effort he forged ahead. The slowness of his progress would have dismayed even the most obstinant climber, but he would not give up, and in the end the mountain yielded in face of his perseverance.

Terray, when his turn came, charged madly ahead. He was like a force of nature: at all costs he would break down these prison walls that penned us in. His physical strength was exceptional, his will power no less remarkable. Lachenal gave him considerable trouble. Perhaps he was not quite in his right mind. He said it was no use going on; we must dig a hole in the snow and wait for fine weather. He swore at Terray and called him a madman. Nobody but Terray would have been capable of dealing with him—he just tugged sharply on the rope and Lachenal was forced to follow.

We were well and truly lost.

The weather did not seem likely to improve. A minute ago we had still had ideas about which way to go—now we had none. This way or that. . . . We went on at random to allow for the chance of a miracle which appeared increasingly unlikely. The instinct of self-preservation in the two fit members of the party alternated with a hopelessness which made them completely irresponsible. Each in turn did the maddest things: Terray traversed the steep and avalanchy slopes with one crampon badly adjusted. He and Rébuffat performed incredible feats of balance without the least slip.

Camp IV was certainly on the left, on the edge of the Sickle. On that point we were all agreed. But it was very hard to find. The wall of ice that gave it such magnificent protection was now ironical, for it hid the tents from us. In mist like this we should have to be right on top of them before we spotted them.

Perhaps if we called, someone would hear us? Lachenal gave the signal, but snow absorbs sound and his shout seemed to carry only a few yards. All four of us called together: "One . . . two . . . three . . . Help!"

We got the impression that our united shout carried a long way, so we began again: "One . . . two . . . three . . . Help!" Not a sound in reply!

Now and again Terray took off his boots and rubbed his feet; the sight of our frost-bitten limbs had made him aware of the danger and he had the strength of mind to do something about it. Like Lachenal, he was haunted by the idea of amputation. For me, it was too late: my feet and hands already affected from yesterday, were beginning to freeze up again.

We had eaten nothing since the day before, and we had been on the go the whole time, but men's resources of energy in the face of death are inexhaustible. When the end seems imminent, there still remain reserves, though it needs tremendous will power to call them up.

Time passed, but we had no idea how long. Night was approaching, and we were terrified, though none of us made any complaint. Rébuffat and I found a way that we thought we remembered, but were brought to a halt by the extreme steepness of the slope—the mist turned it into a vertical wall. We were to find next day that at that moment we had been only 30 yards from the camp, and that the wall was the very one that sheltered the tent which would have been our salvation.

"We must find a crevasse."

"We can't stay here all night!"

"A hole—it's the only thing."

"We'll all die in it."

Night had suddenly fallen and it was essential to come to a decision without wasting another minute; if we remained on the slope, we should be dead before morning. We would have to bivouac. What the conditions would be like, we could guess, for we all knew what it meant to bivouac above 23,000 feet.

With his axe, Terray began to dig a hole. Lachenal went over to a snow-filled crevasse a few yards further on, then suddenly let out a yell and disappeared before our eyes. We stood helpless: should we, or rather would Terray and Rébuffat, have enough strength for all the maneuvers with the rope that would be needed to get him out? The crevasse was completely blocked up save for the one little hole which Lachenal had fallen through.

"Lachenal!" called Terray.

A voice, muffled by many thicknesses of ice and snow, came up to us. It was impossible to make out what it was saying.

"Lachenal!"

Terray jerked the rope violently; this time we could hear.

"I'm here!"

"Anything broken?"

"No! It'll do for the night! Come along."

This shelter was heaven-sent. None of us would have had the strength to dig a hole big enough to protect the lot of us from the wind. Without hesitation Terray let himself drop into the crevasse, and a loud "Come on!" told us he had arrived safely. In my turn I let myself go: it was a regular toboggan-slide. I shot down a sort of twisting tunnel, very steep, and about 30 feet long. I came out at great speed into the opening beyond and was literally hurled to the bottom of the crevasse. We let Rébuffat know he could come by giving a tug on the rope.

The intense cold of this minute grotto shriveled us up, the enclosing walls of ice were damp and the floor a carpet of fresh snow; by huddling together there was just room for the four of us. Icicles hung from the ceiling and we broke some of them off to make more head room and kept little bits to suck—it was a long time since we had had anything to drink.

That was our shelter for the night. At least we should be protected from the wind, and the temperature would remain fairly even, though the damp was extremely unpleasant. We settled ourselves in the dark as best we could. As always in a bivouac we took off our boots; without this precaution the constriction would cause immediate frost-bite. Terray unrolled the sleeping-bag which he had had the foresight to bring, and settled himself in relative comfort. We put on everything warm we had, and to avoid contact with the snow I sat on the movie camera. We huddled close up to each other, in our search for a hypothetical position in which the warmth of our bodies could be combined without loss, but we couldn't keep still for a second.

We did not open our mouths—signs were less of an effort than words. Every man withdrew into himself and took refuge in his own inner world. Terray massaged Lachenal's feet; Rébuffat felt his feet freezing too, but he had sufficient strength to rub them himself. I remained motionless, unseeing. My feet and hands went on freezing, what could be done? I attempted to forget suffering by withdrawing into myself, trying to forget the passing of time, trying not to feel the devouring and numbing cold which insidiously gained upon us.

Terray shared his sleeping-bag with Lachenal, putting his feet and hands inside the precious eiderdown. At the same time he went on rubbing.

Anyhow the frost-bite won't spread further, he was thinking.

None of us could make any movement without upsetting the others, and the positions we had taken up with such care were continually being altered so that we had to start all over again. This kept us busy. Rébuffat persevered with his rubbing and complained of his feet; like Terray he was thinking: We mustn't look beyond tomorrow—afterwards we'll see. But he was not blind to the fact that "afterwards" was one big question-mark.

Terray generously tried to give me part of his sleeping-bag. He had understood the seriousness of my condition, and knew why it was that I said nothing and remained quite passive; he realized that I had abandoned all hope for myself. He massaged me for nearly two hours; his feet, too, might have frozen, but he didn't appear to give the matter thought. I found new courage simply in contemplating his unselfishness; he was doing so much to help me that it would have been ungrateful of me not to go on struggling to live. Though my heart was like a lump of ice itself, I was astonished to feel no pain. Everything material about me seemed to have dropped away. I seemed to be quite clear in my thoughts and yet I floated in a kind of peaceful happiness. There was still a breath of life in me, but it dwindled steadily as the hours went by. Terray's massage no longer had any effect upon me. All was over, I thought. Wasn't this cavern the most beautiful grave I could hope for? Death caused me no grief, no regret—I smiled at the thought.

After hours of torpor a voice mumbled "Daylight!"

This made some impression on the others. I only felt surprised—I had not thought that daylight would penetrate so far down.

"Too early to start," said Rébuffat.

A ghastly light spread through our grotto and we could just vaguely make out the shapes of each other's heads. A queer noise from a long way off came down to us—a sort of prolonged hiss. The noise increased. Suddenly I was buried, blinded, smothered beneath an avalanche of new snow. The icy snow spread over the cavern, finding its way through every gap in our clothing. I ducked my head between my knees and covered myself with both arms. The snow flowed on and on. There was a terrible silence. We were not completely buried, but there was snow everywhere. We got up, taking care not to bang our heads against the ceiling of ice, and tried to shake ourselves. We were all in our stockinged feet in the snow. The first thing to do was to find our boots.

Rébuffat and Terray began to search, and realized at once that they were blind. Yesterday they had taken off their glasses to lead us down and now they were paying for it. Lachenal was the first to lay hands upon a pair of boots. He tried to put them on, but they were Rébuffat's. Rébuffat attempted to climb up the chute down which we had come yesterday, and which the avalanche had followed in its turn.

"Hi, Gaston! What's the weather like?" called up Terray.

"Can't see a thing. It's blowing hard."

We were still groping for our things. Terray found his boots and put them on akwardly, unable to see what he was doing. Lachenal helped

him, but he was all on edge and fearfully impatient, in striking contrast
to my immobility. Terray then went up the icy channel, puffing and
blowing, and at last reached the outer world. He was met by terrible
gusts of wind that cut right through him and lashed his face.

Bad weather, he said to himself, this time it's the end. We're lost . . .
we'll never come through.

At the bottom of the crevasse there were still two of us looking for
our boots. Lachenal poked fiercely with an ice-axe. I was calmer and
tried to proceed more rationally. We extracted crampons and an axe in
turn from the snow, but still no boots.

Well—so this cavern was to be our last resting-place! There was very
little room—we were bent double and got in each other's way. Lachenal
decided to go out without his boots. He called frantically, hauled himself up on the rope, trying to get a hold or to wiggle his way up, digging
his toes into the snow walls. Terray from outside pulled as hard as he
could. I watched him go; he gathered speed and disappeared.

When he emerged from the opening he saw the sky was clear and
blue, and he began to run like a madman, shrieking, "It's fine, it's fine!"

I set to work again to search the cave. The boots had to be found, or
Lachenal and I were done for. On all fours, with nothing on my hands
or feet I raked the snow, stirring it around this way or that, hoping
every second to come upon something hard. I was no longer capable
of thinking—I reacted like an animal fighting for its life.

I found one boot! The other was tied to it—a pair! Having ran-
sacked the whole cave I at last found the other pair. But in spite of all
my efforts I could not find the movie camera, and gave up in despair.
There was no question of putting my boots on—my hands were like
lumps of wood and I could hold nothing in my fingers; my feet were
very swollen—I should never be able to get boots on them. I twisted
the rope around the boots as well as I could and called up the chute:

"Lionel . . . Boots!"

There was no answer, but he must have heard for with a jerk the precious boots shot up. Soon after the rope came down again. My turn. I
wound the rope around me. I could not pull it tight so I made a whole

series of little knots. Their combined strength, I hoped, would be enough to hold me. I had no strength to shout again; I gave a great tug on the rope, and Terray understood.

At the first step I had to kick a notch in the hard snow for my toes. Further on I expected to be able to get up more easily by wedging myself across the runnel. I wriggled up a few yards like this and then I tried to dig my hands and my feet into the wall. My hands were stiff and hard right up the wrists and my feet had no feeling up to the ankles, the joints were inflexible and this hampered me greatly.

Somehow or other I succeeded in working my way up, while Terray pulled so hard he nearly choked me. I began to see more distinctly and so knew that I must be nearing the opening. Often I fell back, but I clung on and wedged myself in again as best I could. My heart was bursting and I was forced to rest. A fresh wave of energy enabled me to crawl to the top. I pulled myself out by clutching Terray's legs; he was just about all in and I was in the last stages of exhaustion. Terray was close to me and I whispered:

"Lionel . . . I'm dying!"

He supported me and helped me away from the crevasse. Lachenal and Rébuffat were sitting in the snow a few yards away. The instant Lionel let go of me I sank down and dragged myself along on all fours.

The weather was perfect. Quantities of snow had fallen the day before and the mountains were resplendent. Never had I seen them look so beautiful—our last day would be magnificent.

Rébuffat and Terray were completely blind; as he came along with me Terray knocked into things and I had to direct him. Rébuffat, too, could not move a step without guidance. It was terrifying to be blind when there was danger all around. Lachenal's frozen feet affected his nervous system. His behavior was disquieting—he was possessed by the most fantastic ideas:

"I tell you we must go down . . . down there. . . ."

"You've nothing on your feet!"

"Don't worry about that."

"You're off your head. The way's not there . . . it's to the left!"

He was already standing up; he wanted to go straight down to the bottom of the glacier. Terray held him back, made him sit down, and though he couldn't see, helped Lachenal put his boots on.

Behind them I was living in my own private dream. I knew the end was near, but it was the end that all mountaineers wish for—an end in keeping with their ruling passion. I was consciously grateful to the mountains for being so beautiful for me that day, and as awed by their silence as if I had been in church. I was in no pain, and had no worry. My utter calmness was alarming. Terray came staggering towards me, and I told him: "It's all over for me. Go on . . . you have a chance . . . you must take it . . . over to the left . . . that's the way."

I felt better after telling him that. But Terray would have none of it: "We'll help you. If we get away, so will you."

At this moment Lachenal shouted: "Help! Help!"

Obviously he didn't know what he was doing. . . . Or did he? He was the only one of the four of us who could see Camp II down below. Perhaps his calls would be heard. They were shrieks of despair, reminding me tragically of some climbers lost in the Mont Blanc massif whom I had endeavored to save. Now it was our turn. The impression was vivid: we were lost.

I joined in with the others: "One . . . two . . . three . . . Help! One . . . two . . . three . . . Help!" We tried to shout together, but without much success; our voices could not have carried more than ten feet. The noise I made was more of a whisper than a shout. Terray insisted that I should put my boots on, but my hands were dead. Neither Rébuffat nor Terray, who were unable to see, could help much, so I said to Lachenal: "Come and help me to put my boots on."

"Don't be silly, we must go down!"

And off he went once again in the wrong direction, straight down. I was not in the least angry with him; he had been sorely tried by the altitude and by everything he had gone through.

Terray resolutely got out his knife, and with fumbling hands slit the uppers of my boots back and front. Split in two like this I could get them on, but it was not easy and I had to make several attempts. Soon

I lost heart—what was the use of it all anyway since I was going to stay where I was? But Terray pulled violently and finally succeeded. He laced up my now gigantic boots, missing half the hooks. I was ready now. But how was I going to walk with my stiff joints?

"To the left, Lionel!"

"You're crazy, Maurice," said Lachenal, "it's to the right, straight down."

Terray did not know what to think of these conflicting views. He had not given up like me, he was going to fight; but what, at the moment, could he do? The three of them discussed which way to go.

I remained sitting in the snow. Gradually my mind lost grip—why should I struggle? I would just let myself drift. I saw pictures of shady slopes, peaceful paths, there was a scent of resin. It was pleasant—I was going to die in my own mountains. My body had no feeling—everything was frozen.

"Aaah . . . aah!"

Was it a groan or a call? I gathered my strength for one cry: "They're coming!" The others heard me and shouted for joy. What a miraculous apparition! "Schatz . . . it's Schatz!"

Barely 200 yards away Marcel Schatz, waist-deep in snow, was coming slowly towards us like a boat on the surface of the slope. I found this vision of a strong and invincible deliverer inexpressibly moving. I expected everything of him. The shock was violent, and quite shattered me. Death clutched at me and I gave myself up.

When I came to again the wish to live returned and I experienced a violent revulsion of feeling. All was not lost! As Schatz came nearer my eyes never left him for a second—20 yards—ten yards—he came straight towards me. Why? Without a word he leaned over me, held me close, hugged me, and his warm breath revived me.

I could not make the slightest movement—I was like marble. My heart was overwhelmed by such tremendous feelings and yet my eyes remained dry.

"It is wonderful—what you have done!"

from Nanda Devi
by Eric Shipton

While other climbers single-mindedly focused on summits, Eric Shipton (b. 1907; d. 1977) was just as eager to see what lay on the other side. His penchant for charting new ground may have cost him the leadership of the 1953 expedition that put Edmund Hillary and Sherpa Tenzing Norgay atop Everest. But it came in handy in an era when just getting to the targeted mountain was often the crux of the climb. In 1934, Shipton and H.W. Tilman sought a way into the remote basin that guards India's 25,645-foot Nanda Devi.

Two days' rest enabled us to explore Badrinath and its surroundings more fully. On our first view of the town itself we had been greatly disappointed as, upon breasting the last steep rise from Joshimath, our minds filled with the severe grandeur of the country through which we had passed, we looked down on a hideous huddle of tin huts and were grieved by the thoughtlessness of man in introducing such ugliness to the mountains. The roll on the drum, which welcomed all incoming pilgrims and had its length and loudness nicely adjusted to the stranger's probable generosity, was an added irritation and the temple itself did nothing to modify our first impressions. It was of no great height and so hemmed in by houses that little could be seen until close up to it, while even the façade, upon which there was some really fine carving, had a ramshackle appearance.

But on our second visit, when we viewed the temple from the far side of the river, we realised better the extraordinary atmosphere of the place and the lure that had drawn men to it throughout the ages. For at Badrinath, Krishna, probably the best beloved of all Hindu gods and one of nine incarnations of Vishnu (a tenth is expected in the future) was supposed to have "practiced austerities," as the saying goes. Since "he stood here for 100 years on one foot, with arms aloft, subsisting on air, with his outer garments thrown off and his body emaciated and with veins swollen," and since but one of his exploits was to lift a huge mountain on one finger to shelter some milkmaids from the wrath of Indra, the god of the skies and rain, we felt that "austerities" was an understatement to say the least.

On the bank opposite the temple was a bathing pool fed by a hot spring, with steps leading down from it to the leaping, icy waters of the Alaknanda, where a ring-bolt was sunk in the rock so that the pilgrim might cling to it while undergoing his ceremonial bath. By this baptism and by worship by Badrinath a man might obtain whatever he desired and all sins of former births were cleansed if the deity was supplicated through the priest. A legend proving the efficacy of this relates how one Janami Jaya slew 18 Brahmans (whether rivals for or guardians of the lady we are not told), in order to possess a beautiful girl whom he met out hunting. Even for this enormity a visit to Badrinath was sufficient atonement! When one remembers that the Rawal or priest here, and at Kedarnath and other important centres, is usually a Brahman from southern India of the Vaishnava sect, and that he is assisted by a secretary or clerk who is also from these parts, the above story seems all the more remarkable.

The origin of this custom of a Brahman priest seemed very remote, but apparently, at one time the ancient religion was supplanted by Buddhism until there arose the reformer, one Sankara, a native of Mysore. The century in which he lived is doubtful but is thought to be about the eighth A.D., and he was particularly active in Nepal and Kumaon, where he drove out the Buddhists and unbelievers and restored the ancient faith. He displaced the Buddhist priests of Badrinath and Kedarnath and in their places introduced priests from the Dhakin and Mysore. Everywhere through his followers he preached the efficacy of pilgrimage to the holy shrines, and there is no doubt that the consequent—and lasting—influx of orthodox pilgrims prevented Kumaon from a second relapse into Buddhism.

Brahmans, the priestly caste, are thus seen to be very powerful, but in many proverbial sayings the lower castes have published their defects. The most glaring seems to be an eye for the main chance, as hinted at in the saying: "Brahmans and vultures spy out corpses"; while in another instance we see a case of diamond cut diamond or two of a trade when we are told: "The Brahman blessed the barber and the barber showed his glass."

But these legends, if believed in and acted upon wholesale, might lead to results which would tax the forgiving powers of even the Badrinath deities, and to offset this there is another little story which inculcates more desirable conduct. A wealthy trader who had ten sons was told to go to Badrinath with his family and his property, there to give all his possessions to the Brahmans and to make his home, thus securing his admission to Paradise. But while living there his wife (who seemingly had her own views as to property) lost a valuable ivory ring, and the sages then told her that as penance for this duplicity in holding back a valuable article, the family must once more do the round of the "tirthas" or places of pilgrimage. When this had been accomplished and they were back in Badrinath, the elephant whose tusk had provided the ivory for the ring suddenly appeared and conveyed the whole family at once to the paradise of Vishnu.

Of men brought up on such traditional tales, none who believed could resist the promises of desires fulfilled and past misdeeds forgotten, and at some period in their lives the majority of Hindus visit one or more of the holy shrines. Judging by the swarms of pilgrims met with on the road and in the town most of them had chosen Badrinath.

Among the many legends of these parts believed to have been founded on fact is a story that, many hundred years ago, there was no high priest of the Kedarnath Temple, and that the high priest of Badrinath used to hold services in the temples of both places on the same day. The shortest known route between the two temples was well over 100 miles, and over a high mountain pass at that. Tradition has it that a quick way across the watershed was known to the priests of those days. But although the natives believe that the two places are only two and a half miles apart, in actual fact, the distance is some 24 miles as the crow flies.

Our observations from the Bhagat Kharak had suggested to us that if a pass could be found from the head of the Satopanth, it would lead us into the Kedarnath Valley system. If this proved to be the case, we should stand very little chance of getting down on the other side, owing to the immense depth of the valley there. However, a view from the crest of the watershed would solve for us many interesting problems.

We had intended to return to the Rishi Ganga about August 10th, and August had already come round. But by now we were thoroughly absorbed in the manifold problems of this range, and to have come away without investigating the head of the Satopanth Glacier would have left our task only half finished.

We did not have the same difficulty as before in collecting men to accompany us, but on the morning of our departure, the porters, despite an early appearance, had neglected to have any food before they left their homes three miles away. Consequently we had to fume for a full hour while they made good this oversight—an unpropitious start!

A dense mantle of cloud still hung over the peaks, as we began to plod up the valley towards Mana and, remembering our little *contretemps* with the Bhasudhara River of a few weeks earlier, we kept this time to the southern bank of the Alaknanda. This provided us with only a narrow walking space under great perspiring, mossy cliffs, down whose black sides streamed a thousand tiny waterfalls, but luckily there was quite a presentable sheep track which allowed our attention to wander from the main business of getting along to the enjoyment of impressive scenery about us, and, a mile or so further on, the valley widened out and provided a stretch of moderately flat grass-land.

Suddenly, with a shout of joy, the Sherpas dumped down their loads and set to work collecting some small, light-blue berries which grew in great quantities amongst the grass. They brought us handfuls of these with great enthusiasm, saying that the berries were considered a delicacy in Sola Kombu, where they came from. On tasting them we found that they had a flavour remarkably like that of tooth-paste, and were certainly pleasanter to look upon than to eat.

At 3 o'clock we came to a small isolated wood of birch and rhododendron about half a mile below the snout of the glacier. We had seen this from the opposite side and had looked forward with relish to the luxury of a blazing camp-fire. But by now it had started to rain again and the locals were still a long way behind. Before we could get the tents pitched we were wet through. There was no dry wood at hand and it was an hour or so before we had sufficient fire to brew some tea, and that only by dint of continuous blowing on the part of Kusang. The rain having cheated us out of a blissful lounge before blazing embers, we retired to our leaky tents with an unpleasant foreboding of what was in store for us higher up.

Awakening to the song of birds and the exhilarating freshness of a perfect morning, our spirits rose and eclipsed the gloom of the night before. Our meal of satu and tea completed, we were content to sit and dry ourselves and our tents in the slanting rays of the morning sun.

It was with an effort that we packed up and started up the boulder-strewn valley. We found that the locals had spent the night in a nearby cave in company with some shepherds, who when we passed their shelter appeared to have not the least intention of stirring themselves for some time to come. What a delightfully carefree life they must lead, requiring nothing but the bare necessities of life, living always up in this wonderland of Nature, with little to worry about and nothing to hurry about; knowing nothing of the filth and squalor of our modern civilisation!

Shortly after leaving camp we came to the corner of the Satopanth Valley and turning half left we made our way along the grass slopes at the sides of the glacial moraine. The slackness of the morning remained with us and we made frequent halts to gaze up at the huge ice-clad precipices about us.

Soon we came in sight of the head of the glacier, still many miles away, and were able to get an uninterrupted view of the gap we hoped to cross. From now on little else interested us and we talked of nothing but the "col." Was it practicable even from this side? Where would it lead us? Back on to the great Gangotri Glacier? Or over the range to Kedarnath? We argued that point over and over again. I felt most convinced that if we succeeded in reaching its crest we would see a great snow-field descending gently before us, turning northwards and forming eventually the Gangotri ice-stream which we had reached a few weeks before. Tilman on the other hand held the other view, that the main Gangotri-Kedarnath watershed was to the north of us and that if we succeeded in crossing the gap we would find ourselves amongst the Kedarnath valleys. The discussion waxed heated in spite of Tilman's common-sense suggestion that we should wait and see.

As was the case on the Bhagat Kharak Glacier our chief concern now was how far we could go up the glacier before our supply of firewood ended. We could not expect the locals to spend a night above the limit of firewood, though we could transport sufficient for one night. So we had to aim at pitching our camp as near as possible at the upper limits of the dwarf juniper. As the valley ascended at a very gentle angle this line was by no means easy to gauge.

The going was easy and we made rapid progress, walking on the crest of a kindly lateral moraine which ran for miles down the southern end of the Satopanth Glacier.

Late in the day we came upon a lateral glacier flowing into the main ice-stream from the south. This glacier was fed almost entirely by ice-avalanches falling from the ice-cliffs of Nilkanta, and in the angle formed by the junction we found an alp whose attractions as a camp site were irresistible. So we spread ourselves out in the sun and basked until the chill of evening sent us to our sleeping-bags. Mine that night was squeezed in between two rocks, a position which was more suitable for contemplation of the infinite than for sleep.

The Mana shepherds occasionally brought their sheep far up these moraine-covered glaciers, and we came across a great many piles of stones hung with prayer flags as in Tibet. These prayer flags were simply bits of rag on which were written prayers. Each flap was supposed to emit one repetition of the prayer written thereon, and consequently on a windy day the hanger of a flag could get through many thousands of prayers in the course of a few hours.

(A similar, and, I should judge, a more effective praying-machine is the prayer-wheel which is commonly used in Tibet. This consists of a drum wrapped round with paper on which are written countless thousands of prayers. Each revolution of the drum emits one repetition of all the prayers written on it. The large prayer-wheels are worked by water power and must get through sufficient praying in one week to insure for each member of the village a high place in the hereafter.)

The going now became very rough as we had to cross a succession of side glaciers, each bringing down on its surface a perfect wilderness of boulders. This meant the usual wearisome performance. Toiling up a long slope of large stones balanced precariously on the ice, balancing along an edge above a yawning crevasse, jumping from a boulder or slithering down some icy slope beyond.

At about 2 o'clock on August 7th we reached a point at which the moraine-covered surface of the main glacier gave place to bare ice only half a mile or so from the cliffs which enclosed the Satopanth Glacier. Across the valley we recognized our old friend Kunaling, from this side presenting a very much more formidable appearance.

We decided that this was the best point from which to launch our attack on the gap, and dismissing the Mana men, we pitched our tents just before a strong wind descended on us from across the ice.

Shortly after an ominous dawn on the following morning we shouldered our heavy loads and tramped slowly across the ice in the direction of the col.

It appeared to us that there was not much choice of route. A steep ice-fall descending direct from the col seemed to be the only way. The line of rock cliffs which bounded it on the left appeared far too steep in its lower section to offer much chance even of getting a footing on them from the glacier. The ice-fall did not look too difficult, though it was certainly very broken in its upper section. So it was towards the ice-fall that we turned.

Over the level stretch of ice we made quick time, but when the angle steepened up our heavy loads made themselves felt and the straps bit cruelly into our shoulders. It was a sultry, windless morning and we were oppressed by an intense lassitude. The ice was bare of snow and steps had to be chipped, though the angle was quite moderate. Our pace became painfully slow.

Soon the ice became broken and complicated, and we came to a section where climbing with a load on one's back was impossible. The leader had to cut steps up the rickety piece of ice and haul the loads after him. The section was only some 30 feet high, but it cost us a good hour to negotiate, and from here the climbing needed the utmost care and called for much step cutting. However, it had the advantage of taking our minds off our sore shoulders and aching thighs.

We climbed steadily for some hours, making long detours to avoid crevasses and ice-cliffs, and we were within a thousand feet of the crest of the gap when we were brought up by a yawning chasm whose bottom was lost to view, hundreds of feet down the icy depths below us. Dumping our loads, we hunted this way and that, but could find no place which offered the slightest chance of crossing this formidable obstacle.

This was a bitter disappointment. After all that weary toil we had but 1,000 feet to go to learn the solution of the riddle which had been occupying our minds for so long.

We descended for a few hundred feet when it occurred to us that we might be able to find a way off the ice on to the upper part of the rock cliffs to the south. Dumping our loads once more, we worked our way over towards the edge of the ice-fall. Reaching it we saw that just below us was a point at which we could get on to the rocks immediately above the steep section below. We could not see how far the rocks would take us, but it was worth trying, and with fresh hope we returned to our loads and pitched camp in the midst of the tangled mass of the ice-fall.

By now it was snowing heavily, and our small tents soon resembled chips off the great ice-blocks which surrounded them. Night fell to the accompaniment of an almost continuous roar of ice-avalanches from the great cliffs of Kunaling above us, and into the early hours of the morning the thunder of falling ice continued. Though our position was quite safe, being well protected by the crevasses and ice-cliffs about us, several times during the night I was brought to a sitting position, trembling, as some particularly large avalanche fell close at hand.

Snow fell gently all the while, and was still falling when we awoke to a grey and unpromising dawn. In consequence of this we made a later start than we had intended. The tents were wet and the loads were heavier in consequence.

Through the mist we could see only a small section of the face of rock above us. Several of the gullies showed signs of recent stone falls and the rock was damp and slippery. When we reached it, however, we found that the angle was easier than it had appeared from below and we mounted at quite satisfactory speed, hurrying here and there when we were obliged to cross one or other of the stone-swept gullies.

Higher up the mist became really thick and we had to grope our way up the rock face—through the still gently-falling snow as if blind-fold.

On the previous day Tilman had fallen and injured another of his ribs, and climbing under such a heavy load as he was obliged to carry caused him considerable pain.

The route-finding now became complicated and we had to trust mainly to a sense of direction. Ridge, gully and rock-facet followed one another in monotonous series, until after a step round an awkward corner we found ourselves at the base of a blunt ice-ridge which we had seen from below.

Chipping small steps in the ice we mounted to the crest of the ridge. From here we caught a glimpse below us of the ice-fall in which we had camped. We followed the crest along until it landed us on what appeared to be a great ice-plateau. The mist was still thick about us and we could only guess at the direction to be followed. We plodded on for half an hour and then halted and pitched the tents.

Our height was 18,400 feet and we calculated that we must be just about on the crest of the col.

Snow was still falling lightly and a southerly wind was blowing. All five of us crowded into one of the tents and sat huddled up waiting for the Primus stove to melt some ice and heat the water sufficiently to make tea. But the Primus had sprung a leak somewhere and had to be pumped up continuously. We waited for two hours before the water was sufficiently warm to absorb any colour from the tea-leaves, and we began to realise that if we were to have a prolonged sojourn on the glaciers we would not have enough fuel for anything but the simple production of water.

That night we were content with a cup of tepid pemmican soup before we turned into our sleeping-bags. At dusk it started to freeze very hard and we became more hopeful about the weather.

Our cheerless camp had done nothing to damp our excitement at having reached the col, and we could hardly curb our impatience for the view which would tell us where the col was leading us.

I still held to the theory that we were at the mysterious head of the Gangotri Glacier. The level stretch of ice over which we had come seemed to indicate the head of a long, gently-flowing glacier. Shortly after dark there was a momentary clearing of the mists above us and we caught the sight of the great buttresses of Kunaling to the north of us and those of another, unnamed peak to the south. But in front, a great sea of cloud still withheld from us the secret of our whereabouts.

I spent much of the long, cold night praying fervently for a fine morning, which the frost gave me good reason to expect.

I was disappointed, however, and when I looked out of the tent door at dawn it was into the same "pea-soup" as on the night before.

After a cup of warm satu, Tilman and I left the camp and started off in a south-westerly direction to reconnoitre.

The surface of snow we were on soon began to fall away in front of us in an ever steepening curve. Shortly after leaving camp we were jumping over and threading our way through a network of small crevasses, and we had not gone far before we were brought up short by a vertical drop of about 150 feet. Beyond this a great tangle of ice-cliffs showed us that we were on the brink of an ice-fall.

It was useless to attempt to find a way through it with a visibility of only 50 yards, and we sat down on the edge of the cliff and waited. The outlook was pretty hopeless as the glacier was narrow at this point and the ice-cliffs seemed to stretch the whole width.

We had been waiting for half an hour when all of a sudden the fog rolled away from below us, and we found ourselves looking down into the immense depths of a cloud-filled valley at our feet. The glacier we were on descended in a steep ice-fall for about 1,000 feet, then flattened out into a fairly level stretch of ice before it heeled over for its final colossal plunge into the gloom of the gorge 6,000 feet below us.

This was obviously not the Gangotri ice-stream, which at its snout, some 20 miles from here, is 13,000 feet high. Tilman had been right and we were looking down into the Kedarnath Valley system, from the "pass" said to have been known to the ancient high priest of Badrinath.

Our little problem was solved, but the grim aspect of the ice-falls below us offered little hope for our succeeding in our project of finding a direct route between the two temples.

After some search we were able to trace a route through the first ice-fall. We hurried back to the camp, reaching it just as Angtharkay and Kusang were starting out to look for us, fearing that we might have come to grief in a crevasse.

Packing up the tents we shouldered our loads once more and made our way down towards the ice-fall. By now the clouds had enveloped us again and we had a difficult job to find the route we had traced through the maze of ice-cliffs and crevasses of which the ice-fall was made up.

In and out of great ice-corridors, past towers and turrets of all shapes and sizes, we worried our way; balancing across slender ice-bridges, which spanned gaping crevasses whose icy depths seemed illimitable; toiling up some bulge which obstructed our path and clinging our way down the slippery banks of its further side.

At length we found ourselves on the flat stretch of ice we had seen from above. Going to its further edge we halted for a few moments to gaze down upon the head of the second and very formidable ice-fall. It was appallingly steep, and for a long time we could not see any way of attacking it which offered the slightest hope of success.

Immediately in front was a sheer drop of some hundreds of feet to the head of the ice-fall itself.

After a careful examination it occurred to us that it might be possible to descend the ice-fall for some distance on its right-hand side, and then force a way off on to the cliffs which bounded it in that direction. Beyond this we could not see, but these cliffs appeared to fall away vertically to the valley still some 5,000 feet below.

We worked over to the right and descended for some time before we were brought up by an impassable crevasse. Search as we would we could not find a way of descending a yard further or of reaching the rocks to our right; so very slowly we toiled our weary way back to the level section where we sat for some minutes sucking lumps of ice in vain attempt to assuage a burning thirst.

By this time the weather had cleared somewhat and as we made our way over to the left-hand side of the glacier we saw that by traversing along an ice ledge under some evil-looking seracs we might get down 500 feet below the level section. Beyond this the glacier disappeared from view on account of the steepness of the angle.

We started to traverse below the seracs and the Sherpas as usual burst into their monotonous praying chant, evidently beseeching the demons of the ice world not to throw things at us.

Hurrying across the débris of a recent fall, we found ourselves at the brink of the glacier's final downward plunge. So steep was it indeed that we thought that we must be standing on the upper part of a hanging glacier.

We dumped our loads on the ice and set off down on what seemed to be an utterly futile errand. But it was the last chance, and we thought we might as well finally prove the thing to be impossible so as to be able, later, to find comfort in that fact. Also the Sherpas, for some reason, were almost frantically keen to get down, and would not admit that the thing could not be done. Whether this attitude of theirs was an outcome of their extreme loyalty to us, or whether they were taking a personal interest in the exploration I cannot say. But in any case it was typical of the fine spirit of these men that, from the time we had left the Satopanth Glacier, they seemed willing to go almost to any lengths to get over that pass. Their loyalty to the expedition did not cause them merely to carry out our instructions; they understood our aims and did everything in their power to see that we realised them.

With these allies we hope, one day, to reach the summit of Mount Everest; without them we would have little hope of doing so.

I have often found that towards the end of a long, tiring day's mountaineering one gets a sudden rejuvenation, particularly when faced with a problem of unusual severity. It was certainly the case this evening and we set about that ice-fall as if our lives depended upon our getting down.

The work was intricate and needed delicate handling as a slip would have had serious consequences. The further we advanced the steeper became the ice until further downward progress on the glacier itself became an impossiblity.

We worked our way over to the left until we came to the left-hand edge of the ice-fall. Standing on a small promontory we looked down a sheer drop of some 200 feet into a steep gully which separated the ice-fall from the rock cliffs bounding it on that side. We saw that if we could reach the floor of the gully we might be able to work our way down between the ice and the rock. But the 200-foot drop at our feet appeared quite impossible. Tilman and I sat down feeling that we had reached the end of our tether.

But Pasang and Angtharkay refused to admit defeat and asked to be allowed to try the wall below us. We consented; and they roped up on a short rope and gave us an exhibition of calm, surefooted climbing whose equal it has rarely been my fortune to witness.

After some 20 minutes they were back with us admitting that the face below was too much even for them. But Angtharkay's blood was up and no sooner had he recovered his breath than he started traversing to the left and soon disappeared from view behind an ugly ice bulge.

Minutes passed as we waited with bated breath. Then, crash! a great chunk of ice hurtled down and smashed itself into a thousand pieces on the floor of the gully, sending up along the cliffs a rolling echo. I think my heart missed several beats before a shout from Angtharkay assured us that all was well. Presently his head appeared from behind the ice bulge, and we saw that his face wore a broad grin.

He informed us that he had found a ledge from which it might be possible to lower our loads and ourselves.

With this hope we raced up our steps back to the loads. It was beginning to get dark and we had yet to find a suitable camp site and get ourselves fixed for the night. To have attempted to get down into the gully that night would have been too much to expect of them. Also, lower down, the gully was overhung by some ice-cliffs and it would be dangerous to pass under these at any other time than the morning.

I spent most of the night tossing about our uncomfortable perch, though it was not so much the discomfort of my bed as excitement which kept me awake.

＊　＊　＊

We had decided not to bother about food or drink in the morning, and as soon as it was light we were packing up the tents and getting ready to start. It was a fine morning and for the first time we were able to get a view down into the valley we were making for, the upper part of which was now only 2,000 feet below us.

A level stretch of glacier some three miles long ended in what looked like a pleasantly wooded valley. About a mile below the glacier there seemed to be a bit of a "cut-off," and below that dark vegetation stretched away as far as the eye could see. This we took to be pine forest, while far beneath we could see patches of light green interspersed amongst the forest.

Two days marching at the most, we thought, would take us through this pleasant looking country to some habitation. Also it seemed reasonable to suppose that we would strike a forest path or game track and be able to cover, if necessary, some 12 miles a day. We knew that it could be no very great distance from the snout of the glacier to the great Kedarnath pilgrim route.

Working along Angtharkay's ledge, clinging close to the cold clammy walls of glacier ice, we reached the little platform from which we were to lower ourselves and our kit. It was an unpleasant place, enclosed on all sides by walls of sickly green ice, and it required but the slightest slip to send one crashing into the depths below, while the most careful handling was needed to save the loads from a similar fate.

Pasang was lowered down into the gully and he stood there ready to receive the baggage. It was painful work. The rope, wet from contact with the snow on the previous day, was now frozen stiff and cut cruelly into our numb fingers.

It took us two hours of hard work before we were safely assembled on the floor of the gully, and it was with feelings of some relief that we turned our backs upon the scene of our labours.

Now the climbing became more straight-forward and for the first time since leaving the Satopanth Glacier we were able to dispense with the rope. Hurrying over the section threatened from above by the ice-cliffs we were soon able to break out of the gully to the left where the angle of the cliffs eased off about a thousand feet above the level stretch of glacier in the valley. This we managed to reach by means of an intricate zig-zag course down the intervening slopes.

After a few moments "breather" we raced down the glacier at top speed, leaping the crevasses in our stride. We were full of pleasant anticipation of a camp in some grassy meadow below the glacier. We were doomed to disappointment. For on leaving the glacier we found ourselves immersed in a tangle of sappy, green vegetation about eight feet high through which we had to hack our way. So thick was it, that we could not see where we were going and all we could do was to stumble on blindly.

We cleared a small space and sat down for a meal, after which we flogged our way on in the hope of finding a better camping place before nightfall. By now it had started raining and the contact with the sodden undergrowth soaked us to the skin. In addition to this the floor of the valley was made up of large boulders which were completely screened by the undergrowth, and at every few steps one stumbled into some pot-hole between the rocks. Brambles soon made their appearance and added to our difficulties.

Late in the evening, after some two hours of this work, we reached the edge of the great cut-off which we had seen from above. This proved to be a sheer drop of some 1,200 feet in the floor of the valley. There was no time to look for a way down the gaunt crags and we had to make shift for the night. After an hour's work we had cleared a muddy space underneath a boulder and collected some sodden stumps of juniper with which to make a fire.

Squatting huddled up under the boulder which afforded scant protection from the rain, vainly trying to dry our sodden garments before the smouldering logs, we discussed our position. Our supply of food was beginning to run low and we had no idea how far we would have to go before we reached the first habitation where we could obtain more supplies with which to carry on. If the going had been good, there would have been little doubt that we could force our way through, however pressed we were for food. But our experience since leaving the glacier had given us an unpleasant taste of what we must expect lower down. The precipice below us might prove to be impassable or cost us much of our valuable time; and with time went food.

Again: what of the side-streams which we must meet further down the valley? By now we had considerable respect for this form of obstacle, which we knew could not only hold us up but completely block our way.

The only alternative was to struggle back up the ice-fall and over the pass back to Badrinath. The matter had to be decided here and now, for as it was, we would have to go all out to get back over the pass before our food and fuel ran out altogether.

The prospect of retracing our steps and committing ourselves once more to the icy slopes we had just left did not appeal to us in the least. Moreover, the weather showed no signs of improvement and we might quite well be held up by a fall of new snow on the pass.

Starvation high up on the glacier, besides being more unpleasant, would be very much harder to fight against than it would be in a forest, where at least we would be able to make a fire. On the other hand, in going down we were taking a step into the unknown. The difficulties of the forest might easily take us some weeks to overcome, though, of course, we might strike some sort of a path tomorrow, or the next day. It was difficult problem on which to make a decision, and we sat discussing it long into the night before retiring to our damp sleeping-bags.

On visualising the position over again I think undoubtedly the wisest plan would have been to go back up the ice, and several times during the week which followed, we sincerely wished we had done so. I am afraid that the fact that we wanted to make the complete crossing of this most intriguing range weighed too heavily on us all, and the downward course was decided upon.

The rain had stopped by the morning and we optimistically delayed our departure in order to get some of the water out of the tents and sleeping-bags. That this was a mere waste of time we were soon to realise. However, it gave us time to look around and decide on the best course of action for attacking our immediate problem, the descent of the 1,000-foot cut-off.

It was an impressive affair. The river, here of quite sizable dimensions, disappeared underground for a short distance above the bank of the precipice and issued forth in a great waterspout to crash down into the depths below. Owing to this we were able to get from one side of the valley to the other without difficulty and could choose either side down which to make our descent.

A short examination of the left-hand side of the valley convinced us that there was no practicable route to be found there, and so, striking camp, we committed ourselves to a search on the right-hand side. Here we fought our way for a quarter of a mile up and along the side of the valley and then began to descend. Clinging on to handfuls of matted undergrowth we clambered down, cursing our loads the while for their insistence on slipping sideways and often nearly dragging us down with them.

Soon we came to a vertical cliff whose rocky sides were too steep to hold any scrub, but whose cracks and crevices were filled with damp earth and moss. Balancing ourselves precariously above this we lowered Angtharkay, the lightest member of the party, on a rope, until he was able to get a footing on a grassy ledge below. Our loads followed in a similar manner. Then, tying two lengths of rope together and doubling them over a convenient juniper root, we slid down to join Angtharkay on his perch below.

Fortunately the side of the valley on which we were was made up of a series of terraces, which were not too widely separated from each other, and by repeating the process described above we eventually reached the densely forested floor of the valley.

Under the spread of the giant forest trees the undergrowth was not so thick and, walking for once in a normal attitude, we made fairly good progress until we reached the upper limit of bamboo. There, at least, was help against the exhaustion of our meagre food supply, and at one o'clock we called a halt and set about gathering a goodly quantity of the small soft cylinders which form the edible portion of the bamboo shoots. This, and the fact that lately we had not been battling through bramble scrub, put us in better spirits, and we almost forgot to call down curses on the rain which had by now started to fall again.

The bamboo was certainly our ally and was later to prove our salvation, but it was not an unmitigated blessing. Really dense bamboo provides an obstacle second only to thickly matted bramble, and when the valley narrowed and we were forced up on to its steep sides, the bamboo jungle reduced us once more to our weary hack, hacking of a way.

The almost impenetrable density of the jungle down by the river forced us to climb up the steep sides of the valley until we were about 1,500 feet above the stream. There we found ourselves in a zone of tall straight plants about nine feet high. The plants were crowned with a spray of most beautiful blue flowers, in shape rather like snapdragons. The growth was as dense as that of a good stand of corn, and, viewed from above, the general effect closely resembled a forest of English bluebells.

Through these lovely blue flowers we waded for three hours, each taking it in turns to go ahead and flog a path with our ice-axes.

Constantly throughout the day we came across fresh spoor which provided ample evidence that large numbers of bears inhabited the forest we were in. These animals, though not wantonly vindictive, possess very poor senses of sight and hearing and should one stumble upon them by accident they are liable to attack through sheer fright. The Sherpas were very alarmed at seeing the tracks of these beasts, and kept up a continuous shouting to give warning of our approach. They were very anxious too that the party should keep well together.

At about five o'clock the ground in front of us began to fall away steeply and, from the change in the tone of the river's roaring, we realised that we were approaching a sizeable side stream, coming down from the peaks of the Satopanth range. Pressing on through the forest we soon arrived at the edge of a ravine from whose unseen depths the thunder of a mighty torrent reached our ears. Looking up to the right we could see the turbulent white river booming its way down towards the gorge.

Here was a problem the seriousness of which we were not slow to recognise, for, if we could find no way of crossing the stream in front of us, we would be in a sorry plight, as now it was too late to think of a return across the pass by which we had come.

Going to the edge we examined the cliffs below us and saw at once that a direct descent into the ravine was out of the question. Moreover, even if we could get across thereabouts, it would be impossible to scale the sheer walls which formed the opposite side of the gorge.

Two alternatives were open to us. Either we could go down to the junction of this torrent with the main river, or we could follow the stream towards its source in the hope of being able to cross it higher up.

We could see that, above the junction, the stream issued from the confines of the ravine and ran for some 20 yards between moderately sloping banks before emptying itself into the main waterway. But here the stream was very broad and there appeared to be but small chance of bridging it at this point. On close scrutiny of the cliffs above the ravine, however, it seemed to us that there was one point where the opposing walls of rock met high above the level of the water.

At first I was sceptical about this and declared it to be an optical illusion produced by a bend in the river; for, although we had seen many such natural bridges during our travels in this amazing country, such formations are rare. But after studying it for some minutes, I agreed with others that it was indeed a natural bridge.

To reach it, however, would involve a climb of some 2,000 feet, over difficult ground, and we decided to pitch camp as soon as we found any water. This was not an easy matter and we had climbed a long way up towards the "bridge" before we came to a small trickling spring shortly before dark. We were lucky in finding a nice level space on which to camp, and, after pitching the tents and collecting a vast quantity of firewood, we settled down to an evening which for sheer enjoyment would take a lot of beating, despite the fact that five yards from the camp was a bear's lair. Luckily its recent occupant kept well clear of the vicinity during our occupation of the camp.

Growing close at hand we found small clumps of forest fungus, which the Sherpas declared to be edible. We collected a large quantity, but each piece was subjected to a searching scrutiny by Angtharkay, and, for some obscure reason, more than 75 percent were rejected. However, in solidity they made up for what they lacked in taste, and, together with the bamboo shoots, the remainder provided us with a square meal. And this was more than welcome, for on unpacking our sacks we found that what remained of our satu was soaking wet and was rapidly going bad; this in spite of the fact that it had been carefully packed in canvas bags.

Indeed, by now almost all our kit was water-logged and we resigned ourselves to living in a state of perpetual wetness.

By now the rain had slackened, and after Kusang had blown the sodden logs for an hour or so we sat before a blazing fire. But though it blazed and needed no further encouragement, Kusang continued to blow late into the night. Tilman conjured up a pleasant picture when he remarked that should Kusang happen upon a house on fire, while others were fighting the flames, he would be unable to resist the temptation of blowing on them!

Lying on a soft, sodden bed of leaves we basked in the glow of the fire. Warm now and, for once, not hungry, we allowed our tobacco smoke to drug us into forgetfulness of the worry which had seemed so acute throughout the long day.

It is astonishing how quickly warmth and a well-satisfied belly will change one's outlook. We were too happy to question whether the bamboo and mushrooms would remain with us all the way along, or whether kindly nature had provided natural bridges over all the side streams which would cross our path. Considering that we had had the "cut-off" to negotiate that morning our estimated distance of a mile and a half did not seem bad. Later we came to look upon a mile and a half as good progress for a day's labour! Meantime we lay peacefully in a half-doze, watching the firelight flickering on the great gnarled branches above us and making weird play with their shadows.

It was raining more heavily than usual when we shouldered our loads next morning and toiled on and up through the forest. Soon we came to dense bramble and began once more the tedious job of fighting our way through it. Our water-logged kit made our loads doubly heavy, weighing us down and causing us to overbalance as we bent and twisted to rid ourselves of the clinging thorns. Soon a dense mist descended upon us and we had to grope along the ever-steepening side of the nala with only a hazy notion of where we were going. Every now and then a steep-sided gully would bar the way and we would have to scramble up some hundreds of feet before we could find a place at which we could cross it.

After some hours of this, the mist cleared and we saw that we were near to the place where we thought we had seen the natural bridge spanning the gorge. Immediately we realised that we had been mistaken, and that the supposed "bridge" had indeed been an optical illusion!

Leaving our loads where we halted, we clambered on through the still heavily falling rain towards the stream. The rocks were steep and very slippery and we had to exercise extreme caution, for a slip would have deposited any one of us in the turbulent waters of the torrent some hundreds of feet below.

At length we reached a point from which we could command an uninterrupted view of the stream for some considerable distance above and below us. Below us the cliffs dropped sheer to the water's edge, while above, the river, descending in a series of waterfalls, did not permit the faintest hope either of fording or of bridging the stream.

We held a hurried consultation. Either we could go down to the junction in the small hope of bridging the torrent down there or we could work on upstream on the chance of finding better things above the point to which we could see. The Sherpas were very much against going down to the junction. On the other hand, to have gone up even to the spot to which we could see would have involved the best part of a day's climbing, and then what chance would we have had of finding a place to cross up there? Fording was out of the question and higher up we would find no trees with which to build a bridge. Much as I respected the judgment of the Sherpas, which in country of this sort had usually proved sounder than my own, at that moment I just could not face, on such a slender chance, the toil which the upward course would involve.

It was decided, therefore, that we should return to last night's camp site, leave our loads there, go down to the junction to examine the possibilities of bridging the stream, and return to the old camp for the night. This latter prospect was the one bright patch in a gloomy outlook.

We returned to our loads and made our way slowly back down the bramble-covered slopes, reaching our old camp at about 3:30. While Kusang blew upon the seemingly dead embers of the morning's fire we stood shivering in our soaking garments and reviewed our position. This certainly appeared unpleasant enough, for, if we failed to get across at the junction, two more days at least would be wasted before we could hope to find a way across on the higher route, and probably more, if indeed we could manage it at all. The work involved in getting along was heavy, and without food it would be well-nigh impossible.

At four o'clock, after swallowing some tepid tea, we raced off down towards the junction, leaving Kusang to build the fire and prepare a meal of the few bits of fungus which still grew near the camp. We were some 800 feet above the junction of the two rivers, but sliding down on the sodden carpet of leaves which formed the floor of the forest we reached it in a few minutes. That is to say we reached a point about 100 feet above it, for the only way we could get down to the stream itself was by way of a steep gully. From a rock above we surveyed the stream as it issued from the mouth of the ravine. The water was obviously much above its normal level, and carried with it great quantities of mud. In the short stretch between the mouth of the ravine and the actual junction there was only one point which offered the slightest possibility of our constructing a bridge. There two rocks stood up well above the surging water, one close to either bank. If we could balance a tree trunk on these two rocks so that it lay across the stream, we could lay other trees diagonally across it and so make a sufficiently sound structure to enable us to cross. But from above, the rocks appeared much too far apart for us to be able to do this.

We climbed down the gully to the water's edge and, measuring the distance across roughly by means of a rope, we came to the conclusion that the thing must be attempted, then reascending the gully we selected some suitable pines which most luckily happened to be growing in small numbers hereabouts.

As it was growing dark we climbed the steep slope back to camp at a pace set by Pasang which left us with aching lungs and thudding hearts. And so we camped in exactly the same position as on the previous night, but with so much less food, considerably less confidence in our ability to cross the stream and with our sleeping-bags wetter than ever. As we ate our vegetarian meal, therefore, we lacked much of the content that had been with us 24 hours earlier.

The dawn of August 14th saw us sliding once more down the leafy slopes, albeit with more caution than previously by reason of our heavy packs. Dumping our loads at the water's edge, and noting thankfully that the stream was no more swollen than on the previous evening, we clambered back up the gully and set to work on the trees which we had marked the night before.

Pasang gave us a fine display with his *kukri* and after a few minutes the first tree crashed to the ground. Stripping it of its branches we dragged it to the edge and, heaving it to an upright position, tipped it into the gully, down which it crashed its way to the water's edge. Angtharkay and I then descended the gully to make the necessary preparations while the others worked above.

In a surprisingly short time three more trees had arrived at the edge of the stream and Tilman and the other Sherpas began to climb down the gully. Angtharkay and I were engaged in building a rock platform at the water's edge, when all at once there was a crash and looking up I saw a huge boulder hurtling down. The others seemed to be well to the side of the gully and I resumed my work thinking how lucky it was that they had not been lower down where the route lay in the actual floor of the gully.

A few moments later, chancing to look up, I saw Pasang leaning against one of the walls of the gully some way above me. His face was very pale and he was trembling. I scrambled up to him and found that the boulder had hit him a glancing blow on the left arm and left foot. It had even torn the lacing from his boot.

Helping him down to the foot of the gully I examined the dama members. The arm, though temporarily useless to him seemed to be badly bruised. His foot was very badly swollen and he move his toes. It looked as if one of the small bones on the foot had been broken.

It was a nasty blow to us all, though I could not he thankful for his lucky escape, for had he been a fo the boulder would have hit his head and would egg; for the rock weighed a good 200-weight

After treating Pasang's wounds as best more on our task of bridging the strea ing rope round the top of the long on the rock platform we had bui tion. Then taking careful aim we let it fall out across the stream. The top of the log hit the rock on the other side and bounded off into the stream to be swept off by the current. Hanging on to the rope for all we were worth we played it into the side.

Having strengthened the structure of the rock platform, we repeated the process with a similar result, but at the third essay the tip of the log remained balanced precariously on the slimy edge of the rock opposite us. We then placed another shorter pole diagonally across the first. This scarcely reached the rocks on the other side.

On this flimsy structure Tilman, with a rope fastened to his waist, started to balance across the raging torrent. We stood watching him with bated breath as, inch by inch, he crept along the swaying poles. It was obvious that he *must* not either slip or upset the balance of the poles, while the further he went the more difficult was his task owing to the thinning of the tree trunks towards the top and the consequently greater sag of the poles. But at length, with what looked like a cross between a leap and a fall, he landed on the other side. We sent up a cheer which was drowned by the roar of the river.

After Tilman had performed this feat the rest was easy, and with other poles laid across and lashed together with strips of bark, and stretched across as a hand rail we had a bridge over which we could transport the loads without further difficulty. It was now shockam and we halted for about half an hour on the further and Ang, partly to give Pasang more time to recover from his load to the to distribute his load between us. Of course Kusang quite enormou isted upon adding the lion's share of Pasang's hich made their packs of water-sodden gear We followed the yards and were then f the main stream down for a few hundred Here the going was very by cliffs to climb high up into the forest. ingly steep and we had to heed. The side of the valley was exceed-vent ourselves sliding down in to the undergrowth above to pre-he undergrowth below while we hacked our way through. At times it took us as much as an hour to cover 25 yards.

At first I went ahead with the *kukri* in order to cut a passage through. It was gruelling work and my shoulders, already burdened by my load, began to ache fiercely. We soon found that except in a few places we could get along faster without the cutting.

The rain was coming down in torrents, but (while on the march) except for making our loads heavier, it could no longer increase our discomfort.

At about 3 o'clock a small side stream, which had cut deeply into the side of the valley, caused us some trouble and by 4:30 pm, being by a small spring of water, we decided that we had had enough and began to prepare for the night.

This was no easy job. There was no place level enough to pitch a tent on, and we had to dig with an ice-axe into the slope for a long time before we could construct a suitable platform. In the pouring rain it was out of the question to make a fire in the open. Here again the woodcraft of the Sherpas was equal to the occasion. Cutting great quantities of bamboo they set to work to construct a shelter under which to make a fire.

These various jobs kept us busy and warm until dusk. Meanwhile poor Pasang sat huddled under the lee of a tree-stump, shivering with cold—the picture of misery. And small wonder, for his struggle with the undergrowth on that steep slope must have been cruel, and now he was incapable of lending a useful hand.

At length, the shelter finished, we huddled under its scant protection. With numbed fingers (we were still at an altitude of 9,500 feet) we struck match after match. (It was fortunate that we had got a good supply of these stored away in sheep-skin gloves!) In this manner we had got rid of two boxes and had started on the third before we succeeded in lighting a piece of rag steeped in paraffin. Once this was accomplished we soon had a fire going. We found that dead bamboo, however wet it may be, catches fire very easily and makes most excellent kindling. Indeed, without it, in such rain as we were experiencing it would have been impossible to light a fire at all. Thus the bamboo plant was providing us with house, fire and food; and without it our lot would have been a sorry one indeed.

Stripping ourselves of our sodden garments we lay naked before the fire while boiling a large pot full of shoot. With a modicum of "ghee" added after the water had been drained off, these were served and eaten as one would eat asparagus. Indeed Tilman's imaginative palate detected some slight resemblance to that delicacy. Unfortunately we had found no more fungus, and our meal failed sadly to satisfy our all too robust appetites.

It had been the busiest day of a hectic week, and I fell asleep without much difficulty only to be roused by Tilman in what seemed a few moments to find it daylight once more.

from The Ascent of Nanda Devi
by H. W. Tilman

In 1936, two years after H. W. Tilman (b. 1898; d. 1977) and Eric Shipton successfully explored the Nanda Devi Basin, Tilman returned with a British-American expedition intent on climbing 25,645-foot Nanda Devi itself. Like Shipton, Tilman was an explorer. I read his mountain writing more for his witty, laconic descriptions of day-to-day expedition life than for thrills— though thrills aren't lacking. We join Tilman and Noel Odell in a too-small tent on the flanks of the mountain.

I forget the exact dimensions of our tent, but it was very long and narrow and the two occupants lay, literally, cheek by jowl—that is if the human face has a jowl; or is it confined to pigs? It was admirably suited to Odell, who is also long and a bit narrow, and I think this was the first night that he was able to lie at full length since he had left Ranikhet. On this expedition we were experimenting with air beds as insulation when lying on snow, instead of the usual rubber mats, half an inch thick and 3 feet by 4 feet. The extra room they took up was very noticeable in a small tent and apart from that they were not altogether successful. Punctures were numerous and unless they amounted to bursts, as they sometimes did, they were not easy to locate; situated as we were, the method of plunging them into a bath and watching for bubbles was seldom practicable. If your bed did go flat, it was a serious matter because no protection at all was afforded, and the result was a cold and sleepless night. Again, if you blew them up too hard you rolled off, and if they were too soft you were in contact with the ground and therefore cold. The Sherpas used to blow them up as if they were blowing up a dying fire, with the result that one bounded about like a pea on a drum, and if two people sat on it when in that state the whole thing exploded. Pasang got a lot of amusement out of the operation of blowing up and deflating beds by making them produce discordant noises like ill-played bagpipes. Now that only two of the Sherpas were left, and those two incapable of raising even a zephyr, we had to blow our own up, and this process provided yet another example of the perfection of natural laws which can even legislate for the remote association of a mountaineer and an air bed; as we gained in altitude and lost breath, the beds required less air to fill them owing of course to the diminution of pressure.

There was a storm in the night but, packed as we were, it was easy to keep warm and difficult to keep cool. Pasang was still blind and very sorry for himself, but Nima was brighter and offered to come with us to Camp III. Odell and I took a tent and paraffin, and Nima 40 pounds of sugar. Care was required on a short stretch above the camp and an upward traverse on rather shaky snow took us on to the ridge. We left it again where it suddenly stood on end and got into trouble on the rocks which would, when climbed, bring us out above this steep bit which had so frightened us. Odell led over a steep ice-glazed traverse which Nima and I resolved mentally to have nothing to do with, and when he was securely placed we had ourselves more or less pulled up in a direct line.

We were now at the foot of the steep snow arête which was such a prominent feature from below, and we settled down to kicking steps up it very slowly and methodically, the steps made by our forerunners having vanished. It was a narrow ridge, but we were able to stick to the crest, or slightly on the Rishi side, which was now less steep than the east side, though both fell away sharply, and the upward angle was 40 or 45 degrees; it will be remembered that from Camp I to Camp II the route lay always on the east flank and that the Rishi side was a precipice. As might be expected after the persistent falls of the last week, there was a lot of fresh snow to kick through before solid footing was obtained, and when we reached the tent at Camp III Graham

Brown told us exactly how many of these steps we had kicked out, he having counted them. As far as I remember, the figure was disappointingly small for we felt that it must be something astronomical, but in sober fact there were only about 700 feet of snow ridge. Approaching the tent, the angle eased off and we found it pitched snugly under the shelter of a steep snow bank.

It was after midday, but Graham Brown and Houston were still in bed and evidently intended "lying at earth" after their efforts of yesterday. Going back we rattled down in an hour, and this time reversed our upwards procedure by descending the very steep snow patch in order to avoid the rocks. Nobody had come up from below, Pasang was still blind, we both had slight headaches, it was snowing again, and there was a big sun halo; but all this was forgotten in the warm glow of self-righteousness induced by our virtuous activity.

Having thus acquired enough merit for the time being by working while others slept, we sat about next morning until Graham Brown and Houston came down from Camp III for more loads. We found it such a pleasant occupation that we sat about some more until the other three came up from Camp I. As soon as the first man's head appeared round the corner of the bulge below us, a shout went up to know if they had found the tea. They had no tea, but they brought the zinc-sulphate medicine and we now hoped that Pasang's recovery would be speedy; at present his eyes were as firmly closed as ever. Nima too had relapsed into his former state of misery, but even yet we did not despair of getting some useful work out of these two. There was still a load to come up from Camp I, so it was arranged that Carter and Nima should go down tomorrow for this and as much more food as they could carry.

At three o'clock four of us started back for Camp III, Odell and Houston on one rope, Graham Brown and myself on the other. We had the advantage of the steps made by them on the way down and, in spite of heavy loads, were up in two hours. Our tent platform was ready for us, so the others had not been so idle yesterday as we thought, and it was pleasant to have some room again, room outside as well as in. I was sorry we had not got a cat to swing.

As Odell and I lay that night with our cheeks and our jowls at a reasonable distance apart, we wondered happily whether the three below were suffocating in the bivouac tent or succumbing to asphyxiation in the overripe atmosphere of the Sherpas'.

We flattered ourselves that the height of this camp was about 21,500 feet but, if it was, it seemed highly improbable that from here we could put a bivouac within striking distance of the summit. It postulated a carry of 2,000 feet at the very least, 2,500 would be better, and on the difficult going below we had not done a carry of more than 1,500. The climbing was likely to get harder rather than easier and, of course, the increasing altitude would slow us up progressively. Repeated trials with the hypsometer made things appear even more discouraging by giving Camp III a height of only 21,200 feet, and though we knew by now that this instrument was, to put it mildly, subject to error, we had perforce to accept the lower figure in making future plans.

The question of the height of our camps bothered us a lot and, quite early on, the hypsometer had earned for itself an opprobrious name of a like sound which may not be printed. For some reason or other we omitted to bring an aneroid barometer graduated for reading height, possibly our numerous scientists scorned an instrument which even the half-wits of the party could read. I remember in 1934 Shipton and I, having no scientific training, took with us an aneroid barometer out of an aeroplane. I think it cost ten shillings at one of those miscellaneous junk shops in Holborn. Our Sherpas conceived a great affection for it and called it "Shaitan," probably because we consulted it so frequently. It worked very well until we dropped it. But this hypsometer, or boiling-point thermometer, while not giving us any very precise information, afforded everyone a lot of fun and the scientists food for thought. The results it gave were always interesting, sometimes amusing, and seldom accurate. For example, after several hours of exhausting climbing in what we foolishly thought was an upward direction, it was startling to learn that we had in reality descended 100 feet from where we started. The learned scientists explained with bland assurance that such vagaries were to be expected, and were accounted for quite simply by the presence of a "column of cold air;" the unlearned oafs on the contrary thought that it must be something to do with "hot air," and plenty of it.

But there is generally some use to be found for the most unlikely things and so it was with the hypsometer. It had as part of its equipment a small bottle of methylated spirits, and when we ran out of solid methylated for priming the stoves, this came in very handy. Priming a stove with paraffin is both noisome and inefficient.

On the 19th Graham Brown and Houston went down again to Camp II for loads while Odell and I went to spy out the land higher up. At the point we had reached, our ridge had widened out into a great hog's-back, so wide that it was in reality the south face, though up the middle of this face a ridge was still discernible, and 1,000 feet higher up it again stood out prominently. We struck straight up the middle of the face over what we called the "snow saddle," avoiding the steep bank above the camp by a short traverse to the left. The snow was in good condition and the angle of slope about 30 degrees for the first 700 feet, after which it began to steepen. Above this was a sort of glacis of snow-covered rock lying at an angle of 45 to 50 degrees. In the steep places outcrops of rock appeared through the snow. This broad glacis appeared to stretch upward for 1,000 feet until it narrowed again to a sharp ridge. On our immediate right was a forbidding gully, a trap for falling stones and ice, and beyond that the tremendous cirque which forms the connecting ridge between East Nanda Devi and Nanda Devi itself. Some 200 or 300 yards to the left was a wide shallow depression, scarcely a gully, and on the far side of it the horizon was bounded by a very bold and steep ridge, probably the same which we had looked at from Pisgah.

We attacked the glacis in the centre and worked upwards and to the left, making for what looked like a slight ridge overlooking the shallow gully. As we mounted, the angle grew steeper and the climbing more difficult. At first a good covering of snow overlay the rocks, but presently this became thinner and the outcrops of rocks more numerous. For mountaineering as well as geological reasons we were keenly interested to reach the first of these outcrops, for the line we should take, and our progress, depended greatly upon its quality. We hoped that at this height it might have changed to something more honest than the treacherous rock of the lower ridge and that the strata might lie in a more favourable direction. Technically it may have differed, but for a climber it was substantially the same crumbling yellow stuff upon which no reliance could be placed, and though the dip of the strata was now more in our favour, little comfort was to be derived from that on rock of such rottenness.

When we had climbed about 500 feet from the foot of the glacis, it became apparent that the supposed ridge we were making for was no ridge at all. To go straight up was still possible, but with loads on it would be both difficult and dangerous, for nowhere was there enough snow for an anchorage with an axe, or any rock round which a rope could be belayed. We decided to traverse to the left and go for the shallow gully which appeared to offer a safe route on snow for at least 1,000 feet. But shortly after putting this resolve into practice, we contrived to get ourselves into such a mess on the ice-glazed face of a rock outcrop that all our attention was concentrated on getting out of it, and instead of continuing the traverse to the left we were compelled to embark upon a long and tricky traverse in the opposite direction. By sticking wherever possible to snow, and avoiding any rock like the plague, we worked our way back down the glacis until we rejoined our earlier track.

A lower route was obviously the best line for the gully, but it was now too late for any more and we hurried back to camp, where we arrived in time to avoid the start of a blizzard. Two days had elapsed since the warning of the sun halo.

Lloyd and Loomis had come up here to sleep after only one night at Camp II in defiance of our self-imposed rule of two at each camp. No one, however, with experience of the Gîte would doubt their wisdom in making that camp an exception to the rule.

The results of our reconnaissance were mainly negative but not without value. It was clear that a route directly up the glacis should only be tried as a last desperate resort, and also that whichever way we went it was going to be a painfully long carry before a place where a tent could be pitched would be found. The conclusions were that further reconnaissance was needed, that the most promising line was the broad gully and that in any case it would be advantageous to move the present camp to a new site at the foot of the glacis.

✳ ✳ ✳

The night was cold and windy and no one turned out until nine o'clock. Lloyd and Loomis started out to have a look at the way to the gully, and the rest of us went down to Camp II for loads. All the tracks down had to be remade after the blizzard and we had long ceased to expect any tracks to last for 24 hours. To anticipate, they did not last so long today, and when we returned in the afternoon all were once more obliterated.

We found Pasang still blind and Nima not well, and it was pretty clear that neither would be any use. Nima's single journey to Camp III, the highest reached by any of the porters, was but a dying kick. The almost total failure of the Sherpas is easily explained, for, as I have pointed out, we had to take the leavings of several other expeditions. The only two I expected to go high were Pasang and Kitar. Of the others three were past their best and one was too young and inexperienced. Pasang of course was unlucky to be struck down with snow-blindness, but it cannot be said that it was not his own fault. Kitar was a victim to disease.

The medicine seemed to be having little effect on Pasang's eyes, and Nima's cheery grin was a thing of the past. That they should both go down was now the best course, but this was not possible until Pasang could see something. Apart from their rather miserable mode of existence at the Gîte, I was anxious to have them safely down at the Base Camp before we lost touch with them entirely by going higher up the mountain. We left them there, alone now, in the big tent, having told them that two of us would come down again tomorrow, and we started back, Carter with us, taking the small bivouac tent. Carter had a note which he had found at Camp I telling us that Emmons had moved the Base Camp down to the foot of the scree slope and that he was busy with the plane table, but only Kalu was able to help him by carrying loads.

It was cold and windy when we reached Camp III in a flurry of snow. There was a halo round the sun and two mock suns, and I have seldom seen a more ominous-looking sky. The report of the reconnoitering party was more cheering than the weather. Taking a line below and to the left of ours, they had reached a point from where they could see into and up the gully. They had not got into it, but they reported that it could be reached by a route which lay almost entirely on snow, and that the going up the near side of it looked straightforward enough. Like us, they had seen no promise of a camp site higher up, and it was agreed to move this camp to the top of the snow saddle and to press the attack by the gully.

It was a quiet night in spite of all the signs of approaching storm. but the morning of the 21st dawned dull, misty, and snowy. We had a late breakfast and spent the morning in one tent discussing ways and means. Now that the thing was to be put to the test, it was clear that some difficult decisions would have to be made, and the upshot of our talk was that the responsibility for these decisions was put upon the writer. The too frequent use of the word "I" in this narrative will not have escaped the notice of the reader. The reason for this is that up to now I may have had most to say in our affairs; but that was merely through the accident of my being the only one who knew the country or the porters. We had no official leader, and managed very well without, until at this crisis the need was felt for some kind of figurehead.

After a cup of cocoa additional to our lunch which, by the way, was usually a slab of chocolate and nothing else, Lloyd, Carter, and I went down again to Camp I for more loads, and the others took a first instalment of loads up to what would presently be Camp IV.

Pasang and Nima still appeared to be immovable, but I told them that two of us would come down again tomorrow and see them safely over the worst of the route to Camp I. Until they were down they were merely a source of anxiety, and, after tomorrow, we expected to be out of reach. We climbed up again in one and a quarter hours and it was satisfactory to see that our time on the snow arête became faster, indicating that we were still acclimatising and not deteriorating. The other party had found a good camp site on the snow saddle near the foot of the glacis, and had dug out one tent platform.

The sunset was again threatening, with greasy-looking cigar-shaped clouds hanging low over East Nanda Devi, a greenish watery haze to the west, and, to the south, black banks of cumulus tinged with copper.

We woke to find the tent shaking and banging to the blasts of a fierce blizzard. The wind was coming out of the south-east, some snow was falling, but it was impossible to tell what was new snow and what was drift, for outside was nothing but a whirling cloud of driving snow. The three tents were close together and guyed to each other for mutual support. Six of us occupied the two big ones and Carter was by himself (a doubtful privilege under these conditions) in the small bivouac tent, pitched on the weather side. Odell, Lloyd, and I held the baby in the shape of the Primus stove, but it was conceivable that the inconvenience of fetching ice and breathing paraffin fumes was outweighed by the advantage of getting the food hot without having to fetch it. Going from the comparative warmth of the sleeping bag and the tent out into the blizzard was a breathtaking experience. Breathing was almost impossible facing the wind, and nothing could be handled without mittens, while the act of leaving or entering the tent by the small sleeve entrance required the quick co-operation of all, unless the inside was to be covered with a layer of snow.

There was nothing to be done but lie in our bags, with one eye on a book and the other on the furiously flapping fabric and the quivering tent pole. The pole was of very light aluminium and we were rather nervous about it, but it stood the strain well, as did the tents, for which we forgave them all our past discomforts. At five o'clock, when we cooked our evening pemmican, conditions were unchanged. The wind still maintained a steady roar with occasional gusts of gale force, and we discussed the advisability of sleeping with windproofs on in case the tent went in the night. However, we pinned our faith to the fabric and did not resort to these extreme measures.

Morning brought no change in these unpleasant conditions, and we wondered whether it was blowing as hard at the Gîte and how the Sherpas were faring. Anyhow, with the direction of the wind as it was, the rock wall would stop them being blown off their ledge.

The snow was being blown away as soon as it fell, and round our tent it had not accumulated to any great depth. The other big tent had not fared so well and there was a high bank of snow around it by morning. The pressure of this snow had reduced the space inside by half, so that the unfortunate residents were sleeping almost on top of each other. They had the consolation of knowing that their tent was now securely anchored. Carter too, in the bivouac, was experiencing trouble in keeping the snow-laden walls off his face.

Another weary day of inactivity and torpor passed, but towards evening the wind began to moderate and we were able to get outside, clear the accumulated snow away from the doors, and attend to the guys. Snow was still falling lightly and a leaden pall hid everything but the snow at our feet and three forlorn-looking tents.

Followed another cold and stormy night, but the morning of Monday the 24th dawned fine, calm and sunny. Had it been black as night, we would not have complained, for stillness was all we asked for after the battering of the last two days. The loss of this valuable time was disturbing, and though it may seem strange that two days in bed could be anything but beneficial, there was no doubt that the strain and the inaction had done us harm physically. Nor could we tell what effect the blizzard might have had on the snow of the upper slopes. It was imperative now to push on with all speed, and surely after such a snorter we might expect several days of fine weather.

These blizzards which we experienced, three of them lasting for 36, 12, and 48 hours respectively, all came from between east and southeast. Monsoon weather in the hills generally comes from between south and west, but these storms may have been deflected by the mountain. Such blizzards are more to be expected prior to the break of the monsoon, and during two previous monsoon periods in the Himalaya, one in Garhwal and one in the Everest region, I do not recollect one of any severity. This year the monsoon broke early and ended late, and was exceptionally severe in the United Provinces and Garhwal.

At nine o'clock Lloyd and I started out for Camp II in accordance with our promise to the Sherpas, the fufilment of which the blizzard had compelled us to postpone. We left to the others the cold work of breaking out the tents from their frozen covering and digging out the buried stores, preparatory to carrying one big tent and the bivouac to the new Camp IV site. Five of us were to sleep up there tonight in readiness for carrying up a bivouac for the first summit party next day.

The presence of a lot of powder snow made conditions on the arête bad, and we both felt weak and got progressively weaker as we descended. Arrived at the Gîte, we were surprised to find it empty; evidently the Sherpas had tired of waiting for us and left early. It was comforting to know that the tent had weathered the storm, that Pasang's eyes must be better, and that we ourselves had not to descend any farther. Indeed, we were now in such a state of languor that our chief concern was how on earth we were going to get up again. We lolled about on the ledge, assailed by a violent thirst, feeling complete moral and physical wrecks; and it was evident that two days and nights in our sleeping bags had taken more out of us than a hard day's work.

The Sherpas had taken the stove and cooking pot with them, but there was some food here and we opened a tin with an ice-axe—not for the sake of the food but for the tin, in which to catch the elusive drips from the rock wall. We had to sleep at the higher camp that night, so at midday we summoned up all our resolution and, taking with us all the food that was left here, we crawled weakly away from the Gîte.

I should be ashamed to say how long it took us to get back to Camp III, but by the time we arrived we were feeling better and our strength was beginning to return. Graham Brown and Carter, who were spending the night here, came down from Camp IV just as we arrived and informed us that up there it was perishing cold. Carter thought his toes were slightly touched with frostbite.

Adding some more food to our loads, Lloyd and I went off once more and an hour of steady plodding brought us to the new camp. They had evidently started late that morning owing to the frozen tents, and, when we got up, the second tent was just being pitched. There was a bitter wind blowing and Loomis was inside attending to his feet, which also had been slightly affected by cold.

In spite of the cold, it was difficult to turn away from the astonishing picture painted by the fast-sinking sun. Nanda Kot still shone with dazzling purity like an opal, and beyond to the east was range upon range of the snow peaks of Nepal, looking like rollers breaking in white foam on a sunny sea. From the snow slope falling away out of sight at our feet, the eye swept across a great void till arrested by the castellated ivory wall of the Sanctuary, dominated by Trisul, up which the shadows were already stealing. And to the west was the dark chasm of the Rishi gorge, the clear-cut outline of the "Curtain," and the blue-green swell of the foothills.

The height of Camp IV we estimated to be 21,800 feet, and with five of us here and food for nearly a fortnight we were in a strong position. If we could push a bivouac up another 2,000 feet, the summit would be within reach, and, big "if" though this was, the time had come to make the attempt. Of the five now at this camp, it was not difficult to decide which two should have the privilege of first shot. Odell was going very well and his experience, combined with Houston's energy, would make a strong pair. Assuming that we could place the bivouac high enough tomorrow, they were to have two days in which to make their attempt, and on the third day a second pair would take their place, whether they had been successful or not. The form shown tomorrow would indicate which two would have the second chance, and, provided the weather held, it might be possible to send up a third pair.

The 25th broke fine, but it was ten o'clock before we had made up our loads of 15 pounds each, which included food for two men for six days. During the blizzard, not very much snow had actually settled, and since then sufficient time had elapsed for this new snow to consolidate. We found it in good condition. After gaining some height by kicking steps, we approached the gully by a long traverse where steps had to be cut and great care exercised. The snow covering grew thinner and we came to an uncomfortable halt on the steep lip of a minor hollow, cutting us off from the main gully. This was the farthest point reached by Lloyd and Loomis, and they had seen that this difficult little gully could be avoided by working round the head of it, 200 feet higher.

We sat here for a little, but it was no place for a long sojourn without prehensile trousers. There was not enough snow to afford a step, much less a seat, and the angle of the rock was such that mere friction was of no avail—boots, hands, and ice-axe were all needed to prevent the beginning of a long slither which would only end on the glacier 6,000 feet below. Turning up the slope, the next few feet were of the same precarious nature that Odell and I had experienced on the glacis, but this was as yet the only part of the route where we had to forsake the security of the snow for the uncertainty of the rock. Once over this, we settled down to a long steady grind, kicking and cutting our way up very steep snow, and having rounded the head of this minor hollow, we took a line up the true left bank of the broad gully.

We were climbing on two ropes, so by changing the leading rope and also the leading end of each rope, the work was divided among four. It was a beautiful day, but in our perverse way we were not content, and were captious enough to wish the sun obscured so that we could climb in more comfort. Nanda Kot, 22,500 feet, sank below us and we began to cast jealous eyes on Trisul, which still looked down upon us majestically from its height of 23,400 feet. Meantime we began to search the snow above us for the slightest break in the relentless angle of the slope which might afford a site for a tent. We were tempted momentarily by the broken outline of the skyline ridge away across the gully, but we decided it was too far off and the approach to it too steep.

As we gained height, the curve of the face to our right grew rounder and narrower and the central ridge was beginning to stand out again like the bridge of a Roman nose. We edged over towards it, thinking that the rocks might provide easier going than the snow, and aiming for the foot of a rock tower where there might be a platform. Knowing by now the sort of rock we might expect, it was curious that we should so think, but such was the distorting effect on our minds of five hours of laborious step-kicking. The change of course was for the worse and we had some awkward moments before we dragged ourselves to the foot of the tower, to find it sloping away as steeply as the rest of the mountain.

The time was now three o'clock and our height something over 23,000 feet, practically level with Trisul. Loomis had an attack of cramp, but when he had recovered we turned our attention to the rock tower at our backs, on top of which we hoped to find better things. Lloyd did a grand lead up a steep rock chimney with his load on and was able to give the rest of us some much needed moral and, in my case, physical encouragement with the rope. This took some time and it was four o'clock before we were all on top of the tower, where there was barely room for five of us to stand, much less pitch a tent. Looking up the ridge, it was impossible to say where such a place would be found, but it was sufficiently broken to offer considerable hope. Meantime three of us had to get back to Camp IV and at this time of the afternoon of a bright sunny day the snow would be at its worst. With the assent of all, it was decided to dump our loads here leaving Houston and Odell to shift for themselves. It seemed a selfish decision at the time and it seems so now; no doubt we could have cut it a bit finer and yet got down before dark, but it was likely that they would not have to go far before finding a bivouac, and, in any case, with sleeping bags and warm clothing they could not come to much harm.

We learned afterwards that they had an uncommonly busy evening. They had to climb another 150 feet before even the most imaginative could discern the makings of a platform, and then they had to make two journeys up and down with the loads. It was dark before they were finally settled.

Oblivious of this activity and the curses which were being bestowed, rather unjustly, on us for our premature desertion, we climbed hastily but cautiously down, reaching the camp at sundown. There was no sign of Graham Brown and Carter, so we assumed they were having a day off at Camp III.

Discussing the results of this day's work, we decided the bivouac was about 23,500 feet, probably too low for an attempt on the summit, but as high as we could push it in the day. We thought they would probably move it higher tomorrow and make their bid on the following day. The closer view of the upper part of the mountain which we had obtained had not made it look any easier, and it was a puzzle to make out where exactly the peak lay. I began to fear we had not allowed them enough time, but now it was too late to alter plans.

Next day was fine, but mist shrouded the upper mountain from our anxious gaze. We felt slack, and took the morning off before going down to Camp III to give Graham Brown and Carter a hand with their loads. As their tent was the one which had been half-buried by the blizzard, it took them a long time to dig it out, so we returned before them and prepared a platform.

The 27th was to be for us at Camp IV another day of idleness. That at least was the plan, but the event was different, and for some of us it was a day of the greatest mental and physical stress that we had yet encountered.

I had been worrying all night over the waste of this day, trying to devise some scheme whereby the second pair could go up at once to the bivouac. The trouble was that a second tent was essential, and having seen something of the extraordinary difficulty of finding a site even for the small tent, to go up there on the slim chance of finding a site for the big one as well was incurring the risk of exhausting the party to no purpose. While we were having breakfast, debating this knotty point and wondering how far the summit party had got, Loomis disclosed the fact that all was not well with his feet, the toes being slightly frost-bitten, and that henceforward we should have to count him out. The loss of carrying power knocked the scheme for a second tent on the head and a few moments later we had something else to think about.

We had just decided they must be well on the way to the top when we were startled to hear Odell's familiar yodel, rather like the braying of an ass. It sounded so close that I thought they must be on the way down, having got the peak the previous day, but it suddenly dawned on us that he was trying to send an S.O.S. Carter, who had the loudest voice, went outside to try and open communications, and a few minutes later came back to the tent to announce that "Charlie is killed"—Charlie being Houston. It was impossible to see anyone on the mountain, but he was certain he had heard correctly. As soon as we had pulled ourselves together, I stuffed some clothes and a bandage into a rucksack and Lloyd and I started off as fast as we could manage, to be followed later by Graham Brown and Carter with a hypodermic syringe.

It was a climb not easily forgotten—trying to go fast and realising that at this height it was impossible to hurry, wondering what we should find, and above all what we could do. The natural assumption was that there had been a fall, and that since they were sure to be roped, Odell was also hurt, and the chance of getting a helpless man down the mountain was too remote to bear thinking about. As if to confirm this assumption, we could get no answer to repeated calls on the way up.

Remembering our struggles yesterday on the ridge and in the chimney, we took a different line and tackled a hand of steep rock directly above us, in between the gully and the ridge. It proved to be much worse than it looked and, when we had hauled ourselves panting on to the snow above, we vowed that the next time we would stick to the gully, which here narrowed and passed through a sort of cleft in the rock band.

The time was now about two o'clock, and traversing up and to the right over snow in the direction of the ridge, the little tent came in sight not 30 yards away. Instinctively we tried almost to break into a run, but it was no use, and we advanced step by step, at a maddening pace, not knowing what we should find in the tent, if indeed anything at all. The sight of an ice-axe was a tremendous relief; evidently Odell had managed to crawl back. But when another was seen, conjecture was at a loss. Then voices were heard talking quietly and next moment we were greeted with, "Hullo, you blokes, have some tea." "Charlie is ill" was the message Odell had tried to convey!

Lloyd and I experienced a curious gamut of emotions firstly and naturally, of profound relief, then, and I think not unnaturally, disgust at having suffered such unnecessary mental torture, and, of course, deep concern for Houston. While we swallowed tea, tea that reeked of pemmican but which I still remember with thankfulness, we heard what they had done and discussed what we were to do.

They had devoted yesterday to a reconnaissance. Following the ridge up they found, at a height of about 500 feet above the bivouac, a flat snow platform capable of holding two tents comfortably. Beyond that the climbing became interesting and difficult, but they had reached the foot of a long and easy snow slope leading up to the final rock wall. Here they turned back, having decided to move the bivouac next day to the higher site. Both were going strongly, but early that night Houston became violently ill, and in the cramped quarters of the tent, perched insecurely on an inadequate platform above a steep slope, both had spent a sleepless and miserable night. Houston attributed his trouble to the bully beef which both had eaten; Odell was unaffected, but it is possible that a small portion was tainted and certainly the symptoms pointed to poisoning of some kind.

Houston was still very ill and very weak, but it was he who suggested what should be done, and showed us how evil might be turned to good. It was only possible for two people to stay up here, and his plan was that he should go down that afternoon and that I should stay up with Odell, and thus no time would have been lost. We demurred to this on the ground that he was not fit to move, but he was so insistent on the importance of not losing a day and so confident of being able to get down that we at last consented.

We all four roped up, with Houston in the middle, and started slowly down, taking frequent rests. We struck half-right across the snow and joined the gully above the rock hand according to our earlier resolution, and there the two men anchored the party while Lloyd cut steps down the narrow cleft, which was very icy. Houston was steady enough in spite of his helpless state of weakness, and having safely negotiated this awkward bit, we kicked slowly down to the left and found our up-going tracks. Presently Graham Brown and Carter hove in sight, and I imagine their amazement at seeing four people coming down was as great as ours had been at the sight of the two ice-axes. When we met, Lloyd and Houston tied on to their rope and continued the descent, while Odell and I climbed slowly back to the bivouac.

This illness of Houston's was a miserable turn of fortune for him, robbing him as it did of the summit. Bad as he was, his generous determination to go down was of a piece with the rest of his actions.

* * *

Scenically the position of the bivouac was very fine but residentially it was damnable. It was backed on two sides by rock, but on the others the snow slope fell away steeply, and the platform which had been scraped out in the snow was so narrow that the outer edge of the tent overhung for almost a foot, thus reducing considerably both the living space and any feeling one yet had of security. Necessity makes a man bold, and I concluded that necessity had pressed very hard that night when they lit on this spot for their bivouac. Odell, who had had no sleep the previous night, could have slept on a church spire, and, as I had Houston's sleeping bag and the extra clothing I had fortunately brought up, we both had a fair night. Odell, who was the oldest inhabitant and in the position of host, generously conceded to me the outer berth, overhanging space.

The weather on the 28th still held and without regret we packed up our belongings and made the first trip to the upper bivouac. The snow slope was steeper than any we had yet met but, at the early hour we started, the snow was good and in an hour we reached the spacious snow shelf which they had marked down. It was about 20 feet by 20 feet, so that there was room to move about, but on either side of the ridge on which it stood the slope was precipitous. After a brief rest the increasing heat of the sun warned us to be on the move again and we hurried down for the remaining loads. The snow was softening rapidly under a hot sun, nor was this deterioration confined only to the snow. We already knew, and it was to be impressed on us again, that at these altitudes a hot sun is a handicap not to be lightly assessed.

Guessing the height of this camp, aided by the absence of the hypsometer, we put it at about 24,000 feet. Trisul was well below us and even the top of East Nanda Devi (24,379 feet) began to look less remote. The condition of the wide belt of snow which had to be crossed, the difficulties of the final wall, and the weather were so many large question marks, but we turned in that night full of hope, and determined to give ourselves every chance by an early start.

We were up at five o'clock to begin the grim business of cooking and the more revolting tasks of eating breakfast and getting dressed. That we were up is an exaggeration, we were merely awake, for all these fatigues are carried out from inside one's sleeping bag until it is no longer possible to defer the putting on of boots. One advantage a narrow tent has, that at lower altitudes is overlooked, is that the two sleeping bags are in such close proximity that boots which are rammed into the non-existent space between them generally survive the night without being frozen stiff. It worked admirably on this occasion so that we were spared the pangs of wrestling with frozen boots with cold fingers. Frozen boots are a serious matter and may cause much delay, and in order to mitigate this trouble we had, since the start, carefully refrained from oiling our boots. This notion might work well enough on Everest in pre-monsoon conditions where the snow is dry, but we fell between two stools, rejoicing in wet feet down below and frozen boots higher up.

By six o'clock we were ready, and shortly after we crawled outside, roped up, and started. It was bitterly cold, for the sun had not yet risen over the shoulder of East Nanda Devi and there was a thin wind from the west. What mugs we were to be fooling about on this infernal ridge at that hour of the morning! And what was the use of this ridiculous coil of rope, as stiff as a wire hawser, tying me for better or for worse to that dirty-looking ruffian in front! Such, in truth, were the reflections of at least one of us as we topped a snow boss behind the tent, and the tenuous nature of the ridge in front became glaringly obvious in the chill light of dawn. It was comforting to reflect that my companion in misery had already passed this way, and presently as the demands of the climbing became more insistent, grievances seemed less real, and that life was still worth living was a proposition that might conceivably be entertained.

This difficult ridge was about 300 yards long, and though the general angle appeared slight it rose in a series of abrupt rock and snow steps. On the left was an almost vertical descent to a big ravine, bounded on the far side by the terrific grey cliffs that supported the broad snow shelf for which we were making. The right side also fell away steeply, being part of the great rock cirque running round to East Nanda Devi. The narrow ridge we were on formed a sort of causeway between the lower south face and the upper snow shelf.

One very important factor which, more than anything, tended to promote a happier frame of mind was that the soft crumbly rock had at last yielded to a hard rough schistose-quartzite which was a joy to handle; a change which could not fail to please us as mountaineers and, no doubt, to interest my companion as a geologist. That vile rock, schist is, I believe, the technical term, had endangered our heads and failed to support our feet from the foot of the scree to the last bivouac. It was a wonder our burning anathemas had not caused it to undergo a geological change under our very eyes—metamorphosed it, say, into plutonic rocks. But, as had been said by others, there is good in everything, and, on reflection, this very sameness was not without some saving grace because it meant that we were spared an accumulation of rock samples at every camp. A bag of assorted stones had already been left at the Glacier Camp, and I tremble to think what burdens we might have had to carry down the mountain had the rock been as variegated as our geologist, and indeed any right-minded geologist, would naturally desire.

Thanks to the earlier reconnaissance by him and Houston, Odell led over this ridge at a good pace and in an hour and a half we had reached the snow mound which marked the farthest point they had reached. It was a ridge on which we moved one at a time.

In front was a snow slope set at an angle of about 30 degrees and running right up to the foot of the rock wall, perhaps 600 or 700 feet above us. To the west this wide snow terrace extended for nearly a quarter of a mile until it ended beneath that same skyline ridge, which below had formed the western boundary of the broad gully. On our right the shelf quickly steepened and merged into the steep rock face of the ridge between East Nanda Devi and our mountain. We were too close under the summit to see where it lay, but there was little doubt about the line we should take, because from a rapid survey there seemed to be only one place where a lodgement could be effected on the final wall. This was well to the west of our present position, where a snow rib crossed the terrace at right angles and, abutting against the wall, formed as it were a ramp.

We began the long snow trudge at eight o'clock and even at that early hour and after a cold night the snow was not good and soon became execrable. The sun was now well up. After it had been at work for a bit we were going in over our knees at every step, and in places where the slope was steeper it was not easy to make any upward progress at all. One foot would be lifted and driven hard into the snow and then, on attempting to rise on it, one simply sank down through the snow to the previous level. It was like trying to climb up cotton wool, and a good deal more exhausting, I imagine, than the treadmill. But, like the man on a walking tour in Ireland, who throughout a long day received the same reply of "20 miles" to his repeated inquiries as to the distance he was from his destination, we could at any rate say, "Thank God, we were holding our own."

The exertion was great and every step made good cost six to eight deep breaths. Our hopes of the summit grew faint, but there was no way but to plug on and see how far we could get. This we did, thinking only of the next step, taking our time, and resting frequently. It was at least some comfort that the track we were ploughing might assist a second party. On top of the hard work and the effect of altitude was the languor induced by a sun which beat down relentlessly on the dazzling snow, searing our lips and sapping the energy of mind and body. As an example of how far this mind-sapping process had gone, I need only mention that it was seriously suggested that we should seek the shade of a convenient rock which we were then near, lie up there until evening, and finish the climb in the dark!

It is noteworthy that whilst we were enjoying, or more correctly enduring, this remarkable spell of sunshine, the foothills south and west of the Basin experienced disastrous floods. It was on this day that the Pindar river overflowed sweeping away some houses in the village of Tharali, while on the same day 19 inches of rain fell at the hill station of Mussoorie west of Ranikhet.

We derived some encouragement from seeing East Nanda Devi sink below us and at one o'clock, rather to our surprise, we found ourselves on top of the snow rib moving at a snail's pace towards the foot of the rocks. There we had a long rest and tried to force some chocolate down our parched throats by eating snow at the same time. Though neither of us said so, I think both felt that now it would take a lot to stop us. There was a difficult piece of rock to climb; Odell led this and appeared to find it stimulating, but it provoked me to exclaim loudly upon its "thinness." Once over that, we were landed fairly on the final slope with the summit ridge a bare 300 feet above us.

Presently we were confronted with the choice of a short but very steep snow gully and a longer but less drastic route to the left. We took the first and found the snow reasonably hard owing to the very steep angle at which it lay. After a severe struggle I drew myself out of it on to a long and gently sloping corridor, just below and parallel to the summit ridge. I sat down and drove the axe in deep to hold Odell as he finished the gully. He moved up to join me, and I had just suggested the corridor as a promising line to take when there was a sudden hiss and, quicker than a thought, a slab of snow, about 40 yards long, slid off the corridor and disappeared down the gully, peeling off a foot of snow as it went. At the lower limit of the avalanche, which was where we were sitting, it actually broke away for a depth of a foot all round my axe to which I was holding. At its upper limit, 40 yards up the corridor, it broke away to a depth of three or four feet.

The corridor route had somehow lost its attractiveness, so we finished the climb by the ridge without further adventure.

The summit is not the exiguous and precarious spot that usually graces the top of so many Himalayan peaks, but a solid snow ridge nearly 200 yards long and 20 yards broad. It is seldom that conditions on top of a high peak allow the climber the time or the opportunity to savour the immediate fruits of victory. Too often, when having first carefully probed the snow to make sure he is not standing on a cornice, the climber straightens up preparatory to savouring the situation to the full, he is met by a perishing wind and the interesting view of a cloud at close quarters, and with a muttered imprecation turns in his tracks and begins the descent. Far otherwise was it now. There were no cornices to worry about and room to unrope and walk about. The air was still, the sun shone, and the view was good if not so extensive as we had hoped.

Odell had brought a thermometer, and no doubt sighed for the hypsometer. From it we found that the air temperature was 20 degrees Fahrenheit, but in the absence of wind we could bask gratefully in the friendly rays of our late enemy the sun. It was difficult to realise that we were actually standing on top of the same peak which we had viewed two months ago from Ranikhet, and which had then appeared incredibly remote and inaccessible, and it gave us a curious feeling of exaltation to know that we were above every peak within hundreds of miles on either hand. Dhaulagiri, 1,000 feet higher, and 200 miles away in Nepal, was our nearest rival. I believe we so far forgot ourselves as to shake hands on it.

After the first joy in victory came a feeling of sadness that the mountain had succumbed, that the proud head of the goddess was bowed.

At this late hour of the day there was too much cloud about for any distant views. The Nepal peaks were hidden and all the peaks on the rim, excepting only Trisul, whose majesty even our loftier view-point could not diminish. Far to the north through a vista of white cloud the sun was colouring to a warm brown the bare and bleak Tibetan plateau.

After three-quarters of an hour on that superb summit, a brief 45 minutes into which was crowded the worth of many hours of glorious life, we dragged ourselves reluctantly away, taking with us a memory that can never fade and leaving behind "thoughts beyond the reaches of our souls."

If our thoughts were still treading on air, the short steep gully, swept by the avalanche bare of steps, soon brought us to earth. We kicked slowly down it, facing inwards and plunging an arm deep into the snow for support. Followed another exhausting drag across the snow, hindered rather than helped by the deep holes we had made coming up, and then a cold hour was spent moving cautiously, one at a time, down the ice and the benumbing rocks of the long ridge above the bivouac. We paused to watch a bird, a snow pigeon, cross our ridge and fly swiftly across the grey cliffs of the ravine beneath the snow terrace, like the spirit of Nanda Devi herself, forsaking the fastness which was no longer her own.

At six o'clock we reached the tent and brewed the first of many jorums of tea. After such a day nothing could have tasted better and our appreciation was enhanced by our long enforced abstinence. There was but a pinch left and we squandered it all recklessly, saving the leaves for the morning. Food was not even mentioned.

We paid for this debauch with a sleepless night, to which no doubt exhaustion and a still-excited imagination contributed. Each little incident of the climb was gone over again and again, and I remember, in the small hours when the spark of life burns lowest, the feeling which predominated over all was one of remorse at the fall of a giant. It is the same sort of contrition that one feels at the shooting of an elephant, for however thrilling and arduous the chase, however great has been the call upon skill, perseverance, and endurance, and however gratifying the weight of the ivory, when the great bulk crashes to the ground achievement seems to have been bought at the too high cost of sacrilege.

It was very cold next morning when we packed up and started down. Near the bottom of the gully we were met by Lloyd and Loomis, who were coming up to help us down and who were overjoyed when they heard that success had crowned the efforts of the whole party. Houston and Graham Brown had already gone down and we decided to stop the night at Camp IV. There were still three or four days' food left in hand but Loomis and Carter were both troubled with their feet, which must have been touched with frost the day Camp IV was occupied. Lloyd was going stronger than ever and it was much to be regretted that we could not make up a second party.

The weather, which during this crucial period had been so kind, now broke up and on the morning of the 31st it was blowing half a gale out of a clear sky. Lloyd, Loomis, and I started some time before the other two, all carrying heavy loads because we left nothing but the two big tents, some snow-shoes, and two pairs of crampons or ice-claws. The snow-shoes had been lugged up to assist us on soft snow and the crampons for use on hard snow, but the slopes were, of course, all too steep for snow-shoes, and the only time we might have used the crampons was now when they had been abandoned.

It was bitterly cold, and the snow on the arête was hard and dangerous—the mountain had not finished with us yet. We started to descend in the usual way, plunging the heel in at each step with a stiff leg. When one or two "voluntaries" had been cut, we should have taken warning that the snow was not right for such tactics, but we were all pretty tired and in a hurry to get down, and it is in such circumstances that care is relaxed and the party comes to grief. Fortunately before this happened we had another warning which could not well be ignored. The leader's heels went from under him and he slid down the slope pulling the second man after him until checked by the rope belayed round the end man's axe, which fortunately held firm. We all felt rather ashamed of ourselves after this exhibition and abandoned that method in favour of the slower but safer one of cutting steps and moving one at a time, which should have been adopted at the start.

There was another slip, quickly checked, when one of the snow steps above the Gîte gave way, and we reached this camp in a chastened frame of mind and hoping that the mountain had now exhausted its spite. After a brief rest we pushed on, unroped gladly when we were off the snow, and picked our way with great caution down the unstable rocks to Camp I. On the way we noticed with concern that Odell and Carter were still high up on the arête and moving very slowly.

We found here Graham Brown and Pasang. The former's leg was troubling him, so he had spent the night here where there were still two tents, and Pasang had come up from below to take his load. We heard that Graham Brown and Houston too had narrowly escaped disaster on the previous day by the breaking of a step above the Gîte. Pasang had completely recovered his sight, but he was not yet his former bright self, for I think he felt keenly the disability which prevented him from helping his Sahibs at grips with the mountain.

It was now midday and after a drink of cocoa, which served only to bring home to us the loss we had suffered, we continued the descent. The cocoa so wrought upon Lloyd that, with a desperation born of thirst, he turned aside to prosecute a last and unsuccessful search for the tea. On the Coxcomb ridge I met Phuta going up to help Pasang and was shocked to hear that Kitar had died in the night. We got down to the new Base Camp at the foot of the scree at two o'clock and but for the melancholy news of Kitar's death there was nothing to mar our contentment. Twenty-one days had elapsed since we left.

from Endurance: Shackleton's
Incredible Voyage

by Alfred Lansing

Alfred Lansing's (b. 1921, d. 1975) account of the 1915 Imperial Trans-Antarctic Expedition is great adventure writing. When ice crushed their ship, The Endurance, expedition leader Sir Ernest Shackleton and 27 starving men crossed shifting ice and rough water on sledges and small boats to a series of camps. Finally, Shackleton led five men in a boat 800 miles to South Georgia Island. In this excerpt, six months have passed since they lost the Endurance, and the bedraggled party faces a final barrier: the island's mountainous interior.

Sitting on the rocks waiting for morning, Shackleton came to the conclusion that instead of sailing to Leith Harbor, they would remain on the south side of the island and three of the party would go overland to bring help.

By sea it would have been a voyage of more than 130 miles out around the western tip of the island and then along the north coast. By land it was a scant 29 miles in a straight line. The only difference between the two was that in the three-quarters of a century that men had been coming to South Georgia, not one man had ever crossed the island—for the simple reason that it could not be done.

A few of the peaks on South Georgia rise to somewhat less than 10,000 feet, which certainly is not high by mountain climbing standards. But the interior of the island has been described by one expert as "a saw-tooth thrust through the tortured upheaval of mountain and glacier that falls in chaos to the northern sea." In short, it was impassable.

Shackleton knew it—and yet there was no choice. He made his announcement after breakfast, and all of the men accepted it routinely and without question. Shackleton said he would make the journey with Worsley and Crean as soon as it seemed feasible.

But there was work to be done first. McNeish and McCarthy were put to the task of removing the decking and the extra planks from the *Caird*, while Shackleton, Crean, and Worsley went to work leveling the floor of the cave with some loose stones and dry tussock grass. Vincent remained in his sleeping bag, gravely troubled with rheumatism.

By noon, McNeish had dismantled enough of the *Caird's* upperworks to lighten her considerably, so they decided to attempt to get her up. And this time they were able—but just barely so. They shoved her up the beach literally by inches, passing every few minutes to rest. She was safely above the high water mark by one o'clock.

Later in the afternoon, Shackleton and Crean climbed a plateau at the head of the cove, and there they saw mounds of white among the rocks. These proved to be baby albatrosses on the nest. Shackleton went back for the shotgun, and they killed one adult and one chick. They ate them for supper, and Worsley wrote of the older bird: "Good eating but rather tough." McNeish noted simply: "It was a treat."

Afterwards they turned in and slept for twelve glorious hours without a single interruption. By morning they all felt infinitely better. Later in the day McNeish recorded rapturously: "We have not been as comfortable for the last 5 weeks. We had 3 young & 1 old albatross for lunch with 1 pint of gravy which beats all the chicken soup I ever tasted. I have just been thinking what our companions [on Elephant Island] would say if they had food like this."

Shackleton and Worsley, meanwhile, had made a survey of sorts around the area and saw that it was very nearly impenetrable country. Except for the cove in which they were camped, the cliffs and glaciers rose almost perpendicularly.

Consequently, Shackleton decided they would sail the *Caird* to the head of King Haakon Bay, a distance of about 6 miles. Their chart indicated that the terrain there was somewhat more hospitable, and they would also be 6 miles closer to Stromness Bay on the opposite side of the island where the whaling stations were situated.

Short as this journey was, Shackleton felt the men were not yet equal to it, so they spent two days recuperating and eating sumptuously. Little by little, as they gained strength and the tension went out of their nerves, a marvelous feeling of security came over all of them, dimmed only by the knowledge of the responsibility they bore to the castaways back on Elephant Island.

May 14 had been the day set for the trip to the head of the bay, but the weather in the morning was squally with rain, so the trip was postponed until the following day. In the afternoon there were encouraging signs of clearing. McNeish wrote: "I went to the top of the hill & had a lay on the grass & it put me in mind of old times at *Home* sitting on the hillside looking down at the sea."

They were up at dawn the following morning. The *Caird* was loaded and easily shoved downhill into the water. She had cleared the cove and entered the open bay at eight o'clock. A brisk northwesterly wind was blowing, and before long the sun broke through the clouds.

It was an utterly carefree journey as the *Caird* drove smartly across the sparkling water. After a while they even began to sing. It occurred to Shackleton that they could easily have been mistaken for a picnic party out for a lark—except perhaps for their woebegone appearance.

Shortly past noon they rounded a high bluff, and before them lay a sheltered, gently sloping beach of sand and pebbles. It was populated by hundreds of sea elephants, enough to keep them supplied with food and fuel indefinitely. They were ashore by 12:30.

The Caird was hauled above the reach of the water and then they turned her over. McCarthy shored her up with a foundation of stones and when she was ready, they arranged their sleeping bags inside. It was decided to name the place "Peggotty Camp," after the poor but honest family in Dickens' *David Copperfield*.

Shackleton was extremely anxious to begin the journey, primarily because the season was getting on and the weather was bound to turn bad before long. In addition, the moon was now full and they were certain to need its light while traveling at night. However, the next day, May 16, dawned cloudy and rainy, keeping them confined under the *Caird* nearly all day. They spent the time discussing the journey and McNeish busied himself fixing their boots for climbing. He had removed four dozen 2-inch screws from the Caird, and he fixed eight of them into each shoe to be worn by the members of the overland party.

Again on May 17 the weather was not fit for travel with squally winds and sleet blowing. Worsley went with Shackleton to the east, toward the extreme head of the bay, to reconnoiter inland as much as possible. It was not a very successful mission due to the poor visibility, though Shackleton satisfied himself that there appeared to be a snow slope leading from the head of the bay up toward the interior.

They had first thought of hauling their supplies on a small sledge, and McNeish had put together a crude affair out of pieces of driftwood. But when they tried it out, it proved to be clumsy and hard to pull, and the idea was abandoned.

May 18 was another day of disagreeable weather, and Shackleton was almost beside himself to begin the journey. They spent a tense day going over their gear once more, and watching for a break in the weather.

The decision had been made to travel light, even without sleeping bags. Each of the overland party was to carry his own allotment of three days' sledging rations and biscuits. In addition they were to take a filled Primus stove which carried enough fuel for six meals, plus a small pot for cooking and a half-filled box of matches. They had two compasses, a pair of binoculars, and about 50 feet of rope knotted together, along with the carpenter's adz for use as an ice axe.

The only superfluous item Shackleton permitted was Worsley's diary.

At dusk the break came. The sky showed signs of clearing. Shackleton met with McNeish, whom he was leaving in charge of the three men staying behind. Shackleton gave him his final instructions, and he wrote this letter in McNeish's diary:

May 18th, 1916
South Georgia

Sir

I am about to try to reach Husvik on the East Coast of this island for relief of our party. I am leaving you in charge of the party consisting of Vincent, McCarthy & yourself. You will remain here until relief arrives. You have ample seal food which you can supplement with birds and fish according to your skill. You are left with a double barrelled gun, 50 cartridges [and other rations] . . . You also have all the necessary equipment to support life for an indefinite period in the event of my non-return. You had better after winter is over try and sail around to the East Coast. The course I am making towards Husvik is *East* magnetic.

I trust to have you relieved in a few days.

Yours faithful
E. H. Shackleton

* * *

The others turned in, but Shackleton could not sleep and he went outside repeatedly to check on the weather. It was clearing but only very slowly. Worsley, too, got up about midnight to see how conditions were.

However, by 2 am, the moon was shining down brilliantly, and the air was wonderfully clear. Shackleton said the time had come.

A final hoosh was prepared and they ate as quickly as they could. Shackleton wanted to get away with the least possible fuss in order not to emphasize the significance of their leaving in the minds of those who were staying behind. It took only a few minutes to gather up their meager equipment. Then they shook hands all around and Shackleton, Worsley, and Crean crawled out from under the *Caird*. McNeish accompanied them for about 200 yards, shook each of their hands again and wished them luck, then walked slowly back to Peggotty Camp.

It was 3:10 am. The final journey had begun. The three men made their way along the shoreline to the head of the bay, then started upland, climbing a fairly steep, snow-covered slope.

Shackleton was in the lead, and he set a brisk pace. For the first hour or so they trudged upward without a pause. But the snow underfoot was soft to about ankle depth, and they soon began to feel the strain in their legs. Fortunately, when they reached a height of about 2,500 feet the slope leveled off.

On the chart they carried, only the coastline of South Georgia was shown—and a great deal of that was missing. The interior was blank. Thus, they could be guided only by what they could see, and Shackleton was terribly eager to determine what lay ahead. But about 5 am, a thick fog rolled in, shrouding everything in a diffused glow of luminescence in which even the snow beneath their feet was real only when they set foot on it. Shackleton thought it would be best if they roped themselves together for safety.

By daybreak Worsley estimated that they had covered about five miles, and as the sun rose higher, the fog began to thin out. Peering ahead they saw an enormous snow-covered lake, just slightly to the left of their easterly course. The lake was a rare bit of good luck because it promised the opportunity of a level route across its entire length, and they started toward it.

For an hour they followed an easy downhill route, though there was an increasing number of crevasses. At first these were thin and shallow, but before long they grew wider and deeper, and it soon became apparent that the three men were descending the face of a glacier. It was an unusual situation because glaciers rarely emptied into lakes—and yet there it was, stretching invitingly before them.

By seven o'clock, however, the sun had risen high enough to burn away the last traces of the fog, and they suddenly saw that the lake extended all the way to the horizon.

They were marching toward Possession Bay—the open sea, on the northern coast of South Georgia.

They had, in fact, covered about seven miles and almost crossed the island at a narrow neck. But it was of absolutely no use to them. Even if they could have descended the perpendicular headlands below them, there was no shoreline along which they might make their way. The glacier fell sheer into the sea. There was nothing to do but to retrace their steps, and they started back upland.

The worst of it was that it cost them time. Given time, they could have probed and reconnoitered for the best route, resting when they felt the need and traveling only when they were fit, and when the weather was best. But they had dared all for the sake of speed. They had neither sleeping bags nor tents. And if they were caught in these mountains by a change of weather, they would be powerless to save themselves. The blizzards of South Georgia are considered among the worst on earth.

It took two toilsome hours to regain the ground they had lost, and then they set off again toward the east. By 8:30 they saw that a range of small mountains lay ahead, a series of ridges and spurs—four altogether, like the knuckles of a tightly clenched fist. Worsley figured that their route lay closest between the first and the second, and they set their course in that direction.

At nine o'clock they paused for their first meal. A hole was dug in the snow and the Primus stove was placed in it. A mixture of sledging rations and biscuits was stirred up, and they ate it scalding hot. They were on the trail again by 9:30.

From here the ascent became increasingly steep, and they labored upward, a foot at a time, with Shackleton in the lead. They climbed what seemed to be an almost vertical slope, cutting steps in its face with the adz.

Finally, about 11:15, they gained the summit. Shackleton was the first to peer over. He saw beneath him a precipitous drop, ending in a chasm 1,500 feet below. It was strewn with the shattered fragments of ice that had plunged from where he crouched. He waved for the others to come see for themselves. There was no way down. Furthermore, to the right lay a chaotic mass of ice cliffs and crevasses—impassable territory. To the left was a steeply descending line of glaciers dropping away into the sea. But dead ahead—the direction in which their course lay—was a gently rising snow slope, stretching away for perhaps 8 miles. It was this they had to reach—if only they could get down to it.

It had taken more than three hours of strenuous effort to reach the summit, but now the only thing to do was to retreat, to retrace their steps again and try to find a different way, perhaps around the second peak.

They granted themselves five minutes' rest, then started down the way they had come. Physically the descent was relatively easy and took only an hour, but it was a disheartening business. When they reached the bottom, they skirted around the base of the mountain, making their way between the overhanging ice cliffs and a truly gigantic bergschrund—a crescent-shaped gully, 1,000 feet deep and a mile and a half long, cut out by the wind.

They paused at 12:30 to have another ration of hoosh, and then they started up again. It was a tortuous climb, much steeper than the first, and they had to cut steps with the adz beginning halfway up the face of the slope. The height and the exertion were a terrible strain and they found it impossible to keep going steadily. Every 20 minutes or so they sprawled on their backs with their legs and arms flung out, sucking in great gulps of the rarefied air.

But finally, about three o'clock in the afternoon, they were in sight of the ridge—a cap of blue-white ice.

The view from the top revealed the descent to be every bit as frighteningly impossible as the first had been, only this time there was an added menace. The afternoon was getting on, and heavy banks of fog were beginning to form in the valley far below. Looking back, they saw more rolling in from the west.

Their situation was starkly simple: Unless they could get lower, they would freeze to death. Shackleton estimated their altitude at 4,500 feet. At such a height, the temperature at night might easily drop well below zero. They had no means for obtaining shelter, and their clothes were worn and thin.

Hurriedly Shackleton turned and started down again with the others following. This time he did his best to keep as high as possible, cutting steps in the slope and working laterally around the side of the third peak—then up again once more.

They moved as quickly as they could, but there was very little speed left in them. Their legs were wobbly and strangely disobedient.

Finally, well after four o'clock, they struggled to the top. The ridge was so sharp that Shackleton was able to sit astride it, one leg on either side. The light was fading fast, but peering warily down he saw that though the descent was steep, it was not so bad as the others had been. Toward the bottom it appeared to slope away toward level ground. But there was no telling for sure because the valley now was thick with fog and the light was very poor.

Furthermore, the fog creeping up behind them was approaching very rapidly, threatening to obliterate everything, leaving them blinded and trapped atop this razorback.

The time for hesitation was past, and Shackleton swung himself over the side. Working furiously, he began to cut steps in the face of the cliff, descending slowly, a foot at a time. A bitter chill had come into the air, and the sun was nearly down. Gradually they were getting lower, but it was maddeningly slow progress .

After 30 minutes, the ice-hard surface of the snow grew softer, indicating that the grade was not quite so steep. Shackleton stopped short. He seemed to realize all at once the futility of what he was doing. At the rate they were going it would take hours to make the descent. Furthermore, it was probably too late to turn back.

He hacked out a small platform with the adz, then called to the others to come down.

There was no need to explain the situation. Speaking rapidly, Shackleton said simply that they faced a clear-cut choice: If they stayed where they were, they would freeze—in an hour, maybe two, maybe more. They had to get lower—and with all possible haste.

So he suggested they slide.

Worsley and Crean were stunned—especially for such an insane solution to be coming from Shackleton. But he wasn't joking . . . he wasn't even smiling. He meant it—and they knew it.

But what if they hit a rock?, Crean wanted to know.

Could they stay where they were?, Shackleton replied, his voice rising.

The slope, Worsley argued. What if it didn't level off? What if there were another precipice?

Shackleton's patience was going. Again he demanded—could they stay where they were?

Obviously they could not, and Worsley and Crean reluctantly were forced to admit it. Nor was there really any other way of getting down. And so the decision was made. Shackleton said they would slide as a unit, holding onto one another. They quickly sat down and untied the rope which held them together. Each of them coiled up his share to form a mat. Worsley locked his legs around Shackleton's waist and put his arms around Shackleton's neck. Crean did the same with Worsley. They looked like three tobogganers without a toboggan.

Altogether it took a little more than a minute, and Shackleton did not permit any time for reflection. When they were ready, he kicked off. In the next instant their hearts stopped beating. They seemed to hang poised for a split second, then suddenly the wind was shrieking in their ears, and a white blur of snow tore past. Down . . . down . . . They screamed—not in terror necessarily, but simply because they couldn't help it. It was squeezed out of them by the rapidly mounting pressure in their ears and against their chests. Faster and faster—down . . . down . . . down!

Then they shot forward onto the level, and their speed began to slacken. A moment later they came to an abrupt halt in a snowbank.

The three men picked themselves up. They were breathless and their hearts were beating wildly. But they found themselves laughing uncontrollably. What had been a terrifying prospect possibly a hundred seconds before had turned into a breathtaking triumph.

They looked up against the darkening sky and saw the fog curling over the edge of the ridges, perhaps 2,000 feet above them—and they felt that special kind of pride of a person who in a foolish moment accepts an impossible dare—then pulls it off to perfection.

After a meal of biscuit and sledging ration they started up the snowy

slope toward the east. It was tricky going in the dark, and extreme caution was needed to watch for crevasses. But off to the southwest a hazy
glow silhouetted the mountain peaks. And after they had spent an
hour in anxious travel, the glow rose above the ranges—the full moon,
directly in their path.

What a sight it was. In its light the edges of the crevasses were now
easily discernible, and every ridgeline in the snow cast its shadow.
They kept on, guided by the friendly moon, until after midnight,
stopping at intervals to rest, for their weariness was now becoming a
real burden, relieved only by the knowledge that surely they were getting close.

At about 12:30 they had reached a height of perhaps 4,000 feet and
the slope leveled off; then slowly it started to descend, curving slightly
toward the northeast—exactly as it should toward Stromness Bay. With
great expectation they turned to follow it down. The cold, however, was
increasing—or perhaps they were beginning to feel it more. So at 1 am
Shackleton permitted a brief halt for food. They were up and moving
again at 1:30.

For more than an hour they traveled downhill, then they came in
sight of the water once more. There, outlined by the moonlight, was
Mutton Island, sitting in the middle of Stromness Bay. As they made
their way along, other familiar landmarks came into view, and they
excitedly pointed them out to one another. Within an hour or two they
would be down.

But then Crean spotted a crevasse off to the right, and looking
ahead they saw other crevasses in their path. They stopped—confused.
They were on a glacier. Only there were no glaciers surrounding
Stromness Bay.

They knew then that their own eagerness had cruelly deceived them.
The island lying just ahead wasn't Mutton Island, and the landmarks
they had seen were the creations of their imagination.

Worsley took out the chart and the others gathered around him in
the moonlight. They had descended to what must be Fortuna Bay, one
of the many coastal indentations on South Georgia lying to the west of

Stromness Bay. It meant that once more they had to retrace their steps. Bitterly disappointed, they turned and began to plod uphill again.

For two miserable hours they kept at it, skirting the edge of Fortuna Bay and struggling to regain the ground they had lost. By five o'clock they had recovered most of it, and they came to another line of ridges similar to the ones that had blocked their way the previous afternoon. Only this time there appeared to be a small pass.

But they were tired now to the point of exhaustion. They found a little sheltered spot behind a rock and sat down, huddled together with their arms around one another for warmth. Almost at once Worsley and Crean fell asleep, and Shackleton, too, caught himself nodding. Suddenly he jerked his head up right. All the years of Antarctic experience told him that this was the danger sign—the fatal sleep that trails off into freezing death. He fought to stay awake for five long minutes, then he woke the others, telling them that they had slept for half an hour.

Even after so brief a rest, their legs had stiffened so that it was actually painful to straighten them, and they were awkward when they moved off again. The gap through the ridges lay perhaps a thousand feet above them, and they trudged toward it, silent with apprehension of what they would find on the other side.

It was just six o'clock when they passed through, and the first light of dawn showed that no cliff, no precipice barred the way—only a comfortable grade so far as they could see. Beyond the valley, the high hills to the west of Stromness stood away in the distance.

"It looks too good to be true," Worsley said.

They started down. When they had descended to a height of about 2,500 feet they paused to prepare breakfast. Worsley and Crean dug a hole for the Primus stove while Shackleton went to see if he could learn what lay ahead. He climbed a small ridge by cutting steps in it. The view from the top was not altogether encouraging. The slope appeared to end in another precipice, though it was hard to tell for sure.

He started down—and just then a sound reached him. It was faint and uncertain, but it could have been a steam whistle. Shackleton knew it was about 6:30 am . . . the time when the men at whaling stations usually were awakened.

He hurried down from the ridge to tell Worsley and Crean the exciting news. Breakfast was gulped down, then Worsley took the chronometer from around his neck and the three of them crowded around, staring fixedly at its hands. If Shackleton had heard the steam whistle at Stromness, it should blow again to call the men to work at seven o'clock.

It was 6:50 . . . then 6:55. They hardly even breathed for fear of making a sound. 6:58 . . . 6:59. . . . Exactly to the second, the hoot of the whistle carried through the thin morning air.

They looked at one another and smiled. Then they shook hands without speaking.

A peculiar thing to stir a man—the sound of a factory whistle heard on a mountainside. But for them it was the first sound from the outside world that they had heard since December 1914—17 unbelievable months before. In that instant, they felt an overwhelming sense of pride and accomplishment. Though they had failed dismally even to come close to the expedition's original objective, they knew now that somehow they had done much, much more than ever they set out to do.

Shackleton now seemed possessed with urgency to get down and though there was an obviously safer but longer route off to the left, he elected to press forward and risk the chance of a steep grade. They gathered up their gear, except for the Primus stove which was now empty and useless. Each of them carried one last sledging ration and a single biscuit. And so they hurried forward, floundering through the deep snow.

But 500 feet down they discovered that Shackleton had indeed seen a precipice at the end of the slope. And it was terrifyingly steep, too, almost like a church steeple. But they were in no humor to turn back now. Shackleton was lowered over the edge, and he cut steps in the icy face of the cliff. When he had reached the 50-foot limit of the rope, the other two descended to where he stood and the cycle was repeated over again. It was progress, but slow and dangerous.

It took them three full hours to make the descent, but finally, about ten o'clock, they reached the bottom. From here there was only an easy grade down into the valley, then up the other side.

It was a long climb, however, nearly 3,000 feet in all, and they were very, very tired. But with only one more ridge to go, they drove their weary bodies upward. At noon they were halfway there, and at 12:30 they reached a small plateau. Then at last, just at 1:30, they gained the final ridge and stood looking down.

Spread out beneath them, 2,500 feet below, was Stromness Whaling Station. A sailing ship was tied up to one of the wharfs and a small whale catcher was entering the bay. They saw the tiny figures of men moving around the docks and sheds.

For a very long moment they stared without speaking. There didn't really seem to be very much to say, or at least anything that needed to be said.

"Let's go down," Shackleton said quietly.

Having got so close, his old familiar caution returned, and he was determined that nothing was to go wrong now. The terrain below demanded caution. It was a severe, ice-covered grade, like the sides of a bowl, sloping in all directions down toward the harbor. If a man lost his footing, he might plunge the entire distance, for there was almost nothing to get hold of.

They worked along the top of the ridge until they found a small ravine which appeared to offer a footing, and they started down. After about an hour the sides of the ravine were getting steeper and a small stream flowed down the center. As they made their way along, the stream increased in depth until they were wading through knee-deep water that was frigidly cold from the snowy uplands that fed it.

About three o'clock they looked ahead and saw that the stream ended abruptly—in a waterfall.

They reached the edge and leaned over. There was a drop of about 25 feet. But it was the only way. The ravine here had grown to the size of a gorge, and its sides were perpendicular and offered no way of getting down.

There was nothing to do but to go over the edge. With some trouble they found a boulder large enough to hold their weight and they made one end of the rope fast to it. All three of them pulled off their Burberrys, in which they wrapped the adz, the cook pot and Worsley's diary, then pitched them over the side.

Crean was the first to go down. Shackleton and Worsley lowered him, and he reached the bottom gasping and choking. Then Shackleton lowered himself down through the water. Worsley was last.

It was an icy ducking, but they were at the bottom, and from here the ground was almost level. The rope could not be recovered, but they picked up the three articles that remained and started off for the station, now only a mile or so away.

Almost simultaneously, all three of them remembered their appearance. Their hair hung down almost to their shoulders. and their beards were matted with salt and blubber oil. Their clothes were filthy, and threadbare, and torn.

Worsley reached under his sweater and carefully took out four rusty safety pins that he had hoarded for almost two years. With them he did his best to pin up the major rents in his trousers.

* * *

Mathias Andersen was the station foreman at Stromness. He had never met Shackleton, but along with everyone else at South Georgia he knew that the *Endurance* had sailed from there in 1914 . . . and had undoubtedly been lost with all hands in the Weddell Sea.

Just then, however, his thoughts were a long way from Shackleton and the ill-fated Imperial Trans-Antarctic Expedition. He had put in a long work day, beginning at 7 am, and it was now after four o'clock in the afternoon and he was tired. He was standing on the dock, supervising a group of his men who were unloading supplies from a boat.

Just then he heard an outcry and looked up. Two small boys about 11 years old were running, not in play but in terror. Behind them Andersen saw the figures of three men walking slowly and with great weariness in his direction.

He was puzzled. They were strangers, certainly. But that was not so unusual as the fact that they were coming—not from the docks where a ship might come in—but from the direction of the mountains, the interior of the island.

As they drew closer he saw that they were heavily bearded, and their faces were almost black except for their eyes. Their hair was as long as a woman's and hung down almost to their shoulders. For some reason it looked stringy and stiff. Their clothing was peculiar, too. It was not the sweaters and boots worn by seamen. Instead, the three men appeared to have on parkas, though it was hard to tell because their garments were in such a ragged state.

By then the workmen had stopped what they were doing to stare at the three strangers approaching. The foreman stepped forward to meet them. The man in the center spoke in English.

"Would you please take us to Anton Andersen," he said softly.

The foreman shook his head. Anton Andersen was not at Stromness any longer, he explained. He had been replaced by the regular factory manager, Thoralf Sørlle.

The Englishman seemed pleased. "Good," he said. "I know Sørlle well."

The foreman led the way to Sørlle's house, about a hundred yards off to the right. Almost all the workmen on the pier had left their jobs to come see the three strangers who had appeared at the dock. Now they lined the route, looking curiously at the foreman and his three companions.

Andersen knocked at the manager's door, and after a moment Sørlle himself opened it. He was in his shirt sleeves and he still sported his big handlebar mustache.

When he saw the three men he stepped back and a look of disbelief came over his face. For a long moment he stood shocked and silent before he spoke.

"Who the hell are you?" he said at last.

The man in the center stepped forward.

"My name is Shackleton," he replied in a quiet voice.

Again there was silence. Some said that Sørlle turned away and wept.

g l o s s a r y

abseil. A method of descending a slope or cliff using rope with a friction device to slow the descent. (see *rappel*).

alpine-style. A method of climbing that calls for fast, light-weight, small-scale assaults. In recent years this style has become routine even on peaks and routes once attempted only by expeditions employing multiple camps, fixed ropes and large teams of porters.

anchor. Natural features or manmade devices that hold climbers and gear on a mountain slope or cliff.

arête. A steep narrow ridge.

belay. A method of using a rope and friction device to soften the likely consequences of a climber's fall.

bergschrund. The gap or crevasse between a glacier and the upper part of a climb.

bivouac. An impromptu or sketchy overnight camp consisting of light-weight, minimal shelter at best—a snowhole or "bivvy sack," for example.

carabiner (also *karabiner*). A metal snap-link used for purposes such as attaching climbers to anchors.

chimney. A crack in the rock or ice wide enough to enter and climb from inside.

col. A pass or dip in a ridge.

cornice. A mass of snow projecting over the edge of a ridge or cliff. Climbers have been known to step through cornices.

couloir. An open gully.

crevasse. A crack created by movement in a glacier. Crevasses are especially dangerous when snow covers them.

cwm. A rounded hollow at the head or side of a valley.

fixed ropes. Ropes left in place during a climb to protect or assist team members as they move up and down a long mountain route.

jumar. Friction device to help climbers ascend fixed ropes on steep terrain.

moraine. Gravel, rocks, sand, and the like carried by glacial movement.

pitch. A stretch of climbing between two belay stances.

piton. A metal peg hammered into a rock crack to serve as an anchor or protection.

protection. Pitons, natural features or other devices used to make a pitch safer to lead. A lead climber who is ahead of a belayer can safeguard himself or herself by placing protection in the rock, ice or snow, then letting his or her rope run through a carabiner attached to the protection.

rappel. A method of descending a slope or cliff using rope with a friction device to slow the descent. (see *abseil*).

serac. A large block, pinnacle or tower of ice.

spindrift. Powder snow carried by wind or small avalanches.

verglas. A thin layer of ice.

acknowledgments

Many people made this anthology. At Balliett & Fitzgerald, Sue Canavan searched the climbing world for photos and with Tom Dyja helped come up with the subtitle; Rachel Florman, Margaret Hanscom, Aram Song, Ben Welch, and Paige Wilder helped with inputting the excerpts; while Maria Fernandez helped with production. At Thunder's Mouth Press publisher Neil Ortenberg liked the text enough to take a risk along with us. At the Writing Company, April Boyle worked on permissions and text.

Greg Child, Jon Climaco, Jon Krakauer and Stephen Venables provided photographs; as did Arlene Blum, Scott Darsney, Harish Kapadia, Mick Fowler, Dan Mazur, and Beth Wald.

This book belongs to these writers, living and dead: Robert Bates, the late Peter Boardman, Greg Child, Art Davidson, Maurice Herzog, Thomas Hornbein, Charles Houston, Jon Krakauer, the late Alfred Lansing, Peter Matthiessen, David Roberts, the late Eric Shipton, the late Joe Tasker, the late H. W. Tilman, and Stephen Venables.

I am grateful to my friends Vincent Hanley of New York City; Susan Kohaut of Cape Elizabeth, Maine; Mike Jewell of the Mountain Guides Alliance in Intervale, New Hampshire; and the late Harold Brodkey.

Another friend, Will Balliett of Balliett & Fitzgerald, deserves more credit than anyone for making this book happen and for making the work a pleasure.

Clint Willis

b i b l i o g r a p h y

The works excerpted from books for this anthology were taken from the editions listed here. In some cases, other editions may be easier to find. Two sources worth trying are The Adventurous Traveler Bookstore in Williston, Vermont (800/282–3963) and Chessler Books in Evergreen, Colorado (800/654–8502).

Boardman, Peter and Joe Tasker. *The Boardman Tasker Omnibus.* London: Baton Wicks Publications, 1995.

Child, Greg. *Thin Air: Encounters in the Himalayas.* New York: Dell Publishing, 1993.

Climaco, John. "Dangerous Liaisons". *Climbing Magazine*, March 15–May 1, 1997.

Davidson, Art. *Minus 148°: The Winter Ascent of Mt. McKinley.* Seattle: Cloudcap, 1986.

Herzog, Maurice. *Annapurna.* New York: Lyons & Burford, 1997.

Hornbein, Thomas F. *Everest: The West Ridge.* San Francisco: Sierra Club, 1965.

Houston, Charles S. and Bates, Robert H. *K2: The Savage Mountain.* New York: McGraw-Hill Book Company, Inc., 1954.

Krakauer, Jon. *Eiger Dreams.* New York: Dell Publishing, 1990.

Lansing, Alfred. *Endurance: Shackleton's Incredible Voyage.* New York: McGraw-Hill Book Company, Inc., 1959.

Matthiessen, Peter. *The Snow Leopard.* New York: Penguin Books, 1978.

Roberts, David. *The Early Climbs: Deborah and The Mountain of My Fear.* Seattle: The Mountaineers, 1991.

Shipton, Eric. *The Six Mountain-Travel Books.* Seattle: Diadem/The Mountaineers, 1985.

Tilman, H. W. *The Seven Mountain-Travel Books.* Seattle: Diadem/The Mountaineers, 1983.

Venables, Stephen. *Everest: Alone at the Summit.* Bath (England): Odyssey Books, 1996.